Peter Verhezen & Tanri Abeng
The Boardroom

Peter Verhezen & Tanri Abeng
The Boardroom

A Guide to Effective Leadership and
Good Corporate Governance in Southeast Asia

DE GRUYTER

ISBN 978-3-11-078751-1
e-ISBN (PDF) 978-3-11-078763-4
e-ISBN (EPUB) 978-3-11-078782-5

Library of Congress Control Number: 2022934649

Bibliographic information published by the Deutsche Nationalbibliothek
The Deutsche Nationalbibliothek lists this publication in the Deutsche Nationalbibliografie;
detailed bibliographic data are available on the Internet at http://dnb.dnb.de.

© 2022 Walter de Gruyter GmbH, Berlin/Boston
Cover image: nala_rinaldo/RooM/Getty Images
Typesetting: Integra Software Services Pvt. Ltd.
Printing and binding: CPI books GmbH, Leck

www.degruyter.com

Dedicated to Linda and my close family members and all those who help "to steer" me in the right direction

Peter Verhezen

Dedicated to the "family of Indonesian state-owned enterprises", in which leadership partnership hopefully steers the organization to succeed

Tanri Abeng

Foreword: Improving Board Functioning

Any organization requires a board to govern and represent its shareholders to steer it "away from threatening risks and to explore new business opportunities". The functioning of a board is often "taken for granted". However, as any policy maker or shareholder understands, some boards are much more effective than others. A lot depends on the processes, procedures and defining of the specific duties of board members. The additional unique structure of a two-board structure in Indonesia which we inherited from the Dutch colonizer may complicate the functioning of boards.

"The Boardroom" – a book written by my predecessor Dr Tanri Abeng and his co-author Prof. Dr. Peter Verhezen who both combine practical experience and academic in-depth research – gives a good overview of what can and should be expected from a board. The authors describe the generic accepted governance principles, but rightfully claim the need to translate them into specific rules and regulations that make sense for Indonesian and other Asian companies. At our ministry, I see a direct relationship between the notion **Akhlak** and the governance principles and the board's fiduciary duties which are well documented and described in this book. Akhlak reflects those principles of transparency, fairness, accountability, responsibility and the board member's duties of care, loyalty and prudence. Akhlak is also an acronym that stands for **A**manah (to follow or to execute), **K**ompeten (the ability of skills, experience and intelligence), **H**armonis (emphasizing the Asian culture of harmony), **L**oyal (loyalty as an expression of integrity to organizational values and leaders), **A**daptif (that is directly related to the knowledge of leadership to remain agile or entrepreneurial and innovative), and **K**olaboratif (collaboration as a way to form effective and competitive teams).

Governance is a fundamental tool to help organizations to look after the interests of the firm in terms of economic prosperity, but it also encompasses the need to embrace a broader socio-ecological and cultural context in which the firm operates. Pursuing both financial goals and optimizing efficiency is still part of the fiduciary duty of a board and its management, but should not take place at the expense of environment or social harmony. It is also true that state-owned enterprises or any corporation will need to adapt to an increasingly digital economy. Our economy has shown some resilience with this latest pandemic crisis. Understanding and implementing the message of "an effective boardroom" will prepare us at state-owned enterprises – but equally true at any company – for a promising and prosperous future, starting with good leadership at the board level.

Erick Thohir, The Minister of State-Owned Enterprises of the Republic of Indonesia
July 2022

Contents

Foreword: Improving Board Functioning —— VII

Prologue: Why Good Corporate Governance Practices? —— XIII

Chapter 1
A Brief Journey of Corporate Governance —— 1
1   The Agency Dilemma Across Borders and Across Time —— 1
1.1   Entrepreneurial Capitalism —— 2
1.2   Managerial & Institutional Capitalism —— 4
1.3   How to Resolve the "Traditional" Agency Problem? —— 6
2   A Western Versus Asian Governance Context —— 9
2.1   Corporate Governance Across Borders: Two Worlds Apart —— 10
2.2   How to Resolve the "Asian" Corporate Governance Challenge? —— 14

Chapter 2
Universal Corporate Governance Practices Across Borders? —— 22
1   "Good" Corporate Governance Principles —— 23
1.1   The Four Generic (OECD) Governance Principles —— 24
1.2   International Investors Pursuing Good Governance while Reducing Entrenchment —— 26
2   Contextualizing those Governance Principles in an Asian Context —— 32
2.1   Global Competition for International Funds based on Good Corporate Governance Practices? —— 32
2.2   An Institutional Perspective on Corporate Governance in Indonesia —— 35

Chapter 3
Creating an Effective Boardroom —— 43
1   Fiduciary Duties of Care, Loyalty and Prudence —— 44
1.1   Some Generic Duties, Making a Board Accountable to Whom? —— 45
1.2   Fiduciary Duty of Care —— 46
1.3   Fiduciary Duty of Loyalty —— 47
1.4   Fiduciary Duty of Prudence —— 48
2   Improving the Functioning of a Boardroom: Structures, Processes and Composition —— 57
2.1   Assessing the Boardroom —— 57
2.2   The Right Oversight and the Right Guidance —— 60
2.3   Fiduciary Duties in an Indonesian Context —— 73

Chapter 4
Two-Tier Boards Versus Single-Tier Boards —— 83

1	Single-Tier Boards Versus Double-Tier Boards —— 84	
1.1	Principles of One-Tier Versus Double-Tier Boards —— 86	
1.2	Advantages and Disadvantages of Both Board Structures —— 91	
2	How to Initiate Dual-Tier Boards to Collaborate more Closely? —— 93	
2.1	The National Carrier Garuda: From being saved to Doom again —— 95	
2.2	The "Telkom" Case in Indonesia: A Unified Board that makes the Right Decisions —— 97	
2.3	PT Pertamina in Indonesia: An Attempt to Reform in spite of Patronage —— 99	
2.4	Concluding Remarks on the Dual-Tier Board Structure —— 107	

Chapter 5
Accountable and Responsible Leadership —— 115

1	From Maximizing Shareholder Value to "Sharing" Created Value —— 115	
1.1	Firms are both a *Nexus of Contracts* and a *Nexus of Relationships* —— 116	
1.2	Re-interpreting Fiduciary Duties aligned with Enlightened Ownership —— 120	
2	From *Stock-holding* Primacy to *Stake-holding* Engagement, resulting in ESG Impact —— 123	
2.1	Stake-holder Engagement —— 124	
2.2	ESG-Reporting and ESG-Impact —— 125	

Chapter 6
Is Your Boardroom Future-proof? —— 141

1	Preparing for the Future and its Risks —— 142	
1.1	Openness for Technological [digital] Innovation and Implementation —— 142	
1.2	Establishing a Clear Purposeful Narrative —— 145	
1.3	Consensus on Trust and *Thumos* that Underpin an Appealing Narrative —— 146	
1.4	External [Technological] Forces Putting Pressure on Governance Principles —— 148	
1.5	Do Firms Lack a Vision to Invest in Promising Projects? —— 150	
2	Development of the Next Leadership with the Aim to "Innovate or Die" —— 151	
2.1	The Global War for Talent —— 152	

2.2	Boards Overseeing Top Executives to make Organizations Competitive —— 155	
3	Addressing Sensitive Socio-Cultural and Eco-systemic Risks —— 158	
3.1	Practical Wisdom should Prevail Over Short-Termism —— 158	
3.2	Boards Being Sensitive and Inventive —— 160	

Concluding Remarks —— 165

Epilogue: The Relevance of Leadership in a Changing World —— 177

Bibliography —— 179

About the Authors —— 197

Index —— 199

Prologue: Why Good Corporate Governance Practices?
A More Effective Leadership in Southeast Asia/Indonesia

> Strategy without tactics is the slowest route to victory. Tactics without strategy is the noise before defeat.
>
> Sun Tzu, *The Art of War*

What is corporate governance exactly? And why do we bother? Some people see governance as mere legal compliance, as a way to have control over the assets of the organization and making sure that executives comply with the prevailing rule of law. That may be true, but only partially. There is much more to corporate governance and what boards are expected to do. We aim to highlight the crucial features of good corporate governance principles and practices as they are applicable in most jurisdictions. But we also will emphasize some unique characteristics of good corporate governance in an Indonesian context, and by extension some other Asian emerging markets. It is widely agreed among practitioners and academics that corporate governance involves both *supervising* and *coaching* top management whereby board members appointed by the owners function as the *custodians* of an organization. Hence why boards have specific tasks to fulfil in order to steer the organization in the right direction.

The Asian financial crisis of 1997 was a real wake up call for most Asian markets. Many Asian firms suffered from this grave crisis. Both government, regulator and shareholders became aware of the importance of proper guidance in making risky strategic bets. Business constraints – as in "the rules of the game" – determine to a high extent how business decisions are made at boards. Research clearly shows why governance is making organizations less risky and often more competitive in a global open economy. About ten years later, a similar crisis hit the Western hemisphere in banking, almost grinding the global financial economy in 2008, barely saved and bailed out by government intervention in cooperation with central banks that functioned as the trusted beacons which drastically injected additional liquidity into the economy, effectively increasing the money supply. Again, one of the major causes of this global financial crisis was the lack of proper risk management and good corporate governance – especially in the banking sector that had become a high risk-taking player instead of an economic intermediary.

Gouverner, c'est prévoir. Governance is about fore-seeing. It's about directing and creating a meaningful future. Corporate governance funds its etymological meaning in the Latin *gubernare, steering the ship away from rocks into open waters*. This book is about governing organizations under high uncertainty and 'foreseeing' and experimenting how to *steer* organizations to create value and to subsequently capture some of that value by optimizing the return of invested capital. In that sense, the main function of an effective board is to safeguard the organization from negative threatening risks and to provide the resources for top executive leadership to exploit current assets to its fullest potential while exploring and therefore investing in new business opportunities. Primary, boards are assumed to create trust by guaranteeing a form of honesty or trustworthiness that includes the disclosure of financial and non-financial information and being transparent about processes behind achieving (audited) performance. Yet, boards should also be focused to the future and take a much more active role in discussing overall strategy with top leadership while at the same time coaching them in preparing the execution of the strategy. Obviously, their traditional main function of avoiding agency problems by monitoring the CEO and the top leadership team is still a major part of their fiduciary duties. That supervision includes hiring the appropriate CEO for the firm *hic et nunc*. Equally, it also involves to fire the CEO if deemed necessary in case of ethical and or legal violations, or consistent underperformance of the firm vis-à-vis the industry average. Finally, boards should be concerned about future trends that may affect the organization. Such changing contexts can be social in nature like stake-holders asking more responsibility from boards to safeguard an ecological equilibrium, not to add pollution to the environment, and to stimulate more inclusive diversity. Or it may be investors who put pressure to firms to explore and to embrace investments in new innovative technology like artificial intelligence or the use of the i-cloud and digitization that potentially may disrupt numerous industries, or plainly, to improve the firm's financial performance with the industry average return on investment as the benchmark.

This may sound straightforward and rather easy. In reality, however, more than 70 percent of the board's time is focused on auditing and compliance issues. In other words, boards spend a lot of their valuable time to verify *past* activities, be it in terms of complying to the international and national accepted accounting standards, or other legislative and legal requirements – especially when it concerns a public listed company. Aside of the banking industry which always has been heavily regulated in comparison with other sectors, we believe that compliance remains a crucial part of good corporate governance, but the real contributions of an experienced board is to prepare top leadership for the *future* where the company will thrive or perish in fierce (and often global) competition. In essence, wherever the company is legally based, corporate governance – as practiced by an effective and responsible board – is meant to reduce risks and to optimise opportunities. Both are forward looking. That should be the focus of a board indeed. It goes without saying that supervision of past and present activities remains a duty, but better management practices and board practices may provide more time for the essential task to steer the organization to "open waters".

That is why this book focuses on leadership development while explaining the obligations and authority of board members who govern and steer these organizations. Indeed, we attempt to decipher "good corporate governance" practices in general, but equally how these generic guidelines may need to be adopted and contextualized to a specific legal and social-economic reality. Be it in Indonesia or in any other Asian emerging market. This book is a timely update of an earlier work ten years ago by Peter

Verhezen and his co-authors Erry R. Hardjapamekas and Pri Notowidigdo, "*Is corporate governance relevant (in Indonesia)?*"

Who should read "*The Boardroom*"? Anyone who is excited about the future opportunities of organizations to become more competitive while collaborating with others; anyone who is interested in firms and their strategy that enables them to potentially sustain their performance over a longer time horizon, especially in an Asian non-Western context. Most governance books are written for a Western public about Western multinational firms. This book claims to provide information to practitioners and scholars alike who want to obtain a deeper understanding of an Asian context, and how these Asian boards attempt to implement best international governance standards.

The book is the result of both solid academic research and teaching of global corporate governance and actual expertise derived from almost nine decades of joined practitioners' experience – directly or indirectly to boardroom functioning – behind the belt of the two authors. This book assesses (1) *how boardrooms and their leaders are expected to govern their organizations* and (2) *how boards can be more effective in seeking and achieving organizational financial and non-financial performance amidst global competitive turbulence, socio-economic volatility and geopolitical uncertainty*. With a special focus on some Indonesian (and other Asian) cases in chapters three and four.

The different chapters of the book aim to answer (1) *why* corporate governance is crucial for investors and executives alike, (2) *what* is expected from a board; (3) *how* boards and their corporate leadership can become more effective, (4) what is so *unique* for boards in Indonesia and other emerging markets, (5) how the Anglo-Saxon *shareholders' primacy* in mainstream (Western) economics, and the prevailing international Anglo-Saxon governance norms are increasingly under critical scrutiny, and finally, (6) how will boards address socio-ecological, digital innovative technological and organizational cultural challenges in *the [near] future*.

In our first chapter, we make a small historical detour explaining why corporate governance became so important in the last couple of years, and why despite the universally agreed governance principles there still exists some substantial differences in the implementation of those principles. Historically, governance finds its roots in the legal interpretation of [British Commonwealth and Dutch civic] corporate law, treating the corporation as a separate legal person. However, over the last three or four decades, the strict legal interpretation of corporate governance has come under pressure where complex questions of agency, attribution and risk-bearing has come to the fore. We may not dwell in all details of this interesting scholarly debate, but we emphasize the importance of a changing context that requires a slightly different interpretation of corporate governance principles. This is definitely the case for boards, its organizations and their investors in Indonesia and Asia.

In the second chapter, we assess the basics of good corporate governance practices across borders and time as defined by the OECD governance principles. This chapter analyzes how board members can and should use their legal power and informal networks to positively influence decisions within the company. If governance is about effective decision-making as a prerequisite for good corporate financial (and non-financial) performance, having experienced and knowledgeable board members selected is crucial. Good corporate governance only functions within a proper ethical organizational culture. That concretely means a climate of consistency, accountability and responsibility, while being transparent and fair in dealing with investors-owners and top executives. Hence why reducing the negative effects of entrenchment at boards and management – often detrimental to the organizational performance – has become a point of focus for many external [new] investors.

In chapter three, we provide an overview of the board's task to govern the organization. Any of the chosen board members, be it non-executive or executive directors (i.e. "directors and officers", or briefly D&O) are expected to discharge [or fulfil] their *fiduciary duties of care and loyalty* – and we are adding the often neglected *duty of prudence* – to the organization. These directors commit to steer and manage the organization with the objective to minimize harmful risks and to optimize business opportunities. And all this while avoiding [personal] *conflict of interest*, and maintaining an attitude of *confident humility to make smart and wise decisions*, including minimizing threats and addressing challenges where applicable. Concretely, boards are supposed to supervise or monitor top executives on the one hand, and to advise and coach them at the other hand. In case of crisis, it is the chair of the board supported by the other board members who directly addresses the challenge and mediate with the different concerned stakeholders. Finding a balance between this supervisory and coaching role – incarnated in the crucial leadership role of the chair supported by the whole board – remains a delicate exercise that requires industry and practical leadership experience, great communication and diplomatic listening skills, and empathetic or emotional intelligence.

Chapter four is crucial for anyone involved with [majority] owners – in particular in Indonesia or Asian countries with similar board structures. Capital providers or investors need to understand the difference between single-tier and double-tier structures. Indeed, we focus on this important difference between monistic board structure as it is prevailing in the USA, UK and other Anglo-Saxon legal contexts and the dualistic board structure that Indonesia inherited from their Dutch colonial past, rooted in a civic law system. To complicate the matter, governance at a national level does affect corporate law (and bankruptcy law) and thus subsequently corporate governance at the firm level. The underpinning legal regulatory authorities stipulate the overall rules of listing requirements for public listed companies and trading regulation of equity or other securities at the respective stock exchanges. The same governance principles apply to privately held enterprises, but in a less 'mandatory' manner. One could interpret these governance rules as more or less formal business constraints. It is obvious that changes by law makers and court rulings by judicial authorities also affect or determine the corporate law (including bankruptcy law) that constitutes 'corporate governance'. Yes, we question whether particular jurisdictions show the political will to reduce corruption, cronyism and nepotism. Contexts are historically and culturally bound, and never remain the same. Changes in socio-economic environments force firms to adapt. Boards are expected to take charge to adapt the organization to those changing trends and new challenges.

In chapter five, we focus on one new important trend: the increased scrutiny of firms by stake-holders who are concerned about firms' *ecological* and *socio-ethical* performance. When we both did our MBA many decades ago, our respective business schools did not teach us about business ethics or corporate social responsibility. Today, an obvious shift has taken place in most business schools and faculties of business and economics, forced upon by a changing public mindset – reflected in the social media and by upset [activist] stakeholders who feel that firms should take more responsibility in preserving the eco-system. There are plenty examples around of firms being chastened for inappropriate behaviour or contributing to climate change concerns. Today, no CEO can omit those non-financial objectives. We claim that sharing the creation of value makes strategic sense. We don't believe in mere [add-on] altruistic corporate social responsibility, but we are strong proponents to take [built-in strategic] responsible decisions that include non-financial objectives to make the company a better competitor. These ESG criteria require a slightly different view on what a company stands for. That probably means a clearly communicated narrative by the board of how the firm makes "profit through purpose". Now we also see that Asia-based companies may have a slight advantage to Western firm because of the Asian longer term view and their inherent "community" perspective as in the Javanese notion of *gotong royong* for example – especially family based firms but potentially also state owned enterprises. Western companies, however, are under pressure to continuously perform on a quarterly or annual basis. This also explains why quite a number of companies may not decide to go public or even decide to delist to avoid this quarterly pressure. The idea is to adapt and embrace these ecological and socio-ethical criteria without losing competitiveness.

Our final sixth chapter revisits the three fundamental tasks of a boardroom, but this time amidst global uncertainty and ambiguous turbulence: (1) how to address future risks, especially with a focus on *digital innovation aligned to a potential organizational transformation*, possibly to be best captured in an appealing narrative synthesizing short term profitability and long term vision; (2) how to secure board continuity through leadership development and more diversity for improved decision-making; and (3) how to address some new social-cultural and eco-systemic risks. We suggest that pragmatic and sensitive wisdom should prevail over short-termism at boards. What can be expected in the next two decades?

We conclude with re-iterating the importance of *effective* and down-to-earth *mindful leadership* at the Boardroom engrained in a strong organizational culture. Only a culture of 'intrapreneurial' innovation and corporate responsibility will enable a revigorated leadership to potentially play a crucial role in the continuous virtuous but also more sustainable growth circle of business in the USA and other

Western organizations. We see similar trends and practices unfolding in Southeast Asia, and greater Asia in general. At the end of the day, good corporate governance in an effectively functioning boardroom all boils down to trust that generates investments, wealth creation for its share-holders. Part of that created value is shared with employees and suppliers, but also with customers, and enhances the well-being and welfare for its involved stake-holders. Indeed, business is about creating value, shared with its main actors, within a context of global competition. But it is equally about collaboration and increased awareness of a global responsibility to face "the tragedy of commons". Any board member should act like good a parent or guardian who has the duty to safeguard the household, their organization, and prepare them for a promising viable future – preferably not at the expense of these 'commons' or deeply detrimental to future generations. Nothing less can be expected from a board that is elected and entrusted by their owners and shareholders.

"The Boardroom" does not pretend to be a theoretical treatise, but rather a practical book with 'guidance', based on proper academic research that can be used by both practitioners and academic scholars. We hope you'll enjoy it, and be inspired by what can be considered some "food for thought".

Peter Verhezen – Antwerp & Canggu
Tanri Abeng – Jakarta
April 2022

Chapter 1
A Brief Journey of Corporate Governance
From Active Owners to Specialized Custodians

> The boardroom can be a tough place, fraught with disagreements and difficult questions that need urgent answers. But board members can transcend conflict so long as they are united on the basics: that the challenges corporations face are existential, that fundamental change is inescapable in a rapidly shifting business landscape, and that organizations can only survive by leaving behind business as usual.   Dambisa Moyo, (2021), *How Boardrooms work*

Over the last 100–150 years, governing an organization has evolved. Governance is in the middle of another transformation with external pressure mounting to broaden the obligations of a board. Boards are now expected not just to make informed reasonable decisions but also to take responsible decisions. Decisions that go beyond mere optimization of shareholder value and include creating value that is shared with other stakeholders like customers, employees, suppliers and the community. Simultaneously, the international competition and international finance has drawn more interest from any investor to make sure that companies have the right leadership in place to properly govern and to secure proper decision-making in the interest of the organization, both short term as well as over a longer period. Mere compliance to short term investors' goals or regulations won't safeguard the competitiveness of the organization over a longer period. We basically want to figure out to what extent the prevailing corporate governance practices in relatively huge and very liquid Western capital markets, New York and London, are applicable in other jurisdictions, especially in a context like Indonesia. But first, how did we get there? What is the meaning of corporate governance? Why do we need corporate governance? The book will take an institutional-related perspective with the additional assumption that invidiual leaders elected to a board can nonetheless make a significant difference. The joint expertise of the elected board members and their partnering at the board – basically the chemistry among themselves executing their respective fiduciary duties – will definitely influence the decision-making that determines the future of their organization.

1 The Agency Dilemma Across Borders and Across Time

Enterprises are incorporated in corporate deeds. To reduce personal liability, the notion of *limited-liability company* was invented and spread through the British empire of the late 19th century.[1] This notion of limited-liability company was elegantly simple and successful in quite a number of nations which adapted the notion into their legal system. Limited liability remains crucial in contemporary company law in most countries.[2] Initially, those Ltd companies were public companies which could invite the public to subscribe for their shares, with the main aim to raise capital to finance growth and innovation. With a legal limited liability, the owners of these public listed firms would not become individually liable for their company's debt. Early 20th century, this form of limited liability became also popular among family and other private businesses, though their main initial aim was not to get access to additional capital, but to seclude company debt from the family holdings. In other words, this notion of limited liability allowed individuals to separate their own possessions from the investments made in legal corporate entities. This notion of limited liability and the court rulings that confirm the protection of these legal accepted entities have thereafter greatly determined the meaning of corporate governance in our capitalist system.

1.1 Entrepreneurial Capitalism

Capitalism – with investors providing capital for new ventures – has been seen as engine of growth for our society over the last two hundred years. However, this notion of limited liability does not abduct investors and owners and their representatives at boards from fulfilling their fiduciary duties. Over time, governance scholars and investors established a common understanding in the functioning of a boardroom in which they determined three major functions: (1) establishing basic objectives, corporate strategies, and board policies, (2) asking discerning questions, and finally (3) selecting the CEO and COO. Not much has changed in terms of the boardroom responsibilities over the last half a century. What did change over time are the expectations of society and stakeholders on the commercial legal entity.[3] However, we first want to delineate some clear lines between the different forms of capitalism in which corporations thrive within a certain institutional context and jurisdiction. We focus first on the modes of historical stages of capitalism and then on the major geographical differences in terms of governance characteristics.

Almost always, an individual or a group of individuals decide to set up an enterprise or organization with specific goals to produce a certain product or serve a particular group of people. The ultimate objective of any commercial organization is often expressed in financial terms, as in optimizing the net return on investment or equity. In practice, in almost all these ventures, the founder(s) were directly involved in the management of their venture. In the USA and to a lesser extent in Continental Europe, organizations evolved from entrepreneurial ventures into family dynasties, and eventually through an IPO and right issues became professional run publicly listed organizations, owned by a variety of people beyond the initial founding family members. Through growth, and consolidation of the market in which companies merged or were acquired, and further through overseas subsidiaries and international joint ventures, these companies grew to what has been colloquially labelled multinational organization (MNO). In the late 19th and early 20th century, these organizations were initially often based in the USA or UK, though a few European and Japanese MNOs emerged as well in the 20th century. Today, that situation is changing with the emergence of Chinese and other Asian companies who even list their stock on foreign exchanges, like Alibaba on the NASDAQ,[4] or attempt to acquire overseas Western companies. The presence of huge Latin American and African firms in the top 500 Fortune list remain limited. Indeed, some [non-Asian] emergent companies have followed suit like the Brazilian Natura company that took over Body Shop from l'Oréal in 2017 for more than USD 1.1 billion. The South-African beer company, SAB Miller, was growing fast, till acquired for Pound 78 billion in 2016 by the Belgian-Brazilian AB Inbev, the no1 beer producer in the world.

Research shows, however, that there are major differences between US-based MNOs and Asian-based Transnational firms or MNOs. The latter usually remains controlled by the founding family owners or the state. The US-based MNOs have become characterized by dispersed ownership where the founding families may still be around but have no substantial controlling veto power in these MNOs. The exception are the newer tech companies like Google and Facebook for instance where the founder(s) through preferred B-shares could keep vetoing voting power – and thus actual decision power at the board over the strategy of the organization. Their cash flow rights, though, have been diluted as result of a few private capital rounds and or an initial public offering (IPO).

In the early days, limited liability companies were relatively small and simple. The initial founders owning most if not all of the shares in the company remained very close to the actual management of the company. Early 19th up to 20th century, sophisticated financial intermediaries, pension funds, brokers, or agents between the investor-owner and the boardroom hardly existed. By early 20th century, growth in these mainly Western companies started to demand a higher degree of sophistication to allow generating continuous growth. For that, capital became crucial. Listing of companies on the New York stock exchange (NSYE) and the London stock exchange (LSE), as well as other exchanges in economically advanced markets became popular. That lead to a separation of owners and those managing the company on their behalf. With the growth of the economy, those owners who had invested in corporations now became more numerous than ever and geographically widespread. It were Berle and Means (1932) who drew attention to the growing separation of power between the executive management and the boards of major public companies in the USA and their dispersed owners.[5]

For our purpose, it is important to note that as long as the founder and or original owners are directly managing their organization, there is no discrepancy between those who own and those who manage the company – because they are one and the same. We colloquially call this "*entrepreneurial capitalism*" where the entrepreneur is the main capital provider ánd the general manager of the enterprise – as visualised in Figure 1. The enterprise thrives on the reputation of the founding family and their hereditary members who not only own but also manage the organization as they see fit. Usually, these family business have a very strong value system that goes back to the founder. It often is strongly oriented to create and capture value and to [pre]serve particular customers.

1.2 Managerial & Institutional Capitalism

The separation between ownership and management caused what is colloquially labelled a (traditional) "agency problem". The professional managers pursue other objectives than the owners. The latter aims for a high stock price and or optimal profitability, whereas the former seeks to maximize the remuneration package while in power as top executive officer for an increasingly limited tenure.

When the founder or owner leaves daily management to other people who are not part of the family, one can expect that objectives between the newly appointed managers and the more distant owners may not always be fully aligned. This clash is known as the **"agency problem"** that lies at the origin of having certain corporate governance standards implemented that aim to reduce this potential risk. The agency power is caused by asymmetric information in the hands of the manager who has more information at hand than the off-hands owners. When the access to *asymmetric information* is not fully absorbed in the stock price, possible power clashes and diverging goals between owners and managers can occur. This agency-principal clash sits at the root of the growing importance of having good processes and procedures in place that guide the decision-making at the boardroom. In other words, corporate governance principles, standards, policies and practices become crucial to safeguard that the interests of different players are aligned as much as possible in the interest of the organization and their shareholders.

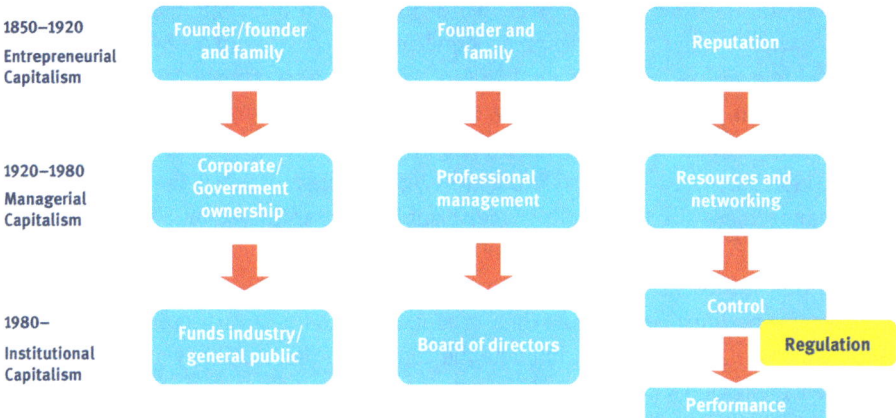

Figure 1: Evolution of corporate governance.

In the USA, the initial academic debate about ownership versus management leadership started when Mr. Sloan became one of the first hired professionals to run a big public listed corporation like General Motors, on behalf of the owners in the early 1920s. It was around the same time that business schools became popular as well. They were expected to churn out professional administrators and skillful managers to run these businesses for their hands-off owners. These highly trained professionals became quite powerful over time in the USA, using their personal networking and the availability of enormous resources of these firms, especially after their organizations became publicly listed companies with plenty of cash to invest. Call it "*managerial capitalism*" as found mainly in the USA and the UK (cf. Figure 1). These professionals used the newly provided capital and other resources to invest as they saw fit, but still with the understanding that their goals should be aligned with the goal of profitability maximization of the owners and or investors. Unfortunately, that was not always the case. Often those managers and executives would use their power as result of privileged access to asymmetric information to optimize their own "sub"-objectives – their own remuneration or salary package. Such clear distinctions in pursuing [different] objectives potentially leads to an agency-principal problem and a growing interest in corporate governance academic research. Corporate governance is assumed to rectify this agency problem by instilling strict control, and supervisory methods within the decision-making at the highest level, the boardroom.

Over the last three or four decades, another shift took place on two major stock capital hubs, the New York Stock Exchange and the London Stock Exchange, but also increasingly on other international oriented exchanges: institutional investors[6] – such as pension funds, private equity funds, hedge funds and other professional investors – became increasingly more influential in most of the public listed companies in the USA and UK. The proportion of shares held by individual investors in the UK for instance is only 13 percent today, down from 66 percent in 1957. Nowadays, individual equity holders own shares inside [institutional] funds. Similarly, over 75 percent of all stock on the NYSE and the London Stock Exchange is owned by institutional investors. Even when individuals are technically still owners of stock, they have delegated their voting rights to the big institutional players. The asset management industry in the US and UK is dominated by some "institutional" titan investment funds managing trillion of dollars,[7] leaving private investors more marginalized than two or three decades ago.

Obviously with such an enhanced clout, those institutional investors have become potential primary movers on numerous boards. Hence why a shift from managerial capitalism to "*institutional capitalism*" has been noticed on those exchanges in the last 20–30 years (see Figure 1). Despite the growing power of those US- and UK based institutional investors, their *activist agenda* on most boards has been limited, and remained rather passive, till recently. In other words, in spite of the growing legal involvement of institutional investors in securities on various stock exchanges, boards and their members have remained quite in charge of the functioning of the company without too much interference by those institutional investors. However, these boards regularly face an agency dilemma. Still, with powerful CEOs, one did not resolve the agency-principal dilemma yet, especially in the USA where about 65 percent are also combining that powerful executive position with the chairmanship of the company.

1.3 How to Resolve the "Traditional" Agency Problem?

Corporate governance aims to control and minimize the potential agency costs of hired [alleged] professional management experts. As result of the discrepancy of having access to confidential information by these professional managers, decisions can be easily manipulated in their own favour at the expense of the owners, creating the so-called agency-principal problem. The prevailing corporate governance theory or agency theory claims that there exists a contractual agreement between the principal and an agent. "Agency theory involves a contract under which one or more persons (shareholders) engage other persons (the directors) to perform a service on their behalf which includes delegating some decision-making authority to the agent. If both parties to the relationship are utility maximizers there is good reason to believe that the agent will not always act in the best interest of the principal.[8]" There are plenty of cases in the Anglo-Saxon but also in continental Europe to prove this point: Enron, WorldCom, Parmalat, and the list is long. Too long. All cases where boardrooms failed with disastrous consequences for organizations, its shareholders, employees and customers.

Managers or agents contractually working for the principal want to optimize their own remuneration package when they have the chance, whereas the principal or owner want to maximize the profitability in short and long term. The bonuses of those managers were initially linked to the quarterly or annual financial performance of the organizations. However, this creates an additional potential challenge: short term performance that is used to calculate these bonuses versus long term sustainable value that safeguards the economic competitive sustainability of the organization.

In order to resolve this agency dilemma, choosing between the fiduciary task to optimize the actual value of the organization in the short term – as reported by the quarterly or annual financials – but also over a longer period by investing in innovative ventures that secures future cash flow, a clear link between financial performance and the remuneration package was necessary. Still, bonuses aggravated the existing discrepancy between agents' and principal's objectives by actually encouraging a short term mindset on behalf of those professional executives. All efforts aim at beating investors' expectations by maximizing annual profitability to placate these institutional investors and to optimize the bonuses of top management.

That is where a few seminal papers on value maximization and corporate objectives by Harvard Professor Jensen[9] – and to a different degree Harvard legal scholar Bebchuk and Yale Professor Macey – had a huge impact on corporate governance and remuneration in particular.[10] What Professor Jensen basically managed to do was aligning the objectives of both professional executives and owners or shareholders by making the executives "owners" themselves through a stroke of conceptual genius with one simple "unified" objective: maximize profitability (through enlightened value maximization). This was the introduction of stock options as part of the remuneration package of executives and occasionally board members. Those stock options became part of the incentive system for executives to optimize their performance as if they were owners themselves – having the option to earn this given company equity. However, it also has contributed to some outrageous salary packages of CEO agents working for huge MNOs in the USA – and those stock options did not necessarily dramatically improve the long-term performance as was theoretically envisaged. What is crucial for our objective here is that the agency dilemma has only been partially resolved without a clear conclusive guideline how to proceed further to reduce the existing agency problem. The scholarly legal and governance debate is ongoing.

Governance today involves a number of entities, with a central role played by the Board – our point of focus. Basically, the owners of the company install or reconfirm a board during the annual shareholders' meeting. It is the board who takes the ultimate decisions – probably on behalf of the owners, but ideally in the interest of [the long term value of] the organization – but remaining accountable to the shareholders, at least once a year. For publicly listed companies, the financial performance and accounting will need to be verified through an official auditing process. Designated auditors are seen as third independent and thus trusted intermediaries who will execute this auditing process. The executive team and management will provide all the necessary accounting information to the auditor to allow them to perform the audit. The CEO and Chair of the company will sign off the audited report that then will be disclosed to the public at large in case of a publicly listed company, or to its shareholders in case of a privately owned company.

Because more than seventy percent of the US based companies are incorporated in Delaware in the USA with a clear pro-shareholder ownership perspective as stipulated by some of the court rulings, the interpretation of fiduciary duties has veered over the years towards profit maximization. Although not explicitly written in corporate US common law, this pro-shareholders' interpretation in the USA has become mainstream for most Western organizations over the years.[11] It now seems that public listed US companies 'belong' to their shareholders with the single 'purpose' to maximize shareholders' wealth. The US common law should be clearly distinguished from continental civic law that clearly provides more social cushions for involved stakeholders, like strict protection of labor rights.

In fact, executives have a fiduciary duty of care, loyalty and prudence to the organization and its long-term value.[12] As far as the organization's objective is to create value, "there is no difference between shareholder and stakeholder capitalism[13]". Creating and sharing value is simple good business practice. It is the board's and leadership freedom to decide how to share the value the organization creates. There

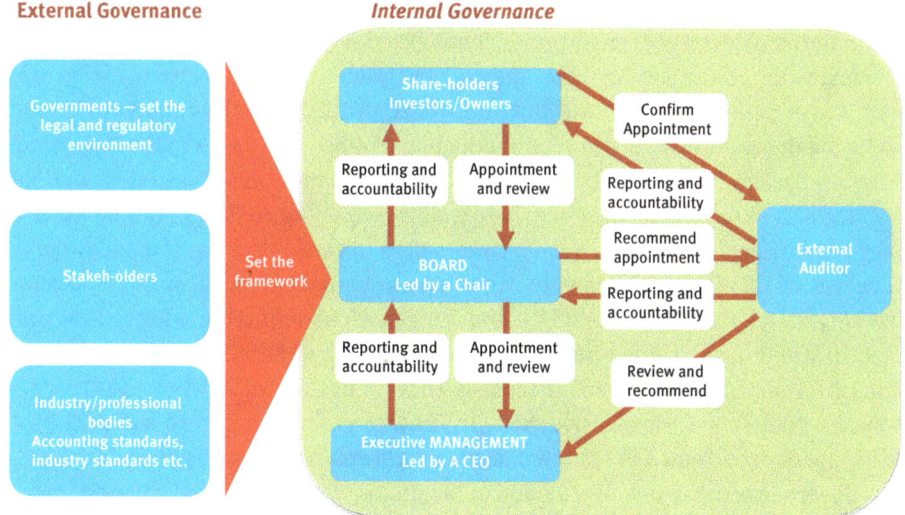

Figure 2: Governance today.

is no [legal] reason stipulated to be believe that organizations need to be beholden to stock-holders only. All depends on the chosen perspective, either giving primacy to capital providers or investing "owners", or to all those who have a real stake in the organization.[14] Highly motivated investor groups with a particular agenda – higher returns, sharper strategic focus on concerns for environmental or social issues – have become a familiar topic of debate in many Western boardrooms, especially in those where small minority can leverage influence with relatively small portion of stock-ownership. It should also be noted that discussions among those (Western) activist investors are increasingly dominated by some big (institutional) players – who do not necessarily have a clear majority on the board – represented by professional analysts and or investors who want to push their agenda.

If we assume that business is about value creation, then the question begs for whom is the board creating value? Economics and management studies can help us to answer that question. Business strategies focus on value creation for customers who are willing to pay a [fair] price for the product or service, and the customers' loyalty may result in higher margins for the company. In a way, focusing on the relations with your customers, but also employees and suppliers helps your organization to differentiate itself, and to become economically and potentially also socio-ecologically more sustainable. These value-focused companies are often also better at spotting the true relationship between new technologies and legacy products because they are keenly aware where and why customers benefit from those potential technological changes.[15]

Focusing on creating value in both the strategy as well as in the daily operational activities and choices managers make for your customers, employees and suppliers will benefit the organization. Most likely, with such an emphasis on creating value through your valuable (but often invisible) relationship with these stakeholders, your organization will rather "easy" make the link with a broader societal value creation, and "share value" – of an increased pie – as much as possible, leveraging these relationships that function as a powerful flywheel. Fairly sharing created value with customers, employees, and suppliers – and possibly the community at large – then becomes and creates a virtuous cycle of trust and loyalty. So far, so good. But what about the different contexts in which corporate governance is applied?

2 A Western Versus Asian Governance Context

The mainstream corporate governance theory claims that top executives need to be closely supervised and monitored to prevent particular agency costs as result of possible opposing objectives between executives and managers who likely will attempt to maximize their remuneration package during their increasingly shortened tenure in power on the one hand and shareholders whose aim is to optimize or maximize stock value and dividend pay outs on the other hand. This discrepancy allows top executives – having privileged access to confidential organizational information – to take decisions that benefit short term results, allowing them to optimize their own packages, often at the detriment of long value creation. Hence why good *corporate governance practices – and the legal entity of an appointed independent board with preferably independent board members –* is perceived by investors as reducing these information asymmetries. Such an (alleged) independent board is therefore assumed to limit risk and improve performance. As mentioned before, well-governing boards steer top executives to enhance business opportunities on the upside and to reduce potential threatening pitfalls on the downside. However, the corporate governance challenges in Indonesia and other neighboring Asian countries constitute a different nature because of a completely different socio-political business context, while additionally 'constrained' by institutional voids.[16]

Strategists rightly claim that investment in innovative products and technology is necessary to explore new business opportunities, while exploiting the current assets to its fullest. However, what may be seen as good board practices in the USA – governing and supervising strategies – may potentially clash with some specific cultural features in Europe or Asia, more particularly Indonesia. We will briefly provide some ideas how political changes affect business perspectives.

A lack of good corporate governance practices can partially explain the existential experience of the "Asian flu" of 1997, and to a lesser extent the global financial crisis of 2008 and even the current pandemic crisis. The globalization of finance and capital investment has become a reality. How will this affect Indonesia and other Asian economies? There is still a long journey ahead to compete with the best in class in reducing risk and optimizing strategic choices for the future.

2.1 Corporate Governance Across Borders: Two Worlds Apart

The institutional background of corporate governance in the US and the UK hardly looks like anything happening in Asia. When comparing corporate governance across borders, we find two worlds apart with fundamental different contexts in which firms operate. On one hand we have the well-known Anglo-Saxon investment model that prevails at Wall Street (New York) and the financial center of London and among venture capitalists in the Western hemisphere such as in the San Fransisco Bay area or Boston area where you have a lot of new entrepreneurial activities looking for financing their projects. On the other hand, we have the more "conservative" family businesses and state owned enterprises that constitute the economic backbone of wealth creation in Europe and Asia, and to a certain extent in Latin America.

Obviously, there are distinctive and more subtle institutional differences between contintental Europe and Asia for instance, but both continents share the focus on family-oriented businesses (either SMEs or bigger international ones) and the prevalence of state owned enterprises. The existence of the latter can be brought back to a political-historical background explaining their importance in these economies. It is true that the dispersed ownership in the USA market hardly exists in Asia or in Europe for that matter as shown in Figure 3. Although the ownership in the US and UK can be described as "dispersed" in comparison with most Asian jurisdictions, the arguments stands that capital itself in the USA is now also increasingly concentrated in the hands of a small group of major institutional players like Blackrock and Vanguard.

Most Asian companies – be it family or state-owned enterprises – have very concentrated ownership. Even after an IPO, those families or state owned firms remain controlling majority owners that determine the strategy of the firm, definitely in terms of voting rights and often even in terms of cash-flow rights[17] – a distinction that is not always made in an Asian context.

Despite these obvious institutional governance differences between the USA – UK and Europe-Asia, corporate governance shares some commenalities that allow us to speak of corporate governance principles that when implemented properly positively affect the functioning of boards. It can be easily argued and empirically proven that firms that have implemented proper governance structures and processes run distinctively less risk of finding themselves in a reputational crisis situation.[18] Mainly because the implementation of good corporate governance minimizes

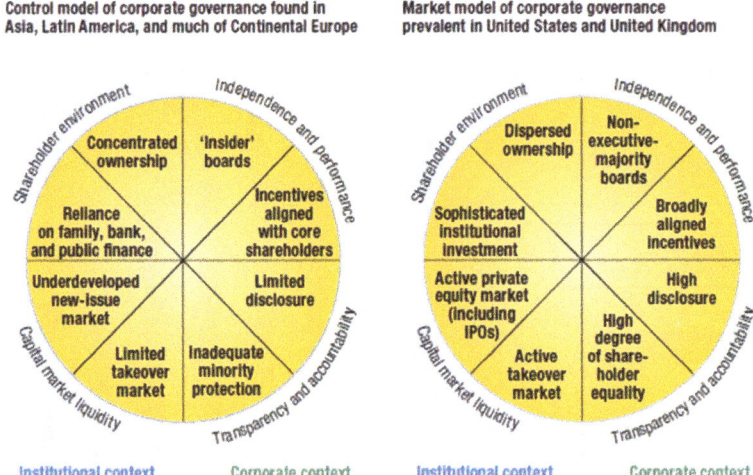

Figure 3: Two corporate governance models, two worlds apart.
Source: Coombes & Watson, (2001), "Corporate Reform in the developing world", *McKinsey Quarterly*, no4: 90

those kind of risks that could excite bad behavior, and strictly imposes certain procedures and processes that reduce or eliminate certain operational risks. That is true for both Western or Asian firms.

Well governed firms usually have an easier time to attract capital – both national as well as international – to finance their strategic growth plans. Alternatively, the greater global competition for the same capital sources will incite companies to implement proper corporate governance. Moreover, having well governed organizations implies an expected higher level of accountability of their top management and board. The result is that overall, well governed firms have a better reputation among stakeholders that matter, be it customers, employees and suppliers. It is probably true that communities can expect more responsible decisions from firms that have implemented proper governance practices. Finally, during the Asian crisis in 1997, it has been documented that more than 75 percent of all investors believe that good board practices were at least as important as financial performance. These lead investors were willing to pay a premium between 18 percent and 28 percent on the existing stock value for organizations that had the reputation to be well governed – as hereunder visualized in Figure 4. Just after the 1998 crisis, investors were willing to pay up to 28 percent premium for firms who were perceived to be well governed. Indeed, quite a number of studies confirm investors will pay a premium for well-governed companies as they tend to perform better. The perceived volatility or risk has been dramatically decreased in almost all companies because of better governance standards today.

12 — Chapter 1 A Brief Journey of Corporate Governance

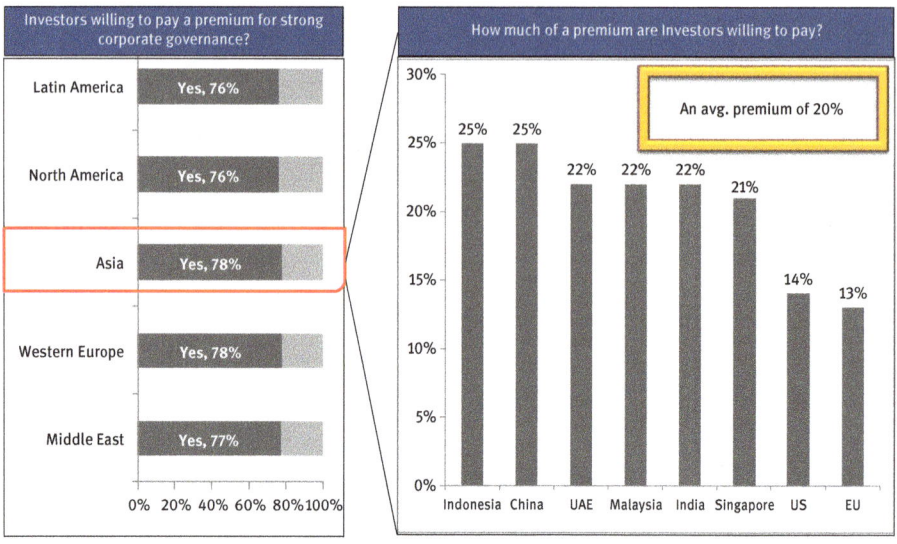

Figure 4: Premium for well governed firms during Asian Crisis.
Source: McKinsey, (2002, 2005, 2020), Global Investor Opinion Survey on Corporate Governance

Obviously, during normal times, that premium on the stockprice will disappear to a great extent – assuming all information is well absorbed in the stock price and therefore already includes risk perspectives on the firm under "normal circumstances". Again, with higher volatility during periods of tension and crisis, that search for well governed and thus safer firms that most often are well managed as well in risky situations. That the risk is relatively higher in Asia in comparison to Europe or the USA is an understatement, mainly because the instutional voids in those Asian markets.[19] Hence why foreign (but also local) investors will require higher profit potential or a above average return on investment on these stocks in order to "neutralize" the higher perceived risks. In general, investors interpret good corporate governance on two levels, the national institutional level and the firm level. The higher market risk can be partially "neutralized" by investing in a well-governed organizations that significantly reduce corporate risk. Indeed, investors, unfortunately, cannot rely on well functioning institutions in these emerging market contexts – be it through neutral objective and effective courts, or reliable police and regulators' force to impose the rule of law. It therefore boils down to the firm level, where investors assess the organisational level of governance standards. It is this firm level governance, as expressed through the functioning of the boardroom, that is the focus of this book.

Overall, we argue that implementing good corporate governance practices has huge advantages for the firm – independent of the institutional level of governance. Indeed, numerous studies have confirmed the importance of good corporate governance (1) on firm performance and *access to finance*. In addition, good corporate governance most often leads (2) to *improved operational performance*: for instance,

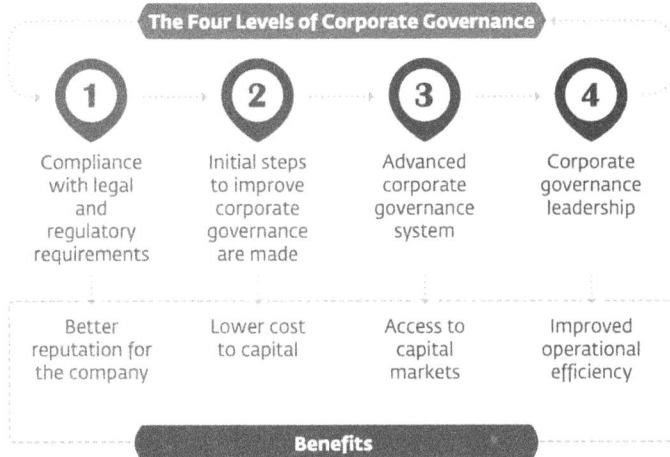

Figure 5: The benefits of Corporate Governance.
Source: IFC World Bank Report: The Indonesian Corporate Governance Manual, (2018), 2nd edition: p38

emerging market companies with good governance rated 8 percentage points higher versus peers in terms of economic value added,[20] and (3) results in *improved risk management*, i.e. companies with superior governance had much lower risk profiles.[21] Furthermore, (4) it often leads to *higher firm valuation* and *share performance*. And good corporate governance (5) often guarantees *better access to capital* since a strong correlation between good governance and lower capital costs can be proven.[22] Finally, good governance practices (6) result in *improved sustainability* as in helping address family governance issues for family-owned enterprises and ease succession to future generations.

IFC's corporate governance manuel summarizes four major benefits of well governed firms – as visualized in Figure 5 that indicate (1) better reputation and less overall risk, (2) a lower cost of capital, (3) easier access to capital markets because of higher trust and improved operational efficiency, including less corruption and other deficiencies. (4) The improvement in the company's governance practices often lead to a better supervision and more accountability through proper standard operating procedures and processes which minimize the risk of fraud or self-dealing by the company's staff, an often heard deficiency in firms. Indeed, proper accountability for all corporate actions taken, combined with risk management and proper internal control, usually brings potential problems immediately to the forefront before it blows into a real crisis.

In other words, corporate governance provides better oversight and more accountability to executive management, one of the corner stones to reduce the potential agency costs, as well as improving the decision-making processes of the board members to steer and direct the organization. And finally it's about improving the overall organizational reputation by complying to the "rule of the game" [at the institutional level] that subsequently causes less friction or potential lapses. The overall result of a implementing proper corporate governance standards in firms is an improvement of the performance and operational excellence since corners are not cut short. It should not be too difficult to convince any competitive organization that adherence to good corporate governance standards usually strengthens the overall decision-making process of the board and its executive teams. When corporate governance standards are applied, boards usually make more informed and more reasonable decisions in the interest of the firm, ultimately contributing to improving operational performance and lower capital expenditures, and in turn an improved growth potential. It is because of well implemented corporate governance practices at the firm level, that global investment may feel comfortable to seek opportunities in firms in the emerging market, in spite of, or rather, for compensating a riskier 'institutional' environment with a higher return on investment.

Figure 6: Generic advantages of good corporate governance.
Source: IFC World Bank Report: The Indonesian Corporate Governance Manual, (2018), 2nd edition: p39

Important is that corporate governance inherently aims to reduce the agency problems, but also helps to facilitate the resolution of potential corporate conflicts between different shareholders, be it minority versus controlling share-holders or powerful institutional investors. And finally, corporate governance also minimizes the risk of personal liability of the company's executive officers.

2.2 How to Resolve the "Asian" Corporate Governance Challenge?

The Western perception underwrites the strong conviction that corporate governance provides the institutional solution for resolving potential agency challenges that directly results from management having access to asymmetric information allowing them to make decisions in their personal interest instead of the organization, and often unnoticed. This led to the focus on structures and procedures that allowed owners to supervise and monitor management more closely and avoid those agency problems to occur.

In an Asian context, however, hired professional managers or top executives may wield some power within the organization, but much less compared to their Western peers. Taking the hierarchical structures into account in Asian cultures,[23] it is clear that in the traditional Asian family businesses the trust in [hired] top management requires an "unconditional loyalty" in return. Most of the time, the family remains in close control, if not *de iure*, then definitely *de facto*.

There does not exist a patriarch or family owner who would not closely monitor the operations of the family empire. Even in case the increased sophistication or complexity of operations would require outside professionals. We both had first hand experience of the 'invisible' control of the family as either the CEO-advisor, director or in an advisory role. We both have worked with a number of conglomerates and tycoons in Indonesia, Singapore, Malaysia and Thailand. This experience have taught us how families use strong leadership at the board – either by the patriarch or next generation of family owners – to keep control. It may be true that the younger generation may slightly adapt a more "international" view – i.e. less Asian patriarchical (or matriarchical) patronage or hierarchical management approach – but that does not preclude them for still having full power over the family business. This is definitely true at the holding company which is almost never made public. But this is equally true for subsidiary levels which may be used by the family to raise "public" capital on a stock exchange to finance some part of the business. The jewels of the family conglomerate, however, will often not be fully exposed or even disclosed to the public at large. The Bakrie saga against James Rothschild[24] a decade ago for instance have made that very clear.[25]

In other words, the typical agency dilemma that owners would face in a Western context hardly occur in Asia because of the strict control that family business holds over assets and resources. Moreover, the family or state almost always remains in relative control in terms of cash flow rights and or voting rights at the annual shareholders' meeting. The major challenge in Asia is situated at the owners' level: how can minority owners' rights be preserved against the *potential misuse of majority power* of the family[26]? It is a typical *majority versus minority shareholders' dilemma*. Ideally, all rights are equally treated. The reality is often very different and more complex.

A family patriarch would have no qualm to protect the family's "own" assets against any potential intrusion by outsiders – even if those 'outsiders' are minority owners of their company (as is the case in publicly listed family business throughout Asia). More, it would not be the first time that majority owners attempt to "expropriate" some of the worthy assets into the family holding structure which remains untouchable to any outsiders.[27] The pyramid structure – often used by families in Southeast Asia, but also in South Korea, and even in Japan – is an ideal tool to camouflage the real intentions of the family. Worse, Peter – who was involved in preparing an IPO of a firm in Indonesia, owned by a powerful Indonesian Chinese tycoon owner, residing in Singapore – witnessed how a newly listed company would not even mention his name in the corporate deeds. In other words, at face value, the *de facto* owner was not explicitly mentioned in the newly listed company, though it was clear that the intention was to use the capital to finance new projects by the company and its related ventures. None of the incoming foreign or even local [minority] owners – the so called public money invested through the IPO – were fully aware of the real power structure behind the veil of apparent ownership. [Deliberate] Opaqueness is hardly a good indicator for strong governance.

What we are saying is that the incredible "discretion" that characterizes Asian culture in general makes business and investments in Asian firms a less than obvious venture – unless if one invests in indices like the MSCI Emerging Markets and even there the higher volatility does not guarantee higher than average returns. It needs to be noted that Indonesia only constitutes a very little portion of this MSCI EM Index. If one looks at Indonesia as a country, then one could argue – from a macro-economic perspective (which is not our focus in this book) – that Indonesia[28] offers great opportunities to foreign investors due to the country's large and young population, rising consumption, abundant natural resources, embracing e-commerce and their digital platforms and cheap labour.

Figure 7: MSCI Emerging Market Index[29] (in USD).

Our interest, however, is to find specific firms within the country or emerging market index that is alluring investors because of its specific business opportunities and organizational governance standards above the average. Finding rough non-polished jewels that are likely under-rated deserve the investors' attention. This was exactly the value-based approach of Marc Mobius, the former executive chairman of Templeton Emerging Markets, who famously would require to get acquainted with the management team and board – and the governance standards applied – before pulling in any investment money.[30]

Admittedly, transparency has never been on the agenda of those Asian companies because family owners often distrust the government and the regulator. And not without reason: these institutions are often weak, and not fully transparent themselves in their decision-making.[31] Worse, these (governmental) institutional voids are correlated with red tape – as in complicating to do business in those markets sometimes to try influencing organizational investment or capex decisions – while corruption remain rive in those emerging markets.[32]

This is one part of the story where family companies are structured like a castle not to be taken over by any outsider. Admittedly, this is a universal characteristic of any family business in the world. The difference is that most US-based family business of the 19th and 20th century have morphed into huge entities with numerous shareholders and often operate as multinational organizations where power of those owners is very dispersed. In Continental Europe, the respective block holding families are a little less dispersed, which means that the family still wield enormous if not "absolute" shareholder [voting] power, be it in Sweden with the Wallenberg family, or the Quandt family in Germany, or the Agnelli family in Italy, or LVMH's empire controlled by the Arnault family in France for example. Even the huge AB Inbev beer conglomerate still remains in the hands of very concentrated ownership of some powerful Belgian [beer founding] families and Brazilian investors. Very similar to what we see in Southeast Asia, though slightly less concentrated in Europe, and compliant to more stringent capital market listing requirements and conditions.

Another very different characteristic in those Asian countries, including China, can be found in the predominant power of state owned enterprises. China is the obvious example where about 70 percent of the assets listed on the Shanghai and Shenzen Stock Exchange are state related. In Indonesia, the biggest companies are still state-owned, be it in the gas- and oil industry, banking, or telcom. And often a number of those state-owned enterprises are publicly listed, though the government would not release "absolute" voting power to the public. The power remains, indeed, very concentrated in the hands of the state, even if publicly listed.

Any Western handbook on corporate governance may briefly mention this unique characteristic of concentrated ownership in Asia, but the profound implications for foreign and local investment make it a very different ball game in comparison with the US- or UK-based more sophisticated investment vehicles. It is because of this lack of fundamental comprehension of the "corporate governance with unique Asian characteristics" that we have written this book on "The Boardroom".

Consider the following Take Away Ideas of Chapter 1:

1. Corporate governance gained prominence in Western firm when historically one moved from entrepreneurial to managerial capitalism in the USA in which professionals took over the management role of the entrepreneurs-founders. Corporate governance became a way to reduce the traditional agency problem, where the power of asymmetric information by professional managers could be used at the expense of [hands-off] owners and investors of the firm.
2. In most Asian firms, and Indonesia is no exception, most listed firms are either family controlled or state owned, characterized by concentrated ownership. This is very different from dispersed ownership of most UK and US-based listed firms. The consequence is that corporate governance - that aims to control and monitor while also to coach its professional executives - may need a different interpretation, measurements and even focus, in comparison with a mature and sophisticated capital market like the one that exists in the USA or the UK.
3. The fundamental governance principles of transparency, fairness, accountability and responsibility are valid across borders. However, listed Asian firms do have less of an agency problem, but often potential conflict of interest may arise because controlling family owners or state may take decisions that are not necessary in the interest of the firm – even at the expense of minority institutional or individual investors. Hence why good governance implementation with proper procedures and processes may reduce the risk of [any form of] expropriation by the majority owners at the expense of minority owners in Asia.

Notes

1 Bainbridge, S.M., (2003), *Agency, Partnership and Limited Liability Companies*, New York, Foundation Press; and Macey, J.R., (2008), *Corporate Governance. Promises Kept, Promises Broken*, New Jersey, Princeton University Press.
2 Tricker, B., (2015), *Corporate Governance. Principles, Policies, and P*ractices, Oxford, Oxford University Press; and Farrar, J., (2005), *Corporate Governance. Theories, Principles, and Practice*, Melbourne, Oxford University Press.
3 See chapter five and chapter six.
4 The current debate of "decoupling" economies (between USA and China) make it more likely that fewer Chinese companies will list on Wall Street, and probably [are nudged to] "prefer" more close exchanges like Hong Kong. A similar fate fell on Didi Chuxing, the Chinese taxi hailing company that drove out UBER of the Chinese market: after just 5 months being successfully listed on the NYSE, it is being pushed by CCP to delist from the American Stock Exchange in New York, and move to Hong Kong Stock Exchange (cf Chapter 6).
5 Berle, A.A. & G.C. Means, (1932), *The Modern Corporation and Private Property*, MacMillan, and revised by A. Berle (1967), Columbia University Press. They argue that the rise of modern corporation has brought "a concentration of power which can compete on equal terms with the modern state – economic power versus political power, each strong in its own field. The state seeks in some aspects to regulate the corporation, while the corporation, steadily becoming more powerful, makes every effort to avoid such regulation. . . The future may see the economic organism, now typified by the corporation, not only on an equal plane with the state, but possibly even superseding it as the dominant form of social organization."

6 An institutional investor is a legal entity that accumulates the funds of numerous investors (which may be private investors or other legal entities) to invest in various financial instruments and profit from the process. In other words, an institutional investor is an organization that invests on behalf of its members.Institutional investors are legal entities that participate in trading in the financial markets.Institutional investors include the following organizations: credit unions, banks, large funds such as a mutual or hedge fund, venture capital funds, insurance companies, and pension funds. Institutional investors exert a significant influence on the market, both in a positive and negative way.

7 The Largest Investment Management Companies in 2021: BlackRock with $9.464 trillion under their management; the Vanguard Groupwith $8.4 trillion; the UBS Group with $4.432 trillion; Fidelity with $4.23 trillion; State Street Global Advisors with $3.86 trillion; Morgan Stanley with $3.274 trillion; JPMorgan Chase with $2.996 trillion; and Allianz with $2.953 trillion.

8 Jensen, M.C. & W.H. Meckling, (1976), Theory of the Firm: managerial behavior, agency costs and ownership structure, *Journal of Finance Economics*, Vol. 3: 305–360.

9 Besides the seminal paper by Jensen, M.C. & W.H. Meckling, (1976), Theory of the Firm: managerial behavior, agency costs and ownership structure, *Journal of Finance Economics*, we also like to mention the following influential papers: Jensen, M.C.,(1986), "Agency cost of free cash flow, corporate finance, and takeovers", *American Economic Review*, 76, 323–329; and the influential game changer by Jensen, M.C., (2002), "Value maximization, stakeholder theory, and the corporate objective function", *Business Ethics Quarterly*, 12(2), 235–256.

10 See Jensen, M.C., (2002: 256), "Value maximization, stakeholder theory, and the corporate objective function", *Business Ethics Quarterly*, o.c.. Allow me to quote the *abstract* of one of these seminal and very influential papers of Professor Jensen (2002), examining: "the role of the corporate objective function in corporate productivity and efficiency, social welfare, and the accountability of managers and directors. [. . .] since it is logically impossible to maximize in more than one dimension, purposeful behavior requires a single valued objective function. Two hundred years of work in economics and finance implies that in the absence of externalities and monopoly (and when all goods are priced), social welfare is maximized when each firm in an economy maximizes its total market value. Total value is not just the value of the equity but also includes the market values of all other financial claims including debt, preferred stock, and warrants. In sharp contrast stakeholder theory, argues that managers should make decisions so as to take account of the interests of all stakeholders in a firm (including not only financial claimants, but also employees, customers, communities, governmental officials, and under some interpretations the environment, terrorists, and blackmailers). Because the advocates of stakeholder theory refuse to specify how to make the necessary tradeoffs among these competing interests they leave managers with a theory that makes it impossible for them to make purposeful decisions. With no way to keep score, stakeholder theory makes managers unaccountable for their actions. It seems clear that such a theory can be attractive to the self-interest of managers and directors. Creating value takes more than acceptance of value maximization as the organizational objective. As a statement of corporate purpose or vision, value maximization is not likely to tap into the energy and enthusiasm of employees and managers to create value. Seen in this light, change in long-term market value becomes the scorecard that managers, directors, and others use to assess success or failure of the organization. The choice of value maximization as the corporate scorecard must be complemented by a corporate vision, strategy and tactics that unite participants in the organization in its struggle for dominance in its competitive arena. A firm cannot maximize value if it ignores the interest of its stakeholders. [. . .] a proposal to clarify what [. . .] is the proper relation between value maximization and stakeholder theory. I call it enlightened value maximization, and it is identical to what I call enlightened stakeholder theory. Enlightened value maximization utilizes much of the structure of stakeholder theory but accepts maximization of the long run value of the firm as the criterion for making the requisite

tradeoffs among its stakeholders. Managers, directors, strategists, and management scientists can benefit from enlightened stakeholder theory. Enlightened stakeholder theory specifies long-term value maximization or value seeking as the firm's objective and therefore solves the problems that arise from the multiple objectives that accompany traditional stakeholder theory. [. . .] Balanced Scorecard theory is [also] flawed because it presents managers with a scorecard which gives no score–that is, no single-valued measure of how they have performed. Thus managers evaluated with such a system (which can easily have two dozen measures and provides no information on the tradeoffs between them) have no way to make principled or purposeful decisions. The solution is to define a true (single dimensional) score for measuring performance for the organization or division (and it must be consistent with the organization's strategy). Given this we then encourage managers to use measures of the drivers of performance to understand better how to maximize their score. And as long as their score is defined properly, (and for lower levels in the organization it will generally not be value) this will enhance their contribution to the firm".

11 See Macey, J.R., (2008), *Corporate Governance. Promises Kept, Promises Broken*, New Jersey, Princeton University Press; and Stout, Lynn, (2012), *The Shareholder Myth. How putting Shareholders first harms Investors, Corporations, and the Public*, San Francisco, Berrett-Koehler Publ.

12 One of the authors, Peter, still remembers the clear instruction by his American superior at the IFC-World Bank in Hong Kong that once someone at IFC is sent to the board of an organization to secure the implementation and execution of good governance principles, he or she does not represent the shareholder who sent them – IFC as an investor – but he or she will independently look after the interests of the organization itself. In other words, ideally, a board is a fiduciary who looks after the organization towards fulfilling its financial and non-financial objectives. And the shareholders are expected to be residual beneficiaries after all others have been taken care of.

13 Oberholzer-Gee, F., (2021b: 19), *Better, Simpler Strategy. A value-based guide to exceptional performance*, Cambridge MA, Harvard Business Review Press.

14 As we further explain in chapter five.

15 Oberholzer-Gee, F., (2021a), "Eliminate Strategic Overload. How to select fewer initiatives with greater impact", Harvard Business Review, May-June: 89–97.

16 Verhezen, P.; Riyana Hardjapamekas, E. & P. Notowidigdo, (2012), *Is corporate governance relevant? How good corporate governance practices affect Indonesian organizations*, Jakarta, University of Indonesia Press; Khanna, T. & K. Palepu, (2006), "Strategies that fit emerging markets", *Harvard Business Review*, Vol. 84: 60–69; Khanna, T. & J.W. Rifkin, (2001), "Estimating the performance effects of business groups in emerging markets", *Strategic Management Journal*, Vol. 22: 45–74; and Khanna, V. & Zyla, R., (2013), Survey says. . .corporate governance matters to investors in emerging markets companies, *IFC World Bank Paper*.

17 Bebchuk, L.; Kraakman, R. & G. Triantis, (2000), "Stock pyramids, cross ownership, and dual class equity: the creation and agency costs of separating control from cash flow rights", in Morck, R.K. (ed), *Concentrated Corporate Ownership*, Chicago, University of Chicago Press; Chang, Y.C.; Kao, M-S. & A. Kuo, (2014), "The Influences of governance quality on equity-based entry mode choice: The strengthening role of family control", *International Business Review*, Vol. 23: 1008–1020; Kim, K.A.; Kitsabunnarat, P. & J.R. Nofsinger, (2004), "Ownership and operating performance in an emerging market: evidence from Thai IPO firms", *The Journal of Corporate Finance*, Vol. 10: 322–381; Kim, J.B. & C.H. Yi, (2006), "Ownership structure, business group affiliation, listing status, and earnings management: evidence form Korea", *Contemporary Accounting Research*, Vol. 23(2): 265–276; and Morck, R. & B. Yeung, (2004), "Corporate Governance and Family Control", *Global Corporate Governance Forum – World Bank, Discussion Paper no 1*.

18 Verhezen, P., (2015), *The Vulnerability of Corporate Reputation. Leadership for Sustainable Long-term Value*, Berkshire, Palgrave Pivot Publishing.

19 See Verhezen, P.; Williamson, I.O.; Crosby, M. & N. Soebagjo, (2016), *Doing Business ASEAN markets. Leadership challenges and Governance solutions across borders*, London, Palgrave MacMillan.
20 See a report by Credit Lyonnais, (2001).
21 Brown, (2004); Brown, R.A., (2006), "Indonesian Corporations, Cronyism, and Corruption", *Modern Asian Studies*, Vol. 40 (4): 953–992; and Brown, L.; Caylor, M.,(2006), "Corporate Governance and Firm Valuation", *Journal Accountancy Public Policy*, Vol.25: 409–434.
22 Dyck, A. & L. Zingales, (2004), "Private benefits of control: an international comparison", *Journal of Finance*, Vol. 59: 537–600.
23 See Meyer, E., (2014), The Culture Map, New York, Public Affairs.
24 Bennedsen, M.; Hoffmann, A.; Hoffmann, R.; Hrnjic, E. & Y. Wiwattanakantang, (2013), East meets West: Rotschild's Investment in Indonesia's Bakrie Group, INSEAD Case no 113-065-1.
25 And as a matter of full disclose, both authors have worked for or with the Bakrie Group in various positions Dr. Tanri Abeng briefly worked as CEO and later as advisor to the board of the Bakrie group in the late 80s, whereas Prof. Peter Verhezen was an IBRA official – on behalf of the Ministry of Finance in Indonesia and IMF – mandated to debt restructure some of the debt of the Bakrie group in 1998–2001.
26 See Verhezen, P., (2018), "Is Indonesia serious about corporate governance?" *Strategic Review*, Vol. 8(3): 48–59; and Verhezen, P.; Williamson, I.O. & N. Soebagjo, (2018), "Living less dangerously in Indonesia", *Strategic Review*, January-March: 54–67.
27 Verhezen, P. & G. Martin, (2018), Corporate Governance & Ethical Behavior affecting Performance: Propositions and Peculiarities at Indonesian Firms within its Institutional context, *Melbourne Business School Working Paper, financed by IFC World Bank*.
28 Each year foreign direct investment (FDI) realization in Indonesia tends to grow, mounting to IDR 111.7 trillion (or USD 7.72 billion) in 2nd quarter of 2021.
29 The MSCI Emerging Markets Index was launched on Jan 01, 2001. Data prior to the launch date is back-tested data (i.e. calculations of how the index might have performed over that time period had the index existed). There are frequently material differences between back-tested performance and actual results. Past performance – whether actual or back-tested – is no indication or guarantee of future performance. The Emerging market countries include: Argentina, Brazil, Chile, China, Colombia, Czech Republic, Egypt, Greece, Hungary, India, Indonesia, Korea, Kuwait, Malaysia, Mexico, Pakistan, Peru, Philippines, Poland, Qatar, Russia, Saudi Arabia, South Africa, Taiwan, Thailand, Turkey and United Arab Emirates.
30 Mobius, M. (2003). "Corporate governance", in Cornelius, P.K. & Kogut, B. *Corporate governance and capital flows in a global economy*, New York, Oxford University Press, 401–412; Mobius, M., (2012a), *Passport to Profits. Why the Next Investment Windfalls will be found abroad – and How to grab your share*, Singapore, John Wiley & Sons; and Mobius, M., (2012b), *The Little Book on Emerging Markets. How to make money in the world's fastest growing markets*, Singapore, John Wiley & Sons.
31 See Khanna, T. & K. Palepu, (2000a), "Is group affiliation profitable in emerging markets? An analysis of diversified Indian business groups", *Journal of Finance*, April Vol. 55(20): 867–893; Khanna, T. & K. Palepu, (2000b), "The future of business groups in emerging markets: long-run evidence from Chile", *Academy of Management Journal*, Vol. 43: 268–285; Khanna, T. & K. Palepu, (2006), "Strategies that fit emerging markets", *Harvard Business Review*, Vol. 84: 60–69; and Khanna, T. & J.W. Rifkin, (2001), "Estimating the performance effects of business groups in emerging markets", *Strategic Management Journal*, Vol. 22: 45–74.
32 Verhezen, P.; Williamson, I.O.; Crosby, M. & N. Soebagjo, (2016), *Doing Business ASEAN markets. Leadership challenges and Governance solutions across borders*, London, Palgrave MacMillan.

Chapter 2
Universal Corporate Governance Practices Across Borders?
International Expectations Versus Asian Interpretation of Governance

> Nothing is more important to the well-being of a corporation than its board [of directors]. The board, by law, has the responsibility for the overall performance of the business. It has the power to appoint the management of the enterprise, to delegate to it specific responsibilities and to oversee the strategic decision and the setting of the long-term goals for the company. It is a self-governing body that has the power, within very few limits, to manage its own affairs. In short, the board, by law, is the decision-making body of the corporation.[. . .]. Knowing how and why boards make decisions is fundamental to an understanding of why some corporations succeed and others do not.   R. Leblanc & J. Gillies, (2005), *Inside the boardroom*

What are those best governance practices? We prefer to speak of proven generic principles that underpin good corporate governance and well-functioning boards. When referring to "best corporate governance principles" it sounds we all have figured it out and have reached the desired outcome. In reality, organizational learning is continuously improving our practices. Good corporate governance is therefore a work-in-process, it is an ongoing activity. "Best" practices imply that one has reached an endpoint, instead of willing to look for "better" practices.

Should equity investors limit themselves to well-governed companies only, or should they look for (potentially undervalued) companies with specific governance attributes? In order to answer this question without getting bogged down in detailed legal requirements, we need to first understand what the basics are of those good corporate governance practices, and how actors use their power and networks to influence decisions within the company. This chapter will take *an institutional investment perspective* to find out why and how good corporate governance at a firm makes a lot of sense for any investor, especially to protect them against inappropriate and illegal behaviour at the company. We need to acknowledge why corporate governance has a slightly different interpretation in Indonesia and Asia in general compared to an Anglo-Saxon investment context from which a lot of global investment funds hail.

Because of the ongoing globalization of financial investments and international trade, corporate governance has become a mainstream concern when making investment or trade decisions in boardrooms and policy circles around the globe. Recent corporate debacles and fraud, economic and financial crises, and the growing global interdependency of financial markets have caused the heightened interest in corporate governance. Indeed, the 1997 Asian crisis and 2008 global financial crisis have reinforced how *failures in corporate governance* (and public governance) can harm shareholders and even ruin firms and adversely affect whole economies, both in the developed and emerging markets. Let us get started with assessing those governance principles.

1 "Good" Corporate Governance Principles

Although we clearly argue there does not exist an "one-for-all-best-solution", in-depth research and practical experience indicate that some generic governance principles are still universally valid. However, these governance principles that underpin any well-functioning engaged board need to be contextualized in each individual (national) jurisdiction. The following four principles (1) *transparency*, (2) *fairness*, (3) *accountability*, and (4) *responsibility* reflect all proper governance rules that will need to be implemented by boards at any company, be it Western or Asian, state owned or family owned, publicly listed or privately kept, small or multinational. Those principles are strongly recommended as a guiding beacon to be implemented in any of those specific contexts. This chapter will indicate why and how those four principles – known as the OECD principles of good corporate governance – will help organizations to reduce risk, to comply to the rule of law, to get better access to capital and talent, to enable organization to create trust for additional investment, and ultimately to steer the organization towards new business opportunities with available capital and acquired new knowledge. We will indicate how neighbouring countries – Indonesia, Singapore, Malaysia and Australia, the last three adhering to a common law system – can significantly differ in corporate governance regulation despite the adherence to the same fundamental four principles of good corporate governance. Confusing? Well, as said, those generic principles need to be fit in to the prevailing legal rules and culture, both at a national, cultural and organizational level. The latter is the focus of this book.

Let us not forget that – despite the uniformity of the generic four principles – there is a huge gap between civic law and common law.[1] Civic law as applied in Indonesia is inherited from the old Dutch colonial system. A civic law system is also implemented in many other parts of Asia, which finds its origin in the legal systems of the European continent. Some would refer to the Napoleonistic regulations now 200 years old. At the other hand, the common law system prevails in Singapore and Australia, two relatively young countries that got their legal system inherited from UK-USA. Also Malaysia and Hong Kong adhere to the UK common law system. Under the UK common law system, historically grown as a battle between the English King and the aristocracy[2] and later joined by the "peasant" class, individual property rights (including *in casu* shareholders' rights) are better protected than under a more interventional civic law system.

Corporate governance practices as they are implemented in Indonesia, follow the Dutch legal system, and under such institutional context government interventions cannot be precluded, but hopefully constrained within reasonable limits. Not only the legal historical background and jurisdictional context play an important role in the implementation of those "good corporate governance" principles, the specific organizational perspective will also colour the interpretation of those generic principles.

Let us first define what corporate governance could mean. According to the influential definition by Sir Adrian Cadburry, he interpreted it as "corporate governance is concerned with holding the balance between economic and social goals and between individual and communal goals . . . . The aim is to align as nearly as possible the interests of individuals, corporations and society" (1999). The two influential financial economists Shleifer and Vishny – who worked both for the IMF – describe corporate governance as "way in which suppliers of finance to corporations assure themselves of getting a return on their investment" (1997). Oxford governance expert Professor Mallin defines corporate governance as being "concerned with both the shareholders and the internal aspects of the company, such as internal control, and the external aspects, such as an organization's relationship with its shareholders and other stakeholders. Corporate governance is also seen as an essential mechanism helping the company to attain its corporate objectives and monitoring performance is a key element in achieving these objectives".[3]

We see *corporate governance* as *a set of relationships between a company's board, its shareholders and other stakeholders, providing the structure through which the objectives of the company are set, how the means of attaining those objectives and the monitoring of performance are determined.* Governance may not completely prevent misconduct or misdeeds, but it can actually improve the way a corporation is run. Let us now decipher those *good [international] corporate governance principles.*

1.1 The Four Generic (OECD) Governance Principles

The OECD principles for instance define good corporate governance as a set of relationships between a company's management, its board, its shareholders and other stakeholders. Corporate governance not only provides the structure through which the objectives of the company are set, but also the means of attaining those objectives and the ultimate organizational power to monitor performance of the organization. The OECD's Corporate Governance Principles prescribe that a corporate governance framework should ensure the strategic guidance of the company, the effective monitoring of management by the board, and the board's accountability to the company and the shareholders. Indeed, corporate governance can be perceived as the collection of control mechanisms that an organization adopts to prevent or dissuade potentially self-interested managers from engaging in activities detrimental to the welfare of shareholders and stakeholders.

There is clear consensus on the generic principles of what constitutes good corporate governance.[4] Somehow, these generic guidelines can be brought back to four generic corporate governance principles of *transparency, fairness & equitable treatment of shareholders, accountability* and *responsibility*. This OECD set has been taken over and "contextualized" by the Indonesian code for good corporate governance. How do we translate those into a business context at a board? Good governance assures that:

(1) *a basis for an effective corporate governance framework is ensured* – the corporate governance framework should promote transparent and efficient markets, be consistent with the rule of law and clearly articulate the division of responsibilities among different supervisory, regulatory and enforcement authorities;

(2) *disclosure and transparency* – the corporate governance framework should ensure that timely and accurate disclosure is made on all material matters regarding the corporation, including the financial situation, performance, ownership, and governance of the company. Transparency & disclosure of [audited] information, which is closely related to the listing requirements of stock exchanges across borders which will be the topic of next chapter. Transparency ensures timely accurate disclosure on material matters, including the financial situation and performance, the ownership, and specific corporate governance features.

(3) *accountability and the rights of shareholders and key ownership functions* – the corporate governance framework should protect and facilitate the exercise of shareholders' rights. The basic shareholder rights should include the right to secure methods of ownership registration, to convey or transfer shares, to obtain relevant and material information on the corporation on a timely and regular basis, to participate and vote in general shareholder meetings, to elect and remove members of the board, and to share in the profits of the corporation. Accountability of fiduciary duties by board members to shareholders to be assessed in more detail in next chapter. The feature of accountability refers to the notion that the leadership and management is accountable to the board for its strategy execution and performance, and for all its organizational activities. And as management is accountable to the board, the board itself is accountable to the share-owners;

(4) *fairness and the equitable treatment of shareholders* – the corporate governance framework should ensure the equitable treatment of all shareholders, including minority and foreign shareholders. All shareholders should have the opportunity to obtain effective redress for violation of their rights. Fairness aims to protect the shareholders' right. Investors in those sophisticated mature markets – in comparison with Asian markets – do not have to worry too much about governance principles at the firm level, since the regulator – the SEC in New York for instance – already imposes rather high governance standards on those listed firms. The board is supposed to treat all shareowners – including minority owners – equitably. In addition, leadership should be remunerated fairly according to the industry standards and aligned with the performance of the company. However, in the USA, founders in mainly tech start-ups are often able to keep control over the organization through a special governance structure, as in dual-class share structures.[5] Investors are still lured into such companies because of promised profitability or a potentially much higher share price, as in

the case of Facebook, Google, Twitter, Airbnb and others for instance. Hence why in the USA, such controlling minority shareholder structures commonly occur through the use of dual-class shares – not to be confused with a dual-tier board structure. In such companies, one makes a distinction between voting rights and cash flow rights. Founders are usually keeping a controlling vote in "their" companies although their cash flow rights may likely be diluted in the process of attracting public investment (through an IPO to start with) as in a publicly listed company with many shareholders. The wedge between the prices of the different classes of stock reflects the private benefits of control enjoyed by the high-vote shareholders, most often founders and initial angel investors. However, research shows that controlling minority shareholder structures are associated with increased agency costs and reduced value in the USA.[6] Today, with incredibly highly valued tech stocks at the NYSE/Nasdaq, the earlier research may need to be amended. Having said this, it is also clear that most Asian stock markets do not allow for such dual-class share structures, though being listed in more than one exchange is permitted in most Asian jurisdictions provided the firm complies to the respective listing requirements.

(5) *the role of stakeholders in corporate governance, and the responsibilities of a board* – the corporate governance framework should recognize the rights of stakeholders established by law, societal expectations, or through mutual agreements and encourage active co-operation between corporations and stakeholders in creating wealth, jobs, as well as safeguarding the economic and ecological sustainability of the organization.

It is clear that the four generic principles of transparency, fairness and equality of shareholders, accountability and responsibility is founded on a proper and fertile governance framework that allows them to flourish. Yes, those principles are generic on purpose. They need to be translated into concrete liveable practices that resonate with the employees, investors, and customers of the firm.

1.2 International Investors Pursuing Good Governance while Reducing Entrenchment

Corporate governance refers to the system of check and balances within an organization that takes optimal strategic decisions to create value, and that monitors its executive directors to execute strategies according to the objectives, and to reduce risks where deemed necessary. Creating and sustaining organizational value fundamentally requires trust and cooperation – expressed in the chemistry – among its board members, not just mere [legal] compliance to rules and regulations. Chairmen and CEOs are also aware that they, and not just the regulators, may need to lead the way forward. Massive corporate governance changes have swept through corporate boardrooms, affecting the way companies report earnings, pay executives, and manage board and societal expectations.

All those factors affect the national level of good corporate governance, where the more stringent rules in the USA and the UK – from which a lot of global investment funds hail – have been considered as the benchmark for other countries. Both the New York Stock Exchange (and the Nasdaq) and the London Stock Exchange (as well as other forms of securitization) have been historically seen as major institutional places for liquid global investment. This led them to become two global financial hubs, putting them in a comfortable position to determine the overall mainstream governance principles for global investment. However, Asia has been growing fast with incredible wealth creation in the region, giving them more cloud to start influencing the overall governance "practices" – led by China nowadays, while both Hong Kong and especially Singapore have been seen as safe investment heavens and thus the financial hubs for Asia till recently. But also other ASEAN countries among which their biggest member, Indonesia, start to gain international influence. However, our focus is on the firm level that can attract investment. Indeed, national or international investors can have a direct impact on firms by imposing certain minimal governance standards, independent of the national governance requirements. Usually both the national regulation that determine the overall country's risk in terms of governance, as well as a firm's implementation of particular governance standards is seen as crucial for any investor.

It is important to note that the typical *"agency" problem* – as it is defined in a Western context – is less a concern in Indonesia and other Asian countries. Certainly under managerial capitalism, but also under institutional capitalism, boards in the USA can become quite entrenched[7] in making (sometimes opaquely perceived) decisions that are often aligned with the CEO and its 'friendly' board – the opposite of being independent. Although it is obvious that the top executives may use their privileged position and access to asymmetric information as a way to optimize their own (short term) objectives instead of "maximizing shareholder value", it is exactly the task of a [supervisory] board to oversee and thus monitor the performances of the top executives. Executives at both state owned enterprises (SOEs) and privately held enterprises make decisions on a daily basis that are supposed to serve the organization. However, quite often those decisions may better themselves at the expense of other parties related to the firm: those costs are known as *agency costs*, which find its roots in the separation of ownership and top management.

A system of check and balances – the basis of corporate governance – is assumed to lessen those agency costs by controlling and monitoring top management. In an Asian context, however, the typical agency challenge between managers and owners is often minimized by the relative huge (concentrated) power of an inspiring and revered (founding] patriarch, or a minister of state-owned enterprises. Another important challenge lurks in the Asian shadows when sitting on a board in Asia: how to curb the potential abuse of power of the controlling family or state, the ultimate owners of a public listed company or state owned enterprise, at the expense of minority shareholders, be it local or international and foreign shareholders. Such potential abuse of power by the controlling and entrenched board members undermine foremost the fairness principle but also the other three governance principles.

The entrenchment by controlling shareholders often results in conditions that are ideally suited for possible expropriation of disadvantaged often minority shareholders. Hence why the option of "voicing" concerns has hardly any effect in Indonesia, and "loyalty" may not be a real option for those minority non-equal partners either, making "exit" the only other option for investors, adding to the already inherent volatile market swings.[8] This inherent asymmetry is aggravated by the existence of particular governance structures and relationship-based governance or network culture perspectives in Indonesia and Asia in general that play in the hands of those actors – alias members of both the Board of Directors (BoD) and the Board of Commissioners (BoC) – who can fall back on relationships with the powerful elite.

Academic research indicates that in countries with relatively low legal protection of minority investors, controlling shareholders may be inclined to expropriate assets at the expense of these minority shareholders, resulting in "private benefits of control". This kind of destructive entrenchment can be materialized by both powerful families who disregards minority shareholder rights, as well as political involvement and unnecessary mingling in daily operations by ministers at boards of state owned enterprises. The *risk of expropriation* of minority shareholders by large controlling shareholders is an important *principal-principal* problem in most emerging countries, and even more so in Indonesia where that gap between control and cash flow rights may be less outspoken, and where both voting and cash flow rights are relatively among the highest (concentrated ownership) in Asia. This possible *entrenchment* between owners, boards, and to a lesser extent managers – called the *tunnelling effect* – often outweighs the possible alignment effect in these family businesses. Tunnelling is accomplished when resources from the [listed] company is channeled to the controlling shareholder through intercompany transactions and dealings whose terms favour the company in which the controlling shareholder owns the larger equity stake. When an insider [supervisory] board (BoC) – "following orders from the boss", often the family patriarch – is heavily entrenched with entrenched with top executive management (BoD), there is an increased potential for expropriation of valuable corporate assets into a privately held holding structure far away from minority shareholders, [often illegally] depriving them their legal rights in a family business. In state owned enterprises, the risk of political involvement and entrenchment is always present when the state intervenes or appoints board members as political alliances at those boards. Or when the minister as the "owner" of the organization regularly intervenes in the board's functioning. We believe that the state as owner should limit itself to appoint the right supervisory board members and possibly the CEO (or President Director) who then should properly govern, lead where necessary and make sure that the executive board (the BoD) pursues the best strategy for the firm in a professional and consistent manner – and in line with its fiduciary duties.

In Indonesia – and most Asian contexts – the capital market is characterized by very concentrated ownership: be it by a controlling family[9] or a mighty state, which may potentially squash minority shareholders' rights. Most of the board members of these companies are consequently insiders, and not independent of the controlling shareholders. It is therefore of the utmost importance to safeguard equal shareholders' rights, proper accountability, and transparency or guarantee proper disclosure of [relevant financial and non-financial] information. In these Asian markets, minority rights are often not adequately protected. Moreover, in Indonesia (and in Asia in general), there is a hardly an active take-over market, and new market capitalization is 'underdeveloped' compared to their more sophisticated and more liquid western counterparts.

The use of reputable auditors and exclusion of related party transactions in the shareholder agreement indicate an activity with a clear objective of creating a *signalling effect*. Indeed, our research indicates that the presence of reputable auditors (big *Four Auditors*) has a positive effect on the financial performance, which is likely due to the (perceived) improved transparency and disclosure.[10] Considering the weak legal enforcement and less than stellar protection of individual shareholder rights under Indonesian law, these listed firms on the Indonesian Stock Exchange signal their willingness to be more transparent and thus reliable or trustworthy by engaging a reputable third party intermediary. Similarly, our findings reveal a positive effect on the return of assets with the implementation of strict rules to constrain or forbid *Related Party Transactions* that could be interpreted as a proxy for potential expropriation, collusion or outright corrupt behaviour. In other words, by having proper mechanisms and procedures in place that will limit the potential of corruption or expropriation or tunnelling of cash flow or assets, the Indonesian firm indicates its willingness to limit unfair practices or to curb possible corruption.

Moreover, a potential *conflict of interest* between a [majority] principal versus [minority] principal problem can be detrimental to the long term objectives of the organization, especially in [listed] state-owned enterprises. Obviously, majority owners – be it the family patriarch or state – can make the final strategic or investment decisions, but that should not be at the expense of minority shareholders. How then (1) to reign in this king-entrepreneur who heads the board while still be able to tap into the founder's expertise and experience, or (2) how to limit the potential interventions through "parachuted" politically appointed commissioners at State Owned Enterprises (SOEs)? In other words, *how to make (Indonesian and other Asian) boards more effective while reducing potential entrenchment?*

We are convinced that some firm-specific governance attributes may neutralize the country-level overall weak governance standards in a number of Asian economies, though that requires an intimate understanding of a specific market. And not all international funds have that expertise in house. For instance, the California Pension Fund (CalPERS) is always on the look for global business opportunities to invest their USD 420 billion disposable investment across borders. First they look at the overall attractive governance rating for each country. If a nation on a scale of 5 does not make it the

2 cut for instance, CalPERS will automatically shun that country for being too risky, even with the presence of well governed firms in those governance underperforming countries. In other words, good national standards attract money. Secondly, once a country is seen as "acceptable from a governance perspective", the fund managers will look for specific well governed firm since that provides a double protection against perceived illicit and unethical behaviour. However, with the increased wealth within Asian borders, firms will likely become less dependent on those "Western" investors and make look for intra-Asian trade with a slightly different view on what corporate governance may mean, and what is expected from those firms. The longer time horizon of both family business and state-owned enterprises could lure institutional investors who like to "park" their money in promising and prospective long term opportunities in a growing region with improving corporate governance standards.

Although there does not exist one ideal board structure or composition for all situations, we argue that one can rather easily distinguish "good" from "bad" or even "ugly" boards. Some of those less efficient "ugly" boards are visualised in Figure 9. One of the main objectives of a good board is to function as specialized guardians of the organization and their assets. In case of active owners – as we see in an Asian family context, but equally in state owned enterprises – the board is often affected by the involvement and active mingling of the majority owner, be it the founding patriarch or his siblings, or a minister representing the state. Too much involvement by a board in the daily operations should be avoided at any costs. The board's function is to supervise and to coach top executive management, not to operate on their behalf – unless in the exceptional case of a major crisis that may have implicated top management. On the other hands, boards rubberstamping the decisions by management is not ideal either – because it lacks proper oversight and can easily lead to aggravating the agency problem, even invite selfish behaviour or outright corruption on behalf of top management without proper supervision. Therefore, engaged boards are highly recommendable, in any jurisdiction (cf Figure 8).

Fortunately, especially after the Asian crisis (1997–2001), we see boards making huge strides to improve governance in Southeast Asia and China. No doubt that firms in Indonesia and other emerging markets have dramatically improved their corporate governance, partially under the pressure of the regulators, but also because of the professionalization of the board. A third reason is the increasing pressure of institutional investors in Asian firms that highlights the importance of good corporate governance practices. This improvement may look quite distinctively different from what is expected in US-based firms, but an improvement nonetheless. For instance, US investors will seek to increase the independency of the board, whereas in Indonesia implemented proper corporate governance procedures and processes outweigh the potential impact of a so-called 'formalistic' independent board.

For many decades, Indonesian boards were often claimed as a "trophy" by the members, or a gesture of goodwill from the majority owners to put you on the board

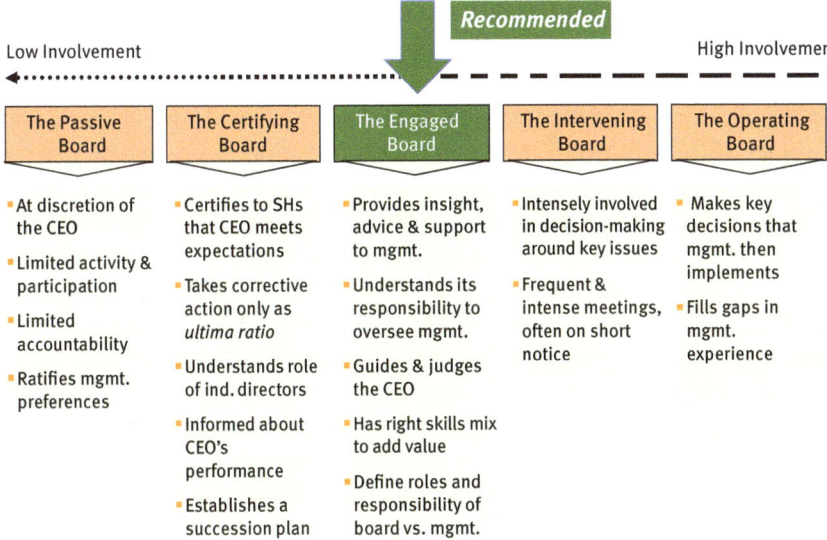

Figure 8: What board to prefer?.
Source: based on Nadler, "Building better boards", *Harvard Business Review*

with the understanding that you'll "comply" with their will, making it a paper-board or a rubber stamp board as seen in Figure 9.

Figure 9: Non-performing and unprofessional boards.

And in all truthfulness, similar "trophy board" perception still continues to exist in some Western elite circles as well. Obviously, it is preferably under any circumstance to avoid the "bad" and the "ugly" and opt for a functioning and engaged board that fulfils its fiduciary duties.

2 Contextualizing those Governance Principles in an Asian Context

The board is expected to accommodate and fulfil three main functions – supervision, coaching and safeguarding leadership continuity. The principles are clear and are widely accepted among the institutional investment and corporate governance scholars' community. However, among certain groups in Asia, corporate governance is seen as a government-related nuisance to which companies need to comply. Yes, most corporate leaders in Indonesia and quite a number of other Asian countries (with the likely exception of Singapore and Hong Kong) see corporate governance as legal governmental regulation to comply with. Governance rules are therefore perceived as an expense rather than an 'investment' to reduce risks and prevent reputational or other disasters (Figure 9). Based on our academic research and personal experience, we believe that corporate governance practices should be perceived as a useful way to assess the performance of the organization while focusing on reducing a variety of potential risks.

2.1 Global Competition for International Funds based on Good Corporate Governance Practices?

The last decade has become fiercer in terms of global competition, while at the same time, we have seen a dramatic shift eastward towards Asian growth markets. What should foreign investors and international corporations be aware of when doing business in Indonesia? What policies and practices will positively affect the competitive advantage of [Indonesian] firms in an ASEAN and even in a more global economic context, and how to enhance their competitive legitimacy? What are the particular pitfalls and challenges international business leaders are facing in Indonesia and ASEAN countries? More particularly, how do executives and supervisory boards (the "Board of Commissioners") effectively deal with or even attempt to strategically take advantage of *institutional weaknesses* without jeopardizing their reputation? And how can good corporate governance help to instil *organizational values and norms* that positively affect its performance, and guide corporate leadership to avoid the usual institutional pitfalls, while at the same time strengthen their organizations? In other words, implementing "good" corporate governance practices may be a necessary first important buffer to safeguard shareholder and stakeholder rights, and reduce potential threatening risks.

Under a narrow definition of corporate governance, the focus is on the rules in capital markets governing equity investments, which includes listing requirements, insider dealing arrangements, disclosure and accounting rules, fair remuneration, and protections of minority shareholder rights. This *Agency Theory* or *Shareholder Model* sees the firm as a **nexus of contracts** between principals or owners and agents each pursuing their own interest which often conflict. The *Agency model* assumes isolated bi-lateral contracts between principals and agents, focusing on contractual efficiency whereby corporate governance mechanisms aim at reducing this agency cost by aligning management to shareholders' interest, providing legal provisions such as information disclosure and accounting requirements to provide control, and efficient markets for corporate control. In addition, in Western countries, stock options were granted to those hired professional executives in order to allegedly make them think like owners. Not with overall success though, as numerous failures and crises in the West testify. However, we could easily ask what kind of shareholders the board is representing? Does the board need to jump to the fancies of short-term investors (as for instance hedge funds) or does it represent the interests of long-term investors? In an Indonesian context, this may not be a big issue since boards of listed Indonesian companies usually represent the power structures of the founding family, big institutional investors, sovereign wealth funds, or the state – who usually have a longer term strategic interest.

A broader definition of corporate governance – as expressed by the OECD principles of corporate governance (2004) –stipulate that all shareholders should be treated equally and that board members should act on a fully informed basis, in good faith, with due diligence and care, and in the best interest of the company. Broadening the stakes beyond shares, allows the stakeholder theory to recognize that the effectiveness of corporate governance practices also depends on the influence stakeholders may have on the firm. Corporate governance then becomes the range of institutions, policies and power decision-making processes that are involved in making an organization function to create value. Institutions become the informal and formal rules of the game which usually serve the interests and ideas of the most powerful groups. Institutions or powerful actors can become a self-sustaining system of shared beliefs about a salient way in which the game is repeatedly played in their own interests. Corporate governance can therefore be conceptualized as a **nexus of the relationships** among *stakeholders and shareholders – or crucial powerful actors – in the process of decision-making and control over the firm's assets and resources.*

International or local investors who focus on emerging markets have to deal with considerable *information asymmetries* in those less transparent emerging markets that could negatively affect the expected long-term income or return on the investment. But asymmetries of a different nature. Good corporate governance practices aiming to reduce those asymmetries assumedly have a positive impact on an enterprise's performance both in the developed world and even more so in rather volatile emerging markets. Particularly in an emerging economy like Indonesia with rather weak legal institutions, the challenge for foreign investors does not lie in the traditional agency problem between ownership and powerful top executives as in most Anglo-Saxon advanced countries, but rather in the tangible and intangible costs resulting from information asymmetry between local majority owners and foreign or local minority owners. The potential conflict may arise as result of concentrated ownership whereby the majority founding family or patriarch, institutional sovereign funds, or state, may not regard minority investors as equal partners. The latter has hardly any recourse within a context that is associated with underdeveloped or not-fully 'functioning' legal institutions under a civic legal system, carrying a significant cost when being operational in or investing in emerging markets.

The single focus of the shareholder model, however, seems to overlook the linkages or complementarities between culture and institutions in contexts that are fundamentally different from the mainstream Anglo-Saxon context. Ideally, the board represents the organization, and not the shareholder who has put them in charge. Indonesian companies within a civic [Continental] law context have adopted a hybrid firm-level formulation of a "bundle" of corporate governance practices[11] that suits their interests, characterized by institutional idiosyncrasies within Indonesia. Sometimes, a set of informal practices. Opaquely structured investments in a pyramid construction for instance keep the holding company outside preying public eyes. These informal practices may shape, constrain and interact with the boundaries of corporate law, and sometimes even substitute in filling certain "institutional voids". Indeed, in the absence of specialist intermediaries, trustworthy regulatory systems, or reliable contract-enforcing mechanisms or an independent court system, the traditional patronage mechanisms so prevailing in Asia, may [continue to] kick in and help the firm to survive. And this, despite all the potential negative side-effects.

The corporate governance definition as applied in emerging markets emphasizes how to protect outside investors against potential expropriation of capital resources by insiders such as the founding patriarch or monopolistic power of the state, or how potential conflicts of interest between various corporate claimholders can be reduced. However, such a corporate governance approach does not say anything about the socio-political, coalition-forming among multiple actors and the institutional embeddedness of a firm in a broader Indonesian or Asian context. In other words, merely looking at the implementation of certain minimum legal corporate governance requirements – for instance, hiring one third independent commissioners on the Board of Commissioners, the existence of an audit subcommittee with an independent chair, the appointment of professional executives, gender diversity, explicit statements on quorum, or having voting procedures explicitly defined in the bylaws etc – does not guarantee proper corporate governance standards. The company may comply to the letter of the corporate law, but not necessarily to the spirit of corporate governance standards. We argue that good corporate governance is definitely not the same as a tick-the-box compliance exercise, or complying to the letter of the rule. Rather good corporate governance reflects a mindset of honesty, openness, accountability and responsible decision-making. That's when it will have a significant effect on the firm's success.

2.2 An Institutional Perspective on Corporate Governance in Indonesia

Unfortunately, quite a number of tycoons still consider corporate governance as a mere [expensive] compliance exercise to legal rules: be it complying with the regulator OJK for listed [financial] companies in Indonesia, or to corporate company law and other specific hard governance rules or "soft" regulations.

The reality is different though. It is clear that the necessary reforms after the Asian crisis of 1997–2001 has been formulized in the Indonesian Corporate Governance Roadmap. Indeed, it is precisely because of the obvious advantages of good corporate governance that the World Bank's IFC has cooperated with the Indonesian regulator OJK – the Indonesian Financial Services Authority – and has done a similar assessment in other Asian countries. IFC co-developed a roadmap for implementing good corporate governance practices in Indonesia in 2004 (with an upgrade in 2018[12]) – broadly seeking to achieve the following: (1) strengthening the supervisory role of company boards; (2) improving quality of disclosure by companies (increased company transparency); and (3) greater protections for shareholders and stakeholders.[13]

Every year, the Indonesian Institute for Corporate Governance and other reputable institutions in Indonesia grant corporate governance awards; we wonder whether all the data should be taken at face value.[14] Let the market determine whether those winners deserve our administration. Let us leave the covid pandemic aside to focus on widely well-governed companies. What does seem to be clear from these annual corporate governance awards though is that among the top 20 best governed listed companies, about half are the strictly regulated top banks in Indonesia.[15]

It is not too difficult to find empirical evidence that stronger corporate governance practices lower the cost of capital, reduce risk, and positively influence firm value. However, we need to slightly shade these findings because high performing Korean firms for instance – as in some form of "reverse governance" – may adopt good governance practices to signal the intention of good behaviour by their powerful insider families or chaebol towards outside minority (foreign) investors. Similarly, our findings in Indonesia seem to also indicate that some organizations applying minimum corporate governance standards want to make a good name for themselves, and use this enhanced corporate reputation to attract additional (foreign) investment.[16] Obviously such a causal relationship is hard to "scientifically" prove. The implementation of particular "best corporate governance" practices could be "signals" to lure [foreign] investors. IndoFood, for instance, – especially after its restructuring since the 1998 Asian crisis – has been deemed as well governed over the last decade and a half. Those familiar with Indonesian history know how the Salim family was able to gain competitive advantage in Indonesia, not the least through cleverly benefiting from a special relationship with those in power, in a context of rather weak institutions, prior to the starting democratization process two decades ago. Nonetheless, the perception of having implemented good corporate governance has helped them to gain a good reputation among foreign investors.[17] The late patriarch's lofty and emotionally appealing narrative to "feed the nation" did obviously not harm this perception either. Today Salim's publicly listed Indofood has a good reputation in terms of good corporate governance and its long term financial prospects and performance. Obviously, two desirable characteristics for any investor.

The institutional context of weak legal enforcement and concentrated ownership in Indonesia often results in potential *conflicts of interest* between majority owners and minority shareholders on the one hand, and in unethical if not *corrupt behavior* and *violations* of *individual property rights* on the other hand. Talking with numerous owners of listed companies, entrepreneurs and foreign investors – and these authors having played an active role in some of those firms – seem to reconfirm the gut feeling that all parties seek to protect themselves from [weak] legal institutions where *potential conflict of interests* between majority and minority shareholders often occur, and where *corruption* and *property rights violations* at all levels of society are still rife.[18] How to address those "voids" of illegitimate rent-seeking behaviour?

Should one apply some universal "context-free" governance principles as recommended by international institutions or (international) law firms? Although legal interpretations may seek to implement some "universal" governance standards or generic road maps, it seems that no "one best corporate governance way" really exists as in minimally complying with certain standards guarantees full transparency, disclosure, equal shareholders' rights or full accountability. Indeed, there is no single global governance standard or codex that could be literally applied to any situation. Hence why "convergence" of corporate governance rules across national borders is not priority for most policy makers and regulators at this point in time.

The effectiveness of corporate governance practices varies due to the institutional and cultural idiosyncrasies of different nations. The legal environment, the ownership structures, systems of governance and the functioning of the board of directors are often intertwined in Indonesia. For instance, Indonesia for instance presents a unique cultural setting in a dynamic economy with the potential to advance the well-being of approximately 270 million people. Yet, we do not have a theoretical framework that explicitly addresses why corporate governance practices differ across countries or over time, and we consequently lack in-depth knowledge concerning the transferability of [global] corporate governance practices assumed to add value. When a country is characterized by an overall low governance quality – as in high opacity of decision-making or a lack of transparency and high levels of perceived corruption – it deters some investors from entering, while high governance quality incentivizes foreign firms to operate or invest in the host country. Due to this potential deterrence, a specific company in Indonesia with its relatively poor country-level governance *de facto* implementation (compared to its neighbours' or international standards) may decide to enhance and adopt its *firm-level corporate governance* to strengthen its competitive attractiveness to lure foreign investors. The reasoning is that applying specific governance mechanisms may improve the firm's performance in the process. Specifically, minority investors could be convinced if conflicts of interest could be reduced or potential devastating corrupt behaviour significantly diminished. We therefore try to understand which dimensions of comparative corporate governance are most critical to affect the operating performance, and therefore potentially attracting investment.

The corporate governance deviance in Indonesia and most other Asian countries with a civic law tradition – with the exception of the common law jurisdiction in Singapore and Hong Kong, and to a lesser extent Malaysia – is socio-culturally rooted in a dominant national relationship-based governance, instead of a rules-based governance system. Admittedly, over the last two decades since the Asian crisis, the rule of law – and thus rules-based-governance – has been significantly strengthened in Indonesia and most other Asian jurisdictions. It is also true that the motivation to potentially expropriate assets from a listed firm is lower in common law countries where there exists a higher investor protection.

Since no reliable universal rules can be taken at face value, foreign investors are advised to distil some generic basic "rules of thumb" when setting up operations in Asia. Here are some suggested heuristics, or rules of thumb: foreign investors who have decided to line up with local partners need to clearly state all the responsibilities of the different (majority and minority) partners in the venture. In addition, they carefully need to choose a reputable and trustworthy partner with similar objectives and goals. Finally, the foreign entity needs to emphasize an effective pro-rata financial investment in the firm's ownership structure in case of a joint venture, based on the fundamental principle of (pro-rata) reciprocity. Moreover, foreign investors may need to adopt a beyond "comply and explain" heuristic to incite long term effectiveness of board practices and adapt to the local socio-cultural context without jeopardizing international standards. For instance, when applying the two main functions of the supervisory board – i.e. a monitoring or control function and an advisory role – its importance may be influenced by institutions, socio-cultural characteristics, and other elements of the corporate governance bundle, such as the reputation of family shareholders attempting to neutralize the weak legal institutional protection of [all] shareholders.

When foreign investors decide to buy stock on the Indonesian stock exchange, our research[19] took into consideration the specific Indonesian institutional setting of *concentrated ownership of both family businesses and state owned enterprises* on the one hand and *institutional voids* at the other hand when analysing which governance variables were affecting financial performance. The main concern is that this combination of weak governance at the country level and potential conflictual owners at the firm-level occasionally results in possible rent-seeking or corrupt behaviour. However, our empirical research did not find the typical assumed agency problems, indicating that other linkages and interdependencies of corporate governance practices are playing a more crucial role in an emerging institutional Indonesian market context. The focus turns to the interactions between insider-outsider conflicts and accountability conflicts in an emerging market context. Obviously, foreign but also domestic [minority] institutional investors are willing to pay a premium for good governance and they search for firms that have good governance practices and promote the adoption of voluntary codes of good governance as in a self-regulatory "comply or explain approach".

The pressure for foreign capital and product markets may not necessarily lead to convergence to international governance standards. Board independence, for instance, is not systematically linked to outright positive performance, and concentrated ownership monitoring its top management functioned as a substitute for independent (non-executive) directors or commissioners who arguably did not have any significant impact on performance. Complying to have a minimal number of "independent" board members on the board seems more a tick-the-box exercise than actually real impacting the financial performance. With a controlling shareholder in most listed companies in Indonesia, the fundamental governance problem is not necessarily opportunistic rent-seeking behaviour by executives and directors at the expense of public shareholders at large, but rather potentially inappropriate or opportunistic behaviour by the controlling family shareholders at the expense of minority shareholders, as indicated above.

Where shareholder rights are not well protected, investors will compensate for this deficiency by taking controlling positions in the firm, or expect clear idiosyncratic governance practices to be put in place to guarantee some minimum level of proper oversight of top management especially over majority shareholders to neutralize for potential expropriation of company property – or *tunneling*,[20] be it cash flow, assets or even equity as in insider trading practices – away of the listed company. We found some form of hybridization[21] in a sense that "good governance practices" are adopted and customized according to their particular circumstances and institutions.

Our empirical research shows that a suspected but not transparently disclosed block-holding family- or state-owned ownership in Indonesia was predicted to negatively affect the net income of the Indonesian listed firms, unless the company explicitly disclosed the beneficial ownership (or block-holding owners).[22] Furthermore, there was a positive relationship between foreign institutional ownership and the firm's return on assets. This is likely due to the perception that these institutional owners would bring or require some sound minimal governance practice into the firm.

From the perspective of the company's management, corporate governance can be interpreted as reducing threatening risks, rather than a mere legal obligation or a pure cost factor. From a corporate governance and international business perspective, we did not find clear evidence that the presence of explicitly disclosed block-holding family or state ownership is undermining financial performance, which provides some comfort to existing and potential investors in Indonesia. Our data offers empirical proof that international trust can be provided by clearly limiting or completely forbidding related party transactions or by emphasizing the presence of [foreign] investors, and reputable foreign third party intermediaries such as trustworthy auditors that positively affect the financial performance of the Indonesian firm.

Understanding and addressing the specific corporate governance attributes may allow equity and debt investors to focus on the most impactful governance mechanisms while enabling to take "advantage" of the usual institutional voids and information asymmetries in Indonesia and other Asian emerging markets, through networks and sometimes collusion with the powerful elite. Similarly, corporate governance provides valuable guidance for boards and corporate regulators in terms of where to focus when instigating corporate governance reform. *Enforcement* is key to making a good corporate governance work. However, merely complying to some "universal" set of corporate governance variables may not be sufficient to convince or secure sustainable investments. Our research strongly indicates the importance of institutional gatekeepers like external auditors, and the strict implementation of measurements that reduce the chance of rent-seeking behaviour such as minimizing related party transactions. Nonetheless, the level of compliance with codes entails significant implementation costs and remains relatively low in most emerging markets.

Foundational corporate governance standards need to be contextualized while individual leadership at (both supervisory and executive) boards should be continuously tested over time. We believe that those boards with impeccable legitimacy – worth the investors' trust – and integrity will prevail in an ambiguous, uncertain and often volatile situation. Such responsible leadership that is grounded in specific firm-level corporate governance practices will continue to attract investments when business opportunities are created. Applying effective and appropriate corporate governance practices that could guide and steer the organization will need to be sensitive to the institutional and organizational characteristics in Indonesia. And equal respect for all capital providers and human talent – through proper [contractual and informal] relationship building – are the first necessary steps to create and sustain a competitive advantage in a global increasingly fierce economy.

What do international and local investors look for? Most of the time, optimizing or maximizing their return on invested capital, return on assets or return on equity either in the short term or over the medium term. What we have found is that there is a direct correlation between well governed organizations and their profitability. And that is not a coincidence. Implementing good governance practices will enhance the boardroom functioning.[23] It likely results in reducing risks and unnecessary decisions that may be too speculative or too "trendy" without proper due diligence or comprehension of all its ramifications.

Should equity investors limit themselves to well-governed companies only, or should they look for (potentially undervalued) companies with specific governance attributes? This book claims that the former is a safer bet, though understanding the latter may likely be more profitable. We recommend any national investment fund or any institutional investment vehicle to look for firms with minimally accepted good corporate governance practices or able to install and improve good corporate governance when investing in a perceived sub-valued firm. That is sensible for any investor, especially to protect them against inappropriate and illegal behaviour at the company. Our experiences inform us that individual engaged and committed leadership can make a difference. Indeed, we need more effective and responsible leadership at boards. Let's turn to the next chapter.

Consider the following Take Away Ideas of Chapter 2:

---

1. The OECD principles of good corporate governance are based on the four principles: transparency, fairness, accountability and responsibility.
   We also claim that an organization is more than a nexus of legal contracts; it is also a nexus of relations which implies that a board needs to take into account the relevant stakeholders of the organization, as in customers, employees, suppliers and the community.

---

2. Both Western and Asian boards can become quite entrenched if members are not thinking independently, and align their decisions too much with the CEO or founding patriarch, instead of focusing on the long-term interests of the organization itself.

---

3. Indonesian and other Asian boards need to make efforts to reduce potential conflicts of interests (between majority and minority shareholders), including the possibility of entrenchment potentially resulting in subtle 'expropriation' of assets away from the listed company (be it by the family or state majority owners).

Notes

1 The literature on institutional governance have proven that legal differences significantly affect national governance structures. See La Porta, R., Lopez-De-Silanes, F. & A. Schleifer, A, (1999), "Corporate ownership around the world", *Journal of Finance*, 54(2), 471–517; La Porta, R., Lopez-De-Silanes, F. Schleifer, A.& R. Vishny, (2000), "Investor protection and corporate governance", *Journal of Financial Economics*, 58, 3–27; and La Porta, R., Lopez-De-Silanes, F. Schleifer, A.& R. Vishny, (2002), "Investor protection and corporate valuation", *Journal of Finance*, Vol. 57; 1147–1170.

2 The historical battle culminated in the important Magna Carta of 1215 that curtailed the absolute power of the English King, for the first time in English history, that would be result over the subsequent centuries in the common law system in which individual rights prevail over state intervention and state power.

3 Mallin, C.A., (2010), *Corporate Governance*, Oxford University Press.

4 After joining the IFC team as a governance expert in Asia Pacific to assist with implementing good corporate governance practices, Peter Verhezen, attended a speech in 2014 by the then Country Manager of IFC in Indonesia, Mr. *Sarvesh Suri. IFC is a member of the World Bank Group and the largest global development institution focused exclusively on the private sector.* He observed in 2014 that companies that practice good corporate governance advance their long-term survival and prosperity. A well-performing company with streamlined internal practices has a positive impact on private sector development. Good corporate governance builds healthy organizations and institutions and leads to sustainable economic growth. "With a young population that needs jobs, it is crucial Indonesia adopts long-term ways of building and sharing prosperity among its more than 240 million people (in

2014). To do just that and place corporate governance front and center of Indonesia's economy, the Financial Services Authority (OJK) recently launched with support from IFC, the member of the World Bank Group focused on private sector development in emerging markets, the Indonesian Corporate Governance Roadmap and Manual. What does that mean? The roadmap defines key principles of governance which will shape the regulatory framework for listed companies. It emphasizes transparency and seeks to strengthen the role of company boards. There is evidence to show that investors gain great confidence in companies that are more transparent and have active boards who are capable of stewarding companies effectively. Complementing the roadmap is the Indonesia Corporate Governance Manual, a benchmark of existing laws and regulations within the context of globally recognized practices. The manual provides practical guidance to Indonesian companies – not just those that are traded on stock markets – on how to implement sound governance practices. Now, as Indonesia's corporates navigate choppy economic waters, is the right time for companies to improve their practices and prepare for the future. Indonesia's companies – and the country as a whole – will be all the more stronger for it", as expressed by Mr. Sarvesh Suri.

5 Bebchuk, L. & A. Hamdani, (2009), "The elusive quest for global governance standards", *University of Pennsylvania Law Review*, Vol. 157(5): 1263–1317; and Bebchuk, L. & M. Weisbach, (2010), "The State of Corporate Governance Research", *The Review of Financial Studies*, Vol. 23(3): 939–961.

6 Gompers, P.A.; Ishii, J. & A. Metrick, (2003), "Corporate Governance and Equity Prices", *Quantitative Journal of Economics*, Vol.118: 107–155.

7 Bebchuk, L. & A. Cohen, (2005), "The costs of entrenched boards", *Journal of Financial Economics*, Vol. 78: 409–433; Bebchuk, L. & J. Fried, (2004), *Pay Without Performance. The Unfulfilled Promise of Executive Compensation*, Harvard University Press, Cambridge MA; and Bebchuk, L.; Cohen, A. & A. Ferrell, (2004), "What matter in corporate governance?", Working Paper Harvard Law School.

8 Hirschman, A.O., (1970), *Exit, Voice and Loyalty. Responses to decline in firms, organizations and states*, Cambridge MA, Harvard University Press.

9 Verhezen, P. & G. Martin, (2018), Corporate Governance & Ethical Behavior affecting Performance: Propositions and Peculiarities at Indonesian Firms within its Institutional context, *Melbourne Business School Working Paper, financed by IFC World Bank*; Claessens, S.; Djankov, S. & L.H.P. Lang, (2000), "The separation of ownership and control in East Asian Corporations", *Journal of Financial Economics*, Vol.58: 81–112; and Claessens, S.; Djankov, S.; Fan, JPH. & LHP. Lang, (2002), "Disentangling the incentive and entrenchment effects of large shareholders", *Journal of Finance*, Vol. 57: 2741–2771. Data seem to suggest (just till the global financial crisis – after which no research has been published on this specific criterium in our knowledge – that about 10 of the biggest families own more than 50 percent of the assets on the Indonesian Stock Exchange. Very high concentrated ownership indeed, much higher as the European family businesses.

10 Verhezen, P. & G. Martin, (2018), Corporate Governance & Ethical Behavior affecting Performance: Propositions and Peculiarities at Indonesian Firms within its Institutional context, o.c.

11 See Aguilera, R.V. & K. A. Desender, (2012), "Challenges in measuring of comparative corporate governance: a Review of the main indices", *Research Methodology in Strategy and Management*, Vol. 8: 289–321; and Aguilera, R.V.; Filatotchev, I.; Gospel, H. & G. Jackson, (2008), "An organizational approach to comparative governance: costs, contingencies, and complementarities", *Organizational Science*, Vol. 19(3): 475–492.

12 See IFC World Bank, (2018), *Indonesia Corporate Governance Manuel, 2nd Edition*:
   https://www.ifc.org/wps/wcm/connect/e66bacdc-07c6-40f3-b094-8d3ca96a77a0/Indonesia_CG +Manual_2nd_Edition.pdf?MOD=AJPERES&CVID=mf8483z.

13 See IFC World Bank, (2018), *Indonesia Corporate Governance Manuel, 2nd Edition*. The recommendations in the roadmap can be summarised as follows: "Corporate governance framework: the enforcement of a code of good corporate governance through a "comply or explain" regime and the implementation of a code of conduct for stakeholders (such as capital market professionals, business

journalists and other media); Protection of shareholders: through transparent preparation, organisation and disclosure of results of the general meeting of shareholders and clearly defined dividend and voting rights; Role of stakeholders (such as employees, vendors, and others): in the implementation of anti-corruption and procurement policies, and long-term incentives for employees. It also includes the roles and qualifications of corporate secretaries and implementation of whistleblowing policies; Transparency and disclosure: disclosure of ultimate ownership and disclosure of independence criteria for commissioners, as well as ensuring the availability of financial and non-financial information on companies' websites; Role of boards: in the nomination and remuneration process of commissioners and directors. It also includes ensuring disclosure of qualifications of board members and providing orientation programmes for board members on their fiduciary duties. The role of boards should also extend to: tenure of commissioners; promotion of board diversity; evaluation of board performance; and implementation of succession planning policies."

14 Verhezen, P., (2018), "Is Indonesia serious about corporate governance?" *Strategic Review*, Vol. 8(3): 48–59.

15 The list changes every year, but among the recurring awarded companies we find a few well-known "Indonesian brands" which are perceived to be reasonably well governed. BCA, CIMB Niaga, Mandiri, Danamon, Maybank, BRI, BTN, OCBC NISP, BNI and BTPN), as well as a number of well esteemed state owned enterprises such as PT Telkom Tbk, PT Aneka Tambang Tbk, and PT Jasa Marga Tbk, while the top 20 list is completed with reputable names as PT Hero Tbk, PT Matahari Tbk, PT XL Axiata Tbk, PT Saratoga Investama Tbk and of course PT Astra International Tbk which has consistently been perceived as among the top corporate governance performers. Other top 30 contenders include PT Garuda Tbk, PT Indosat Tbk, PT Kalbe Farma Tbk, PT Salim Ivomas Tbk, PT Unilever Tbk, PT Indocement Tbk, and PT Wijaya Karya Tbk to name a few.

16 Black, B.S.; Jang, H. & W. Kim, (2006), "Does corporate governance affect firms' market values? Evidence from Korea", *Journal of Law, Economics and Organization*, Vol.22(2): 366–413.

17 For the same of proper transparency, we here note that one of the authors, Peter and a team, advised the board of Indofood on redefining the organizational culture or fine-tuning and updating the purpose, values and mission-vision of this public-listed company, Indofood.

18 Verhezen, P.; Williamson, I.O. & N. Soebagjo, (2018), "Living less dangerously in Indonesia", *Strategic Review*, January-March: 54–67.

19 For more details see Peter Verhezen and Geoff Martin, (2018), a Melbourne Business School paper, and initiated by discussions with the International Finance Corporation in Jakarta; and an academic book and *Strategic Review* essay by Verhezen, Williamson and Soebagjo (2016).

20 Faccio, M.; Lang, L. & L. Young, (2001), "Dividends and Expropriation", *American Economic Review*, Vil. 91(1): 54–71; and Faccio, M. & L.H.P. Lang, (2002), "The Separation of Ownership and Control: an analysis of Ultimate Ownership in Western European Corporations", *Journal of Financial Economics*, Vol. 65: 365–395.

21 Aguilera, R.V. & G. Jackson, (2002), "Hybridization and Heterogeneity across National Models of Corporate Governance", *Economic Sociology: European Electronic Newsletter*, ISSN 1871–3351, Vol.3(2): 17–22.

22 Verhezen, P. & G. Martin, (2018), Corporate Governance & Ethical Behavior affecting Performance: Propositions and Peculiarities at Indonesian Firms within its Institutional context, *Melbourne Business School Working Paper, financed by IFC World Bank*.

23 Verhezen, P. & T. Abeng, (2020), "Boards that Govern and Lead", *Strategic Review*, Vol. 10(2): 42–57.

Chapter 3
Creating an Effective Boardroom
Fiduciary Duties Aimed to Create Trust

> The board is entrusted with the responsibility of providing guidance and oversight to ensure sustainable value creation. While boards do not manage the corporation, they govern by setting the rules; selecting the management; reviewing and approving key decisions; coaching, evaluating and rewarding the management; and ensuring that risk management and internal control systems are effective. The board's success depends on making sound judgments in numerous situations that involve balancing different interests.   Y. Argüden, (2009), *Boardroom Secrets*

What is a board expected to do? Any board has an obligation to govern the organization. This implies that board commissioners need to fulfil the *fiduciary duties of care and loyalty* to the organization by supervising or monitoring and advising and coaching top executive [or the board of directors], and to mediate with different stakeholders that can affect the organization.

This chapter explains that all board members of any organization – be it for profit or for non-profit – have a fiduciary and thus legal duty to make informed decisions that optimise long-term organizational value aligned with the interests of the organization and their shareholders. In most jurisdictions we distinguish a *duty of care* and a *duty of loyalty*, that leads to a third *duty of prudence*. Prudent decision-making reflects the idea that board members make informed and reasonable decisions in the interest of the organization. These duties of care and loyalty are then practically translated in what boards actually do. They focus on *strategy, supervising* and *advising* top executives. In order to be able to discharge board members of their fiduciary duties, a board is characterized by certain structures, procedures and processes that help function the boardroom.

These three fiduciary obligation, translated in the three main functions of a senior board (Board of Commissioners in Indonesian terminology), can only take place through a governance charter that describes the actual structures and specific duties of each of the directors. The charter (or articles of association) also refers to the composition of the board (be it single or dual-tier), its committees chaired by whom, its voting procedures (both at board meetings as well as during the annual shareholders' meeting, its evaluation process of the CEO and the board itself, criteria for calling an extraordinary shareholder meeting, how to organize a potential right issue etc . . .

Adding to the complexity today of governing an organization is the fast changing context in most countries with disruptive events cascading through interdependent ecosystems – environmental, economic, technological and operational. Not adapting or being limited by the firm's non-adapting capacities could be catastrophic. The repercussions of poor decision-making at the board level have never been greater, and board members – colloquially labelled "directors and officers" (D&O) or "commissioners and executive directors" – will try to limit their personal liability[1] by attempting to mitigate or limit some of those risks, including some special insurance policies for board members (D&O insurances). This concern for personal liability plays a role in the Western hemisphere to legally insure oneself against such potential cases – which is less adopted in Asia – with the exception of the more sophisticated exchanges in Singapore and Hong Kong, and for the banking industry where the liabilities can be quite significant. Our focus will be on explaining the duties of a board and its members, which will intrinsically limit the personal liabilities – especially if a board will be able to prove that the decisions were fully informed, reasonable and taken as a unified team. Only in exceptional cases of fraud or misconduct, (non-executive) board members will be prosecuted and effectively penalized (with jail terms).

1 Fiduciary Duties of Care, Loyalty and Prudence

Boards and their chairmen carry the ultimate legal power of an organization. That is true for both dual as well as single-tier boards. However, under single-tier boards that power is even more concentrated because the function of chairman and CEO can be combined. In the USA, in about 68 percent of the cases, the CEO combines this executive title with chairmanship of the board, making him extremely powerful. Cases such as Enron and Disney in the early 2000s have indicated that it is very hard to challenge such powerful chairman-CEOs. Such entrenched boards may be too loyal decision-makers, without being critical enough to optimize the creation of sustainable value for the organization.

The directors' duties of care, loyalty and prudence are well established.[2] The custodian's duties of board members include the obligation to act in good faith, be sufficiently informed, and exercise due care in oversight over strategy, risk and compliance of the management in the organization. In a nutshell, boards steer the organization away from risks to promising business opportunities. The board's obligations are always situated in a particular legal and socio-economic context. A consensus on good corporate governance implies (1) to select and supervise top leadership, (2) to set the overall firm's strategy as well as setting the cultural ethical tone at the top, and (3) to assure that the leadership and the organization comply to the rules imposed and values agreed upon.

In Indonesia, the corporate context[3] is distinctively different from a number of Anglo-Saxon countries. One of the consequences of this unique socio-historical institutional context is that the Indonesian law requires the separation between chairman (President Commissioner) and CEO (President Director) by having installed a dual-tier board structure. Despite the legal separation between those two functions, quite often the founder entrepreneur of the company remains at the helm of the company, usually as President Commissioner or non-executive Chairman of the supervisory board (Board of Commissioners). For State Owned Enterprises, the chair has often been a political appointment, which obviously complicates the economic objective to optimize organizational value creation.

1.1 Some Generic Duties, Making a Board Accountable to Whom?

Organizations can and should expect their board and managers to fulfil their respective fiduciary duties. A fiduciary duty to the organization is essentially a legal relationship of confidence or trust between two or more parties, most commonly a fiduciary or trustee and a principal or beneficiary, who justifiably reposes confidence, good faith, and reliance on his or her trustee. The fiduciary is expected to act for the sole benefit and interests of the principal, with loyalty to those interests. The whole question boils down to "who" is this principal: are we referring to the long term interests of the organization for which one works, or for the capital providers, short term investors or long term owners of the organization? Mainstream financial economics has veered towards 'activist' shareholders whose main function is to optimize profitability over the short term "at any cost". The current saga reflects this antagonistic relationship between different perspectives for example: one of the top 10 shareholders of Unilever claims that its CEO has "lost the plot" by pursuing sustainability medals at the expense of financial performance.[4] This activist shareholder seeks short term profitability over a lofty sustainability story that likely may initially cost some money.

However, this [shareholder] model has resulted in behaviour by the trustees that may not be in the long term interest of the organization as such. Owners or investors seem to be allowed to do anything with "their" organization to which they provided capital, even if that is at the expense of the [long-term] interest of the organization. Of course, the typical debate between financial analysts and concerned stakeholders will not fade away any time soon. Those analysts whose bonuses are directly related to financial performance of the firms work for institutional powerful investors, whereas the other kind of "committed" investors, often less powerful individuals, consider ecological and social goals in organizations as important contributors for future growth. We believe that balancing these seemingly opposing goals may be the right longer term approach – as we'll explain in chapter five. Theoretically, it would make more sense to interpret the fiduciary duties as economic and socio-ecological obligations to the organization. However, this is extremely difficult to materialize in reality, be it in state owned enterprises or in family listed companies. Again, business is messy and definitely not black and white. Corporate governance may help to clarify and clear up some of this "greyness" in business.[5]

Principles of good governance have been a major component of international financial standards, and many regulators view effective corporate governance as "a first line of defence" in their supervisory activities. The functionality of any board is expressed through the fiduciary duties of its executives and non-executive board members as a unified team to optimize this organizational value, often misquoted as maximizing shareholders' value. When someone is elected to a board, two main duties are "imposed" to guarantee that a board functions well: a fiduciary duty of care and a fiduciary duty of loyalty. That usually results in a duty of prudence which implies that risks are taken seriously before making any decision.

The *fiduciary duty* of a board usually includes a *duty of care* that requires directors to make decisions with due deliberation, a *duty of loyalty* that addresses conflicts of interest whereby the interest of shareholders should prevail over the interest of a director, and a *duty of candor* or *prudence* that requires that management and the board inform shareholders of all information that is important in their (risk) evaluation of the company's prospects and its management abilities to deal with those potential risks. These fiduciary duties are often translated in the legal requirement of having at least two or three professionally run subcommittees at the board: (1) a committee of internal audit and an operational internal control organism to contain accounting and other specific risks, (2) a nomination committee that explicitly safeguards that the best professional CEO will be chosen, and (3) a remuneration committee that decides on an appropriate and fair remuneration package for its top managers. Sometimes (4) a subcommittee is added to assess the risks that are allied to the suggested strategy or due to external factors that can be socio-ecological, geopolitical in nature or related to potentially natural disasters. Let us explore those three duties in detail.

1.2 Fiduciary Duty of Care

Any director, be it a full time executive director or a (part time) non-executive director is expected to exercise a duty of care which implies that this executive director or non-executive director (a commissioner under Indonesian law) is expected to make informed decisions after a reasonable inquiry and discussion in good faith within appropriate circumstances and in the interest of the company. And these informed decisions should also be in line with the ethical code of conduct, stipulated in the governance charter of the company.

Board members – its non-executive and executive directors – shall discharge their duties in good faith, and in a manner they reasonably believe to be in the best interests of the company in compliance with the company's code of conduct. If the company does not have a code, it should adopt one. In that sense, compliance with the standard of care can be defined as the obligation of a director to make reasonable enquiry in appropriate circumstances, and taking a decision after reasonable discussion. It means that board members act honestly in the interests of the company; be active and question and challenge management; ensure that the company acts in compliance with the applicable laws; and regularly attend meetings; ensure that the CEO provides sufficient information to the board; and finally that the member exercises adequate control over management.[6]

Unfortunately, we have seen a number of cases where the board members did not take all precautions in making decisions, potentially falling in the trap of groupthink or being misguided by other than the organizational interests, including giving in to external political pressure and allowing non-organizational objectives to prevail. Those members may have acted in their own selfish personal interests while diluting or possibly ignoring their duty of care. We have seen from close by how boards are misguided and even take on unjustifiable projects in the 90s – prior to the Asian crisis. A same phenomenon repeated itself in the USA and even Europe in 2008 when a crisis erupted rooted in a mortgage debacle that affected whole economies in the Western hemisphere.

1.3 Fiduciary Duty of Loyalty

The fiduciary duty of loyalty refers to the obligation to always put the interest of the organization first, which implies that information should be kept confidential, that ethical behaviour is obliged and that any potential conflict of interest should be avoided at any time. The fiduciary duty of loyalty stipulates that the own interests of the elected board members should never prevail over those of the company and their shareholders. To ensure the organization's interests, board members will keep all information confidential and will always avoid or manage conflicts of interest. In other words, a commissioner should not be discharged from his or her duties if there is a conflict of interest between him or her and the company and its shareholders in a single instance or transaction. Board members – both non-executive directors and executive directors – shall discharge theirs by ensuring that their own interests do not prevail over the those of the company and its shareholders; keeping information confidential[7] and avoiding or managing conflict of interest. Commissioners should not disclose confidential information or use their access to corporate information for their personal interests or the interests of third parties. Hence why inside trading is heavily penalised by the law. The personal use of confidential information ultimately damages shareholders. For banks, the definition of conflict of interest is even more stringent.[8]

However, if a commissioner has a general conflict of interest with the company and its shareholders, that board member can blow the whistle and subsequently ought to be discharged from his/her position as commissioner. Loyalty underpins the effective implementation of key corporate governance principles, for example the need to monitor and to limit related party transactions and to establish appropriate remuneration policies for the board members. Duty of loyalty requires commissioners to exercise their powers in the interests of the company as a whole. Simply put, commissioners should not allow personal interests to prevail over those of the company. Again, unfortunately, there exist numerous cases both in Indonesia and elsewhere which seem to confirm the disloyalty of some boards vis-à-vis the organization by serving their political patrons, or worse, their own short-term pecuniary interests.

We can interpret this fiduciary duty as a board member *not* to conduct transactions in which they have a personal interest (that could potentially harm the company); directly or indirectly purchase or sell company shares without disclosure; accept a position in a competing company; enter into contractual relations with a competing company; use assets and facilities of the company (for personal interest);

use information and business opportunities received in their official capacity for personal gain; and finally a board member should not accept gifts that could distort his decisions on behalf of the company.[9]

The duty of loyalty requires commissioners to act in the best interest of the company regardless of who nominated and elected the member, and or pressure from other commissioners, shareholders, or other individuals to take actions or make decisions that are not in the best interest of the company.[10] We all know examples that indicate how difficult it sometimes can be to take decisions that show loyalty to the organizational best interests, and not craving to please the powerful elite who put you in that position at the board.

1.4 Fiduciary Duty of Prudence

A fiduciary duty of prudence explicitly refer to the decision-making process of the board members who at any time need to minimize the potential negative risks affecting the company, especially when discussing substantial investments or M&A related issues.

To create value, a company needs to take certain [strategic] risks and limit operational risks that could be avoided. Corporations should assess, analyze and prepare for external risks. Moreover, although a company cannot avoid external risks, such as political changes or a natural disaster,[11] a board should prepare themselves in case such not preventable external risks would take place. In other words, boards need to make informed and thus smart decisions that can reduce threatening risks. Successful management of risk is central to the success of all organizations. The practice of risk management has evolved significantly from its original emphasis on operational risks. The most effective board risk oversight is not the result of a stringent regulation but rather a good function board or CEO or investor has the experience and expertise to proficiently carry out that important task, both in terms of supervising and execution. A board is often mindful of risk oversight because it has had a negative experience in which it failed to recognize and respond to a risk. It is advised that a board encourages appropriate risk taking while also challenging overly risk-averse or risk-seeking behaviours.[12]

A) Risk Management Process
Key differentiators of the recent international standards on risk management (such as ISO 31000 in COSO Enterprise Risk Management[13] – Integrated Framework, 2009, and visualized in Figure 10) from traditional risk management are the linking of key risks into an organization's strategic objectives, the expansion of responsibility for managing risks across the organization, and a broader definition of risk as "the effect of uncertainty on objectives", which therefore includes strategic, reputational, financial, or IT and cyber-risks, among others, as opposed to focusing solely on operational risks.

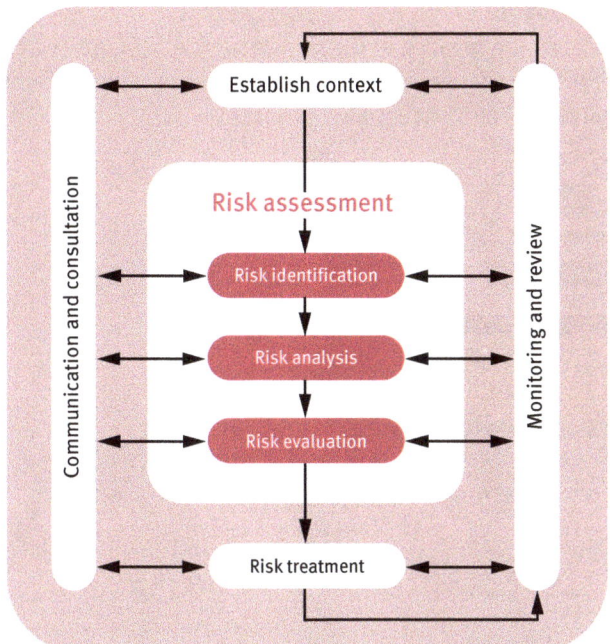

Figure 10: ISO 31000 Risk Management Process.

Boards should therefore be very candid about any potential risk to secure prudent decision-making by ensuring that the board agenda covers key strategic and risk issues; displays maximum care and prudence that be expected from a good director under similar circumstances. We consider the fiduciary duty of prudence as a manner to deal with risks. The board is ultimately responsible for determining the nature and extent of risks that an organization is willing to take to achieve its strategic objectives and for ensuring that these risks are identified and managed properly.[14] Under a dual-tier structure, the Executive Board is responsible for implementing the risk management system while the Supervisory Board is in charge of monitoring and reviewing its implementation – as explained in the next chapter.

The Corporate Governance code recommends the following: (1) the [executive] Board should establish and implement a sound risk management system within the company, covering all aspects of the company's activities – this is often the authority given to the operational *internal audit* who should directly report to members of the supervisory board; (2) each strategic decision taken, including the creation of new products or services, should be carefully considered against its risk exposure to ensure an appropriate balance between benefit and risk, and (3) to ensure proper implementation of risk management, the company should have a work unit or person in charge of this function.

B) Determining Risk and Risk Appetite

In order to better understand risk governance and risk management, figure 11 distinguishes three major risks: preventable or operational risks, strategy risk inherent for the business, and external risks – as visualized hereunder.

Figure 11: Three main risks to address.
Source: Kaplan & Mikes, (2012), "Risk: a new framework", *Harvard Business Review*, June

Once the risks have been identified, the board can start evaluating and managing the risks. Even if one cannot determine the precise probability of external risks, it is highly recommendable to perform crisis scenario games to prepare the organization, but also to encourage all board members to participate in such games to learn in case of likely deficiencies in the level of sophisticated understanding of risks. The [supervisory] board is not involved in the actual management of the risks, but will need to supervise and coach executives that risks are properly dealt with. It is the board's ultimate responsibility to safeguard the existence of the organization, which implies to avoid any preventable risk, or to prepare for risks that cannot be avoided, and to embrace strategic risks with an acceptable risk appetite.

To prepare for a meaningful organizational future, one partially adopts to a changing context, and partially one attempts to influence that future by taking deliberate well informed decisions that strategically can improve the strategic odds to succeed in such a changing environment. Hence why scenario planning (cf. Figure 12) is a useful tool for boards. A better understanding of strategical risks as well as external risks help to reduce negative consequences, or to be ready to embrace potential windfalls.

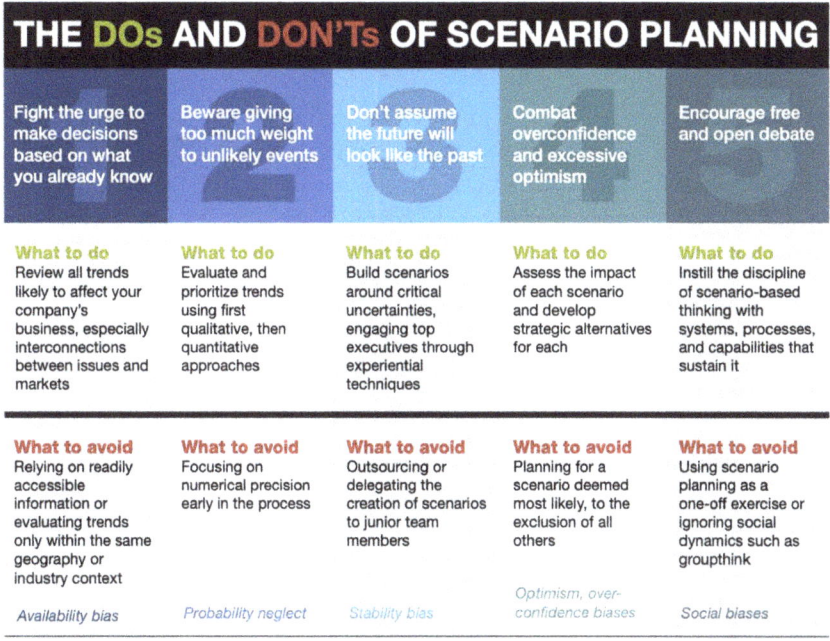

Figure 12: Usefulness of good scenario planning for addressing strategic and external risks/biases. Source: Erdmann, D.; Sichel, B. & L. Yeung, (2015), "Overcoming obstacles to effective scenario planning", *McKinsey & Company*, June.

Preventable operational risks are often mitigated by applying proper "best operating procedures" and standards that have proven their usefulness in similar operating environments. What are the specific tasks of the board in preparing for this "promised planned future"?

Although not a too common practice among many boards, the board determines (1) the *risk capacity*, as in what circumstances a company can be brought down, through stress testing, and (2) the *risk appetite* – as in determining at the board level how much is the firm willing to risk prior to taking any specific risk and or investment decision as can be seen in figure 13. Risk appetite refers to the amount of capital that an organization is willing to lose at any point in time, comparable to 'value at risk' in the financial sector. Indeed, risk appetite is the amount at stake when an organization pursues certain strategic objectives and is directly connotated with a risk-return calculation that is consistent with the competitive positioning and competitive advantage of the firm within a certain industry. The management will translate this risk capacity and risk appetite, determined by the board, into specific risk limits and thresholds, by business line, or by product or geographic locations. The risk exposures of any of these decisions will be managed in real time.

Often, specific risk boundaries are put in place as visualized by the grey rectangular in Figure 13 where one attempts to maximize the positive upside and minimize the negative downside of any potential risk.

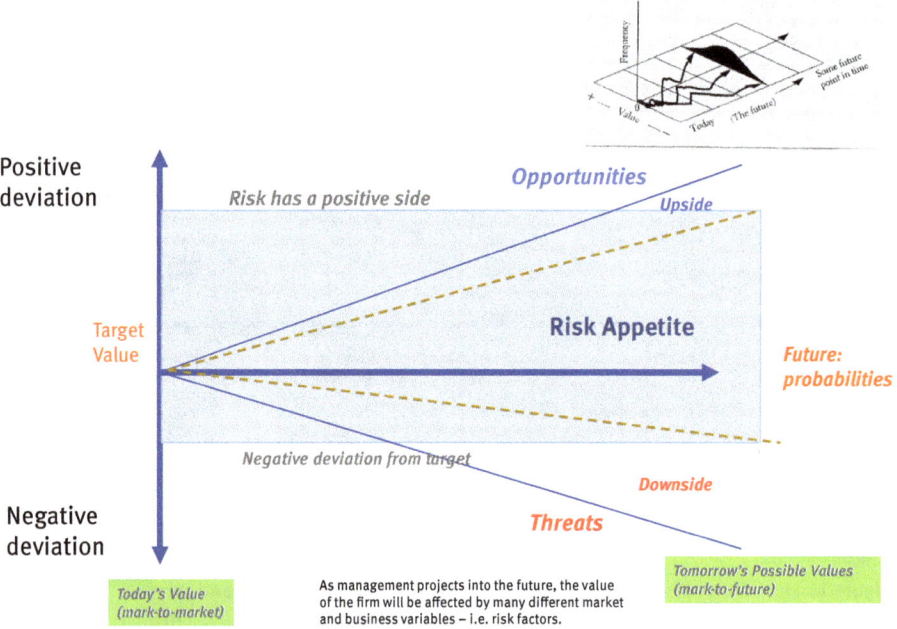

Figure 13: Defining risk appetite.

Once the risk appetite and its boundaries have been defined, a board can make more informed decisions within the agreed limitations. Unfortunately, not many organizations apply this risk methodology, with the exception of financial institutions where this kind of thinking is almost mandatory. These informed decisions often relate to eliminating or avoiding certain risks, or by transferring and mitigating risk, and finally by taking informed risk decisions that potentially result in positive strategic outcomes. How to mitigate those risks? Well, boards and their management team can eliminate some of those risks, or transfer them to other third parties who are willing to buy those risky bets at a 'discount', or mitigate them by cleverly reengineering or moving into a different market and thus diversifying away that risk. In case of strategic risks, they form part of the business model, they are ingredients for risk taking innovation that create (future) value and constitutes the (desired) return on invested (risked) capital.

Well, boards and their management team can eliminate some of those risks, or transfer them to other parties who are willing to purchase those risky bets at a 'discount', or mitigate them by cleverly reengineering or moving into a different market and thus diversifying away that risk. In case of strategic risks, they form part of the business model, they are ingredients for risk taking innovation that create [future] value and constitutes the [desired] return on invested [risked] capital. Our experience is to assess the overall risks of the company by initially focusing on the outliers, or anything that deviates from the normal, in its literal but also statistical meaning. Subsequently, one seeks for any possible tail risk whose probability may look as improbable but its impact could be dramatic. Due diligence should reveal possible breaches in terms of legal and ethical boundaries. And finally, from a strategic perspective, the rapid proliferation of disruptive innovation or the negative effect of a new wave of regulation (an external risk potentially directly impacting a strategy) can require to re-evaluate the strategy of the firm. And yes unforeseen shocks could be life-threatening and need to be taken into account. From personal expertise, one of the authors, Peter, is adamant that the essence of risk management lies in looking for unusual patterns, all those data that fall outside the traditional Gauss curve. When working as an advisor for IBRA-IMF, Peter attempted to first look at or for the "essence" of what was assumed to be "normal" and what the organization stood for, and subsequently his team was always searching for outliners, or data which did not fit the usual, or what was unexpected. That allowed his team to provide proper and quite "accurate" assessment of the current situation and come up with sensible possible solutions. Or, in more extreme cases where his team was confronted with "suspicious" deviations in the financial data on which the team had to base itself to come up with recommendations to restructure bad debt.

Moreover, it is amazing how politicians and business leaders sometimes decide to ignore certain unusual patterns, which at least should have risen red flags, regarding certain behaviour or decisions.[15] Afterwards, one sees too often excuses for not having known those risks, or having ignored those red flags. Managers often misinterpret these warning signs because they may remain blinded by cognitive biases. And worse, management sometimes take the near-misses of possible risk failures – or even catastrophes – as indications that everything is fine. Unfortunately, our experience is that boards need to be more on the ball for understanding the potential operational or external (and even strategic) risks and potential systemic risks.

Researchers believe that managers can recognize and learn from near nisses. A board and management should (1) be on alert when time of cost pressure are high, (2) watch for deviations from the norm, (3) uncover the deviations' root causes, (4) hold themselves accountable for near misses, (5) envision worst-case scenarios, (6) look for near misses or deviations from the usual that may be masqueraded as alleged successes, and (7) reward individuals for exposing near misses and the deviations from the norm, both technological as well as socio-ethical.[16] More generally, Figure 14 summarizes the possible choices to take in order to reduce risks.

- **Eliminate or avoid risk**
    - Diversification
    - Set strict policy
    - Cancel a project
    - Move out of the market
    - Sell off part of the firm
- **Transfer the risk** :
    - Hedging
    - Selling / Contracts
    - Insuring
- **Risk Mitigation**
    - Acquisition or merger
    - Move to a new market
    - Develop a new product/technology in an existing market
    - Business process reengineering
    - Corporate risk management policy
- **Absorb and Manage the risk**

    = risk retention = *a positive decision to accept the risk due to the potential gain it allows*

Figure 14: Risk Mitigation.

In fact, looking for specific differences in patterns constitutes what boards should look for as a potential business opportunity, either as a distinctive trend or a potential negative risk. Making sure that operations do not deviate too much from 'normality' – rooted in what represents the essence of the firm – can be interpreted what management is all about.[17] Spotting abnormal data may be essential for a board to see potential negative risks or to understand what the future may bring. That understanding is often the combination of tacit (experience) as well as explicit knowledge (expertise). Wise leaders spot the essence by grasping universal truths from details. Expanding the particulars to universal principles requires continual interaction between subjective tacit intuition and [explicit] objective knowledge.[18]

At the end of the day, boards and management aim to create value by taking well calculated risks. Indeed, trying to come up with distinctive value propositions that cater to the needs of customers is often founded in sensing different perspectives and future trends. The competencies and character of the board and its management often determine the success rate of an organization. Supervisory and executive boards need to dance together to optimize the return on investment by taking calculated and thus informed decisions. This requires a unified team that respects each other duties and authorities and work together to find appropriate solutions. A checklist is hereunder summarized in Figure 15:

Checklist for Leading Risk (=Probability of occurrence x Impact of event)

- ✓ Is the company's **risk appetite** well defined by directors and disciplined by executives?
- ✓ Is the board **well informed** and accepting of the company's **risk management** strategies?
- ✓ Are non-executive directors regularly updated on company risks via the board's **audit and risk committees**?
- ✓ Does the board include non-executive directors with prior executive experience in **managing risks** = *does the BoC have the experience to determine risk management*?
- ✓ Are the company's **risk management practices preemptive rather than reactive**?
- ✓ Does the company properly **balance downside risks and business opportunities** (upside risks)?
- ✓ Is **excessive risk** well **defined** and properly **avoided**?
- ✓ Is **risk management embedded in operating practices** and in the mind-set of managers throughout the ranks?
- ✓ Has the company prepared for **low-probability but high consequence events**? = Prevent Risks or Prepare for Risks (if cannot be avoided)
- ✓ Does the board lead within management in conducting **due diligence** and deciding on **major acquisitions** and other **highly risky transactions**?
- ✓ Has the board considered **creating an advisory body**?

Figure 15: How boards address risks.

Usually, the [supervisory] board will only focus on monitoring the risks taken by the executives. However, in case of a *crisis,* we suggest, that the chairman steps in and takes a more "leading" role[19] in steering the organizations "out of risky waters towards open opportunities", when the organization is distrusted by its stakeholders or when legal accountability and corporate reputation is at stake – as visualized in Figure 16 hereunder.[20] Over the last four decades, most reputational crises found their roots in unethical behaviour, where "personal" career interests to secure the highest short term target return on investment for instance prevailing over long-term value at the organization. The VW-Dieselgate or the bribery scandal at Siemens a decade ago are such obvious examples in Germany that is known for its rules-based governance and adherence to norms and rules. At most business schools, executives are nowadays trained in ethical dilemmas, and special programs exist for preparing board members to improve applying fiduciary duties. The examples of inappropriate and unethical behaviour at boards in Asia are too long to even start mentioning! Asian executives are not less ethical as their Western counterparts, but are less constrained by those institutional voids.

Probably, unethical behaviour is determined by limited institutional precautionary norms that are not meticulously and unequally implemented, favouring the powerful elite. If this local elite finds a way to escape any form of 'justice', it makes the place rather unpredictable, and probably unfair because no stringent equal implementation of the rules of the game. Such non-implementation of the law aggravated by blatant favouritism definitely makes a number of these emerging Asian economies a rather risky place for investors.

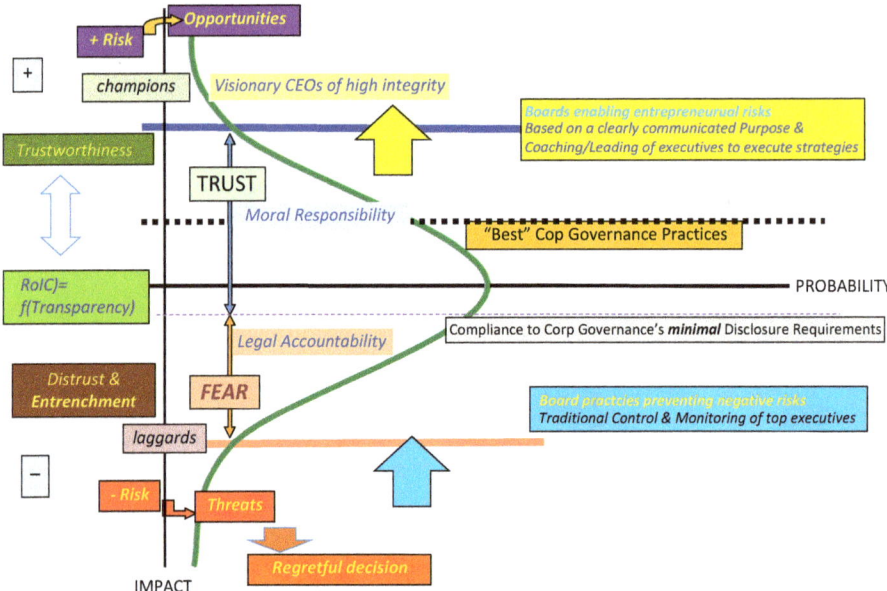

Figure 16: Corporate governance minimizing threatening risks and optimizing entrepreneurial opportunities.
Source: interpretation of Verhezen, P., (2010), "Giving voice to a culture of silence: from a culture of compliance to a culture of integrity", *Journal of Business Ethics*, Vol. 96(2): 187–206

C) Addressing Specific Risks – Cyberthreats and Data Privacy

The scale of possible repercussions of making poor choices has never been greater. Thus fear for making potentially bad decisions is higher in a volatile, uncertain, complex and ambiguous (VUCA) context, just when calm judgment and reasoned decisions are most important. Today, the most obvious issue to point to is cyber risk,[21] whether breakdowns may be the consequence of system disruption, cyber thieves or cyber terrorism. Political uncertainty is also increasing which was already undergoing significant change. Litigation seems to be an ever-increasing threat, whether well founded or not. Regulators, too, are rattling their swords, and activists continue to attack, with some greater credibility in the eyes of some.

As a board, risks need to be taken seriously. And we strongly advocate to install a particular subcommittee for risk management to prepare the organization for the future – a future that becomes increasingly complex and volatile. Quite a number of new risks have arisen, especially those risks related to digitalization which we touch upon in our last sixth chapter. However, we here like to briefly mention the cyberthreats that most organizations face today.[22] Indeed, boards (and their directors and officers) face a more challenging landscape than ever before when it comes to liabilities arising out of *cyber risks*. The risk landscape applicable to companies is shifting quickly and boards need to adapt to this. There has been an increasing number of high profile, adverse cyber incidents that have brought the potential consequences of cyber risks to light. Threats to companies are well known and incidents that have led to loss of profits, reputational damage, regulatory liability and litigation have been reported worldwide.

The landscape for boards continues to evolve in an ever-increasing risk matrix. The extension of the senior managers' regime, shareholder activism, the increasing sophistication of collective actions across Europe, the EU's General Data Protection Regulation (GDPR), data loss, alleged management failings in insolvency situations and cyber security all feature strongly in the risk column. These risks are set against increasing political tension and economic uncertainty, festering trade wars, and geopolitical concerns.

2 Improving the Functioning of a Boardroom: Structures, Processes and Composition

Because a business environment is constantly changing, boards are not static either. The chair and members of a nominating committee for instance have the responsibility of approving the strategy of a firm and of constantly monitoring the manner in which the board is acting and reacting to these inherent changes. Consequently, as the strategic context changes, the board has the obligation of finding and recruiting members whose competencies and behaviours can assist the board in addressing these new situations. For effectively with this varying needs, competencies, behaviour, strategy and recruitment need to be aligned. It makes building an effective boardroom somewhat like solving a simultaneous equation that is unique for each corporate board: the competencies needed at a board vary from firm to firm, and from industry to industry. It may be relatively easy to find a professional, but expecting someone with the appropriate desired behavioural characteristics [of a high level of integrity] may prove to be more difficult. The challenge is to find someone with both characteristics. And finding someone for a board position to have the professional competency, to think strategically within a certain industry, and being able to implement an organizational strategy is quite demanding on anyone. And adding the characteristic of being trustworthy remains crucial for any board.

2.1 Assessing the Boardroom

When addressing the functioning or evaluating a board, we usually look at the major tasks and why is best suited for addressing those fiduciary duties. When governance principles are applied, socio-historical contexts may differ, but the essence is applicable across borders. The key of good corporate governance in any of the firms, wherever incorporated or operational, lies in ensuring that the principles of *transparency, fairness, accountability* and *responsibility* are consistently and effectively deployed throughout the organization. Any serious lapse of these principles can result in failure or even collapse of organizations – as shown in the case of Enron, Arthur Anderson and other international examples. At the same time, it is also well-understood that organizations will need to take risks to create value. So far we argued that this creation of value through risky ventures need to be balanced with proper governance. From a functional perspective boards aim to optimize their duties of supervision, steering and coaching.

Allow us to reiterate: The three fiduciary general duties are translated in roughly two or three specific generic obligations and responsibilities that directors (both executive as non-executive) need to fulfil: Steering to a profitable future of the organization through (1) strategy & risk, compliance, (2) oversight & supervision of performance of top leadership, and finally (3) advising & coaching top leadership on a number of issues that can profoundly affect the organization in one way or another.

To discharge the Board of its fiduciary obligations, the members therefore need (1) to steer the organization strategically, which implies the allocation of resources once the strategic decision has been taken, and it also goes without saying that any potential threatening risk will need to be taken into account and mitigated or prevented if possible. In other words, boards will need to establish a Strategy and Governance committee to discuss those potential investments and how that affects the future competitiveness of the organization, and it is also recommended to also have a separated Risk Committee in which the potential threats (and opportunities) are discussed, such as external risks (geopolitical and international crises, macroeconomic downturns, or de-globalization trends as result of China-US contest), but also operational risks (cyberthreats and data privacy issues, corruption and nepotism tendencies in the operations) that can and should be prevented – often seen as falling under the organizational authority of the operational *Internal Audit* – which reports directly to the [supervisory] board and is charged with looking after safeguarding against or controlling of those specific risks; (2) to make sure that the organization complies with all the rules and regulations, especially when the company is publicly listed, it means that an *Auditing committee* prepares the financials that need to be signed off by all board members after a public audit. The information that leads to the signed off audit or annual report constitutes the basis for a performance appraisal of top leadership by the non-executive board. New is the board's obligation to look after the compliance of data privacy as stipulated by the [Indonesian] law – following the EU's data privacy regulation. For board members at banks, considerable time is taken to make sure that the bank is compliant to those stringent bank regulations. Nomination and Remuneration are usually discussed in a separated committee to make sure that the principle of fairness and transparency is respected – to secure "compliance" to this best practice. Finally, boards (3) also function as the senior elders of the

2 Improving the Functioning of a Boardroom: Structures, Processes and Composition — 59

organizational community, to coach top leaders, to prepare them for the difficult job of making choices in a very uncertain and ambiguous world. The board is a structure that allows top leadership to consult this senior board members, especially when the CEO is preparing strategic options but also with complex specific challenges on which board members may have competence and expertise. To use a sport analogy, the players (i.e. executive leadership) on the pitch execute what the coach (i.e. senior non-executive board members) has discussed and prepared them to do. At any time, the players can and should ask advise in order to make them performing and potentially winning championships.

How to improve the accountability of a collegial board while improving [incentivized] performances? How to avoid the silo-mentality of individual board members? Boards take the final and ultimate responsibility for the performance of an organization, be it a state owned enterprise, or a family company, or a listed company with many different shareholders, or a privately held company, or a NGO, all are bound by evaluating the performance of the board and its executives to the agreed objectives and goals of the organization. These good corporate governance principles, that can and should be contextualized for any specific company, help firms to reduce threatening risks, and guarantee that proper decisions are made according to established procedures and rules to safeguard the integrity of the organization – and not to fall in the trap of particular (often vested) interests at the expense of the organization.

We both had our way to assess, analyse, evaluate, and assist or challenge boards when necessary. Whatever the specific responsibilities given. The matrix-table (figure 17) hereunder reflects an overview of the different focus points that

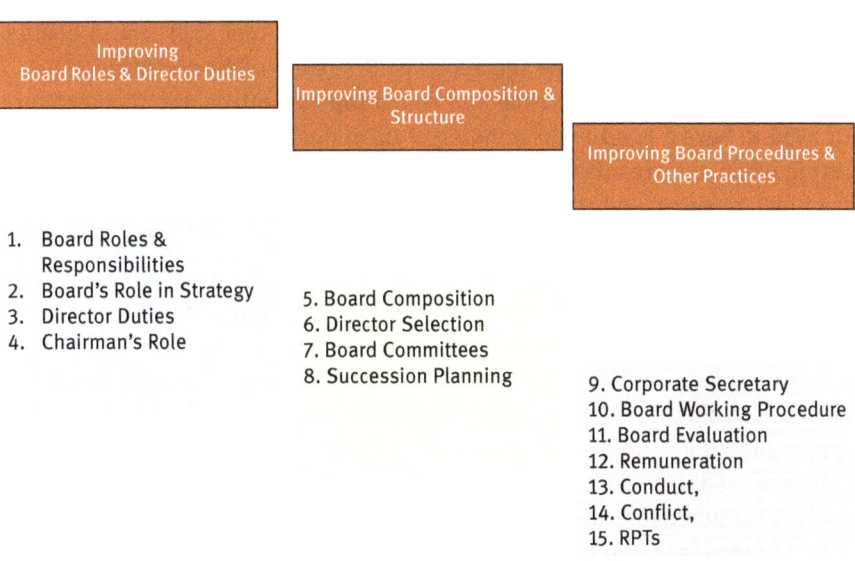

Figure 17: Enacting functioning boards that create trust.

allows shareholders and or advisors to help boards to fine-tune and or to enhance their abilities to perform their respective fiduciary duties. The fifteen items hereunder spelled out function like the instrument board of a car's cockpit screen. Each of those items need to be defined and or explained in detail in the constitution of the organization or spelled out in the specific procedures or processes of the board's functioning, as we will explain the following sections.

For a board to perform properly, executives need the right oversight to secure their expected performance and the right guidance to prepare guidance to prepare the future by making the right strategic decisions and the subsequent investments. That is only possible with having the right people and the right team on board, supported by the right processes and the right culture which ensures the appropriate accountability and responsibility from its board members. And it goes without saying that to measure the performance of a board, the right information should be properly and transparently disclosed to its shareholders and involved relevant stakeholders.

2.2 The Right Oversight and the Right Guidance

Success is to create and to deliver value. In doing so, sustainable success in value creation requires not only to "do the right things" (strategy execution) but also "doing the things right" (as in operational and quality management). To secure this value creation, boards look after the interest of the organization and supervise the major strategists and executers of it. A certain level of formality is required to avoid future misinterpretation.[23] Moreover, compliance is necessary but not sufficient. A board is also expected to challenge, shape and approve the strategy of the organization.

Being able to supervise, advise and coach top executives, the members of a board need to have a good understanding of the industry, the competition and the context in which the organization operates. It requires experience in setting and implementing strategies, and the commitment to demonstrate critical thinking skills. But it also involves the ability to shape a proper organizational culture, by playing an exemplary function in the organization, as chair and or as commissioner at the board. Impeccable integrity is crucial to be able to properly function and to be trustworthy: actions speak louder than words. Being an effective board member also implies a duty to foresee the sustainability of the organization and thus continuity through leadership development, which implies a proper succession planning. Succession involves the training and preparing next leadership.

Effective oversight and internal control for the organization requires establishing a culture of accountability and transparency – beyond a mere mechanistic rule-based retrospective approach. We believe that a pure formalist corporate culture – or worse a monopolistic culture where the patriarch or monarch-like-CEO decides all – should be avoided, because such a culture is ultimately detrimental to the creation and capturing of shareholder value. Similarly, reducing the supervisory role of the board to a mere "control-oriented" (often bureaucratic) mechanism is not advisable. The internal control unit plays a crucial role in assisting and advising the board to supervise. Although the internal [control] audit has an important support function, it should not be seen as acting like the internal prosecutor and or evaluate decisions solely on a result-oriented and or retrospective basis. Decision-making partially remains an artform since we never have 100 percent information available. A balance between risk-aversion and too much risk-taking needs to be established, preferably at the board level – setting the [risk appetite] boundaries in which decisions can be made. The internal audit function should have the goal to bring a systematic and disciplined approach to evaluate and improve the effectiveness of risk management, internal controls, strategic thinking and governance processes. The internal audit should be directly linked to the supervisory board. Financial auditing has a specific function and is conducted to keep the corporate records accurately and up-to-date. These records need to be reliable and verifiable. However, it is well-known that if too many issues need to be approved by the board, it will significantly slow down the decision-process and limit or weaken the learning mechanisms of managers.

It is not unnecessary to emphasize the fact that good operating boards and their committees imply real discipline. Being well informed to make good decisions, and making swift decisions result in organizations outperforming their peers by two times.[24] Enough time need to be foreseen at boards to discuss potential low-likelihood but high consequence [predictable] surprises, or 'black elephants'.[25] All managers are accountable for all the decisions they have made and they need to be able to explain the reasons for their decisions in line with the governance principles of accountability, fairness and transparency. Risk management can be seen as the essence of the flip side of strategic management. The role of a board is to ensure that the processes established are sound and reliable. Hence why prudent risk management practices remain a key to the sustainability of any organization. Yes, business is the art of undertaking calculated risks to gain competitive advantage whereby [negative threatening] risks should be managed, mitigated or avoided all together. Everyone is familiar with the adage that "luck favours the prepared mind". It concretely means that any business and their board should assess, analyse, evaluate and where possible to mitigate these risks, be it financial, operational, strategic, or reputational risks. The latter includes cyberthreats that have lately gained in importance. Assessing and managing those risks while providing the proper oversight is a key board obligation to gain the trust of stakeholders, in particular the important shareholders. The board needs to ensure that management protects and develops corporate assets that are used to create and capture value.

The other crucial important responsibilities of a board is to provide the strategic guidance to the organization. Such guidance includes good decision-making skills, as well as impeccable behaviour and communication that could shape the corporate culture. Walking the talk and openly adhering to good corporate governance principles is a must: consistency in behaving responsibly, being accounted for the behaviour at the board and organization, being fair and effective in motivating management and investors while focusing on the right issues and considering different options and aspects that could increase the effectiveness of the guidance provided, while challenging enough strategic alternatives. Implementing those governance principles is critical in setting the tone at the top with the aim to get it translated into the tune or culture of the organization.

Organizational culture functions as the fundament of an organization because culture expresses the values, vision, mission and purpose. The organizational culture reflects the sum of the actual behaviour of all employees within the firm. It is what you feel, the ways things are done in the organization. Organizational structures and processes – the features developed and approved at a board – either help or constrain strategy. These structures and processes need to be adapted to the long term strategy of the organization which may require education, training, adapting reward systems, all criteria that may affect the ultimate actual behaviour of the people working within the organization. The essence of *strategy is making an informed choice* – which always takes place within a certain organizational context or culture. Hence why the culture that carries the values of an organization is so important. And it is the board who sets the tone, ultimately. Without leaders being an example, they cannot expect the subordinates to stand tall or to do the right thing or do the things right. And thus, choosing the right top management with the right leadership style for the top job is crucial.

Indeed, one could easily argue that good corporate governance can be interpreted and summarized as in providing the right *guidance* and the right *oversight*

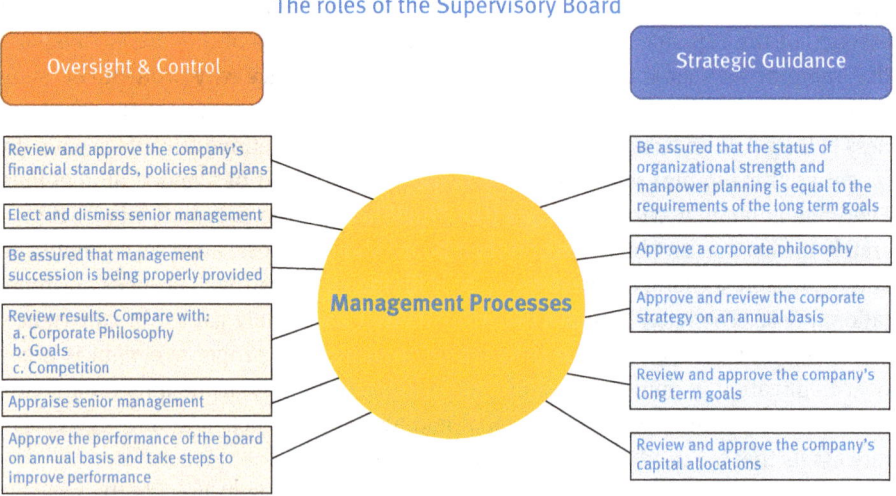

Figure 18: The role of the Board of Commissioners under dual-tier boards.
Source: *Monks and Minow – Corporate Governance, 2004*

(as visualised in Figure 18) through a combination of (1) choosing the right *people* and the right *team*, (2) installing the right *processes*, and the right *culture*, and (3) providing the right *information* and proper transparency and disclosure.

A) The *Right People* and the *Right Team* with an Independent Mind, being Entrepreneurial and Innovative

In choosing a CEO or President Director, the board members need to feel comfortable that they know the candidates well in order to be able to evaluate them from different perspectives. Top executives need to be competent, smart but also wise or ethical, and be able to communicate well with investors, customers, employees, government and the community. Yes indeed, a good functioning board at the end of day is about *good leadership*, about securing that organizations sustain over a longer period, by preparing and executing appropriate strategies, by securing that no excessive risks are taken, that executives remain within the risk boundaries as agreed by the board, that enough liberty is given to executives to take reasonable risks to create value and that all board members and executives can be accounted for their performances according to the agreed objectives in a transparent and fair manner. And although it may sound like a cliché, one of the keys to a successful functioning board is the character and the competencies of the people who make up the board. The simple reason is that those people will exercise judgment on critical dimensions of risk versus reward, short-term versus long-term interests, and of effective oversight versus motivating executives, ethical considerations versus market practices in different jurisdictions and contexts, and balancing the competing interests of the numerous stakeholders who may have opposing views.

It is therefore crucial that board members are trustworthy, think independently and bring experience and diverse opinions and competencies to the table of a board. The notion of independence plays a crucial role on most boards to guarantee some kind of "objectivity" in making reasonable informed decisions. In a Western but increasingly also in an Asian context, *independence* has become a legal requirement to join a board in many instances. However, this legal notion of independence may be overrated since we believe that independence refers to a state of mind that oozes some intellectual independence, as well as political and emotional independence. All to avoid group thinking[26] – that is a type of thought exhibited by group members who try to minimize conflict to reach consensus. Group-thinking is definitely a form of bias[27] that you encounter in Western but also Asian hierarchical places where critical reflection or consensus is naturally sought. In such a consensus-seeking culture, harmony often trumps fierce debates and open discussions. In open organizational cultures, diversity and disagreement is seen as a way to allow innovative ideas to emerge. In cultures where harmony is supreme, a candid and sometimes radical openness is not necessarily fully acceptable.

Having an independent mind is not an easy natural feature in an Asian context where hierarchy and loyalty are woven into most social fabric. Moreover, our empirical research did not immediately see a correlation between independency and return on assets in firms listed on the Indonesian Stock Exchange.[28] A partial explanation may be that most regulators have now imposed a quota for independency at boards. Such minimum level of independence is assumed to pursue the board members to make more informed and reasonable decisions. And yes, Indonesian and other regulators in ASEAN countries have imposed a minimum of at least 30 percent of the supervisory board to be declared "independent"[29], whereas in the USA and the UK, single-tier boards aim to be as independent as possible with more than 50 percent of the members considered to fulfil that label.

From experience we are also strong proponents of appointing experienced members to the board – persons who have proven to be entrepreneurial and innovative, who can bring some risk-perspective to the table, allowing to really prepare the organization for the fast changing future that likely will be more "digital and relational".[30] Would firms survive without innovative perspectives that personalize products and services in the future? Likely not. It will require boldness and foresight to prepare organizations for such a fast changing future.

And it goes without saying that each board member should be able to devote sufficient time and attention to fully assume the responsibilities and duties to serve on the board. Above all, creating a conducive chemistry between these different opinions and perspectives is the task of the chair, for the simple reason that a board functions as a unified team to the outside world.

In reality, board members in Asia (but also elsewhere) are often chosen because of their loyalty towards the family patriarch and family members. Former high state officials are often honoured to sit on the board of state owned enterprises. Over time, we have seen an improvement in the choice of board members at both well-known family businesses and state owned enterprises in Indonesia, and in Asia in general. Having said that, we still believe that more can be done. State owned enterprises would enormously benefit from "*de-politization*", *de-bureaucratization* and a *professionalization* of their boards and managers with clear fiduciary duties to the organization and not being 'informally obliged' to its changing political and often entrenched patrons. Proper functioning boards should guarantee a succession of managerial talent for the future. Only then, we believe, state owned organizations have a chance to survive and thrive over the long term. And that is what would be the duty of any government official who have opted for public office to underwrite a common public good, not their self-interest or political patronage. That applies as well to board members serving on state owned enterprises who are paid to create organizational value, not to destruct it or to pay "patronage" to those who put them in that position. Only people with high integrity, supported by strong and professional structures and governance rules may have a chance to take on those daunting challenge to secure competitiveness and productivity in those organizations, while simultaneously serving the bigger common goals at such state owned enterprises.

Board performance is a team performance and is key to the organizational success. The composition of the board is therefore important to guarantee enough in-depth experience and understanding of what the organization may look like in 10–15 years from now. Each board member with specific expertise, experience and commitment complements the total expertise of a board that supervises, guides and coaches top management. The diversity and complementarities of the skillsets of the individual board members – the composition[31] in other words[32] – all contribute to improving the effectiveness of decisions made. Groups and teams are often better decision-makers than individuals because they can act on error-correcting mechanisms and reduce possible biases.[33]

The chemistry between the individual board members is important in order for a board to be effective, and as mentioned groupthink should be avoided at all costs. Groupthink-bias should be clearly distinguished from a board which is expected to collectively take decisions after serious debate and discussion (reaching a dialectic obtained consensus). It is the collective culture of the board that determines the success or failure of its functioning. The more diverse a board is with the relevant expertise and experience, the higher chance of getting different perspectives and or options that will significantly improve the decision-making, as long as this diversity is not implicitly undermined by trying to merge into group-thinking. Indeed, it is this diversity that likely determines the potential [improved] success of good "informed" decision-making, more so than the precise optimal size of the board whereby the minimal size is often determined by the regulator. Banks on average, because of their complexity in different activities in a heavily regulated industry across borders, have a larger size of board members than other companies. Either way, competencies need to be aligned with desired behavioural characteristics. Different contexts require different kind of leadership.[34]

B) The *Right Processes* and the *Right Culture* (for Accountability and Responsibility at Boards)

Processes and procedures help boards to professionally fulfil their fiduciary duties. And there is no doubt in our mind that the success of an organization depends on the effectiveness of the decisions on its resource allocation and investments. Such decisions requires the process of initiation, approval, implementation and monitoring. All basic functions that apply to the duties of a board and to a lesser extent of management. Indeed, for key strategic decisions the board's involvement is supreme. And to ensure that the board can fulfil its role properly, the right processes and by extension, the right culture is assumed.

When referring to the processes, we think of the way board members but also shareholders are informed, how proposals are considered, discussed and whether guidance is provided by the [supervisory] board. Right processes are helping boards to make informed decisions, where certain responsibilities are assigned to subcommittees in preparing some of those decisions. Processes also refer to the way results are monitored. Although we do not go in detail of how board meetings should be planned and conducted, it is adamant that the chairperson sets the agenda of those meetings, taking into account the recommendations of the CEO and committee chairs, and other experienced board members. The agenda should always focus on the key strategic issues, rather than getting lost in day-to-day operational issues which should be addressed by the management and the executive directors.

When boards make decisions, its members need to be decisive and take responsibility for their decisions, as well to be accounted for the consequences these decisions carry with them. Historically and culturally, one often sees that the members of the board of directors will postpone decisions by pushing the buck to the supervisory board for "approval" because of the increased fear for "doing something wrong". Such boards – especially at state owned enterprises – have become very ineffective and non-decisive, undermining the ultimate task of a board.

Some critical voices in state-owned enterprises comment that the pressure of an external powerful anti-corruption committee can be a cause of non-decisive boards, fearing that a number of decisions could be interpreted as potentially "nepotistic". An intriguing argument that we understand but do not underwrite – for the simple reason that if decisions are properly taken in a transparent manner, the board should not be afraid being accounted for those decisions. Yes, if the roles and duties are clearly defined, and if good corporate governance practices are applied, no member should be worried of nepotism or mis-behaviour. It is because of the decades long pervasive culture of individual loyalty to patronage and expected reciprocal behaviour in all forms and format, that this greyish area often become an arena of "unethical" conduct.[35] In all fairness, when a board does their job, following the proper procedures and processes, nobody should feel threatened or intimidated by anti-corruption officials.[36] In fact, properly implementing good corporate governance will protect board members.[37]

When a board hides being the board out of fear for "wrongdoing", hardly any substantial decision will be made, aggravating the ineffectiveness of boards. Being collegial at a board does not preclude to avoid tough decisions, or to disagree. It is the responsibility of the chair to prioritize the topics on the agenda, and to allocate adequate time for discussion and deliberation on the topic so that the board can comfortably reach a conclusion – with the understanding that these decisions are "recorded in minutes" in a quasi-formal manner. At the end, a board makes a "unified" decision, though individual disagreement could be noted in the board notules/notes, and all board members should be accounted for the decisions made.

How can the functioning of the board (BoC + BoD) be improved to ensure real collaboration and joint responsibility taking? How to create a well-functioning board that takes advantage of a dual-tier board structure while acting as a unified board? By empowering the senior supervisory board to advise, coach and collaborate with

2 Improving the Functioning of a Boardroom: Structures, Processes and Composition — 67

the executive board on strategic decisions, while also monitoring the executive board's (BoD) performances, the Indonesian state-owned PT Telkom for instance was able to significantly improve its overall productivity and become a competitive player in the deregulated telco industry.

The board's structure and composition can help to improve the overall performance of the business. We here describe two "mandatory" (sub)committees at the board, (a) the audit committee (cf Figure 19) and (b) the nomination & compensation committee (cf Figure 20). We here describe two "mandatory" (sub)committees at the board, (a) the audit committee (cf. Figure 19) and (b) the nomination & compensation committee (cf .Figure 20). We add two optional (sub)committees that we highly recommend to put in place at any corporation with a considerable revenues stream: (c) a risk & strategy committee (cf. Figure 21), and (d) a governance and sustainability committee (cf. Figure 22).

The board's audit subcommittee (as detailed in Figure 19) reviews the financial statements and internal controls. This committee recommends, appoints and cooperates with

Audit Committee[142]
- Mandatory for issuers and public companies (OJK)
- Recommended for other companies (OJK CG Guidelines)

Function	Composition
The audit committee should assist the BoC to ensure that: • Financial reports are presented appropriately in accordance with generally accepted accounting principles • The internal control structure is adequate and effective • Internal and external audits are conducted in accordance with applicable audit standards • Management follows up on audit findings In addition, the audit committee will assist the BoC with the appointment, re-appointment, and removal of the external auditors, including approving the remuneration and terms of engagement of the external auditors , as well as assessing the quality of their work.	The audit committee should consist of at least three members, comprising an independent commissioner as well as parties from outside the company. One member should have knowledge and/or expertise in finance and accounting. The audit committee should be chaired by an independent commissioner.

Figure 19: The Audit (Sub)committee.
Source: IFC Indonesian Corporate Governance Manuel, (2018: 173).

an external auditor who will verify and audit the financials and subsequently transparently disclose that audited information. It is expected that this audit committee will also address integrity issues and fraud prevention.

To ensure that the board and top executives (among whom the CEO) are professionally and properly chosen, a nomination committee (as described in Figure 20) assesses the candidates, often with the assistance of an executive search company. As the supervisor of top management, the board is expected to oversee the performance and determine the appropriate and competitive compensation of top management – assuring quality, integrity and continuity of management while also ensuring the motivation and loyalty of this top management.

Like in any profession, board members need to have the necessary skills to govern and to lead an organization or a board. Often, Asian boards are stacked with "friendly" members whose tasks is to protect the interest of the one who put them there, and not genuinely providing guidance to management to enhance opportunities and to reduce risks. What kind of leadership skill set should be ideally expected from board members, both commissioners and executive directors? Above all integrity and trustworthiness has been a characteristic that is valued by investors and stakeholders alike, across borders and time. The other highly demanded feature is the ability to be a critical and creative thinker – similarly to what is expected from the feature of independency. Often industry experience is required to join a board. Sometimes, a particular scientific academic skillset is appreciated, especially in pharma and the bio-industry, but increasingly also in tech companies that develop artificial intelligence algorithms among other technology.

After the board has agreed on a particular candidate, the remuneration is discussed and determined according to the prevailing industry standards.

Let us stop for a moment at state-owned enterprises, and how specific such context can be. Why not installing a Selection Committee with the unique objective of assisting the Minister of State-Owned Enterprises (in Indonesia) to choose the right people in charge of making crucial decision at important state-owned enterprises. It would secure a reasonable and objective process helping the minister of SOEs to appoint the appropriate team at the boards of SOEs. The main reason is to "de-politicise" the process of appointing of boards at SOEs. One should avoid the mentality of auctioning off those powerful positions as a political favour. Indeed, the purpose of this Selection Committee at the ministerial level is to recommend the *right people* to the Minister of SOEs – after a thorough independent "search and select" process of leader candidates with the right skillset, impeccable integrity and proper management or leadership qualifications to govern or to steer, to lead and to execute the proper decisions. These candidates for a position of commissioner [or director] – selected and recommended by this Committee – with the envisaged right skillset and leadership qualifications will help to empower the supervisory board to collaborate with the executive team while also be accountable for monitoring that same executive board. A supervisory board with professionals who know how to

2 Improving the Functioning of a Boardroom: Structures, Processes and Composition

Nomination and Remuneration Committee[143]
- Mandatory for issuers and public companies (OJK)
- Recommended for other companies (OJK CG Guidelines)

Function	Composition

The nomination and remuneration committee is responsible for the following:
 	
• Make recommendations to the BoC on the composition of the BoC and BoD, including required policies and criteria for board nomination and performance evaluation
• Make recommendations to the BoC on training programs to develop the capacities of the BoC and BoD
• Propose to the BoC any candidate who might qualify as a member of the BoC or BoD, to be submitted to the GMS
• Make recommendations to the BoC on remuneration structure, remuneration policy, and amount of remuneration
	OJK requires the nomination and remuneration committee to have at least three members, who must fulfill these requirements:
	
	• The chairman of the committee must be an independent commissioner
	• Other members of the committee may be:
	  1. Members of the BoC
	  2. Persons from outside the company who:
	    • Have no affiliated relationship with that company, any members of its BoC or BoD, or with any principal shareholders
	    • Have experience related to nomination and remuneration
	    • Not hold any position in any other committees of the company
	  3. Persons who hold a managerial position in human resources under the authority of the BoD (should not be the majority members of the committee)

Figure 20: Nomination & Remuneration Committee: leadership development to install board skills. Source: IFC Indonesian Corporate Governance Manuel, (2018: 173).

govern and to lead an organization will likely make better decisions in terms of risk management, strategy and development & selection of capable qualified people who are able to lead and execute major decisions.

Let us return to the board in general, selecting and developing future leadership talent. The process of selecting new board members should ideally be initiated by the corporate governance subcommittee who determines the prospective candidates and present them to the board for approval. Let us not forgot that it is the Nomination & Remuneration Committee (as seen in Figure 20) that actually nominates the top executives and their compensation package. However, it is the Corporate Governance

Risk Policy Committee	
Recommended for all companies (OJK CG Guidelines)	
Function	**Composition**
The risk policy committee should assist the BoC in: • Setting the risk governance structure, determining levels of risk tolerance, and monitoring key risk indicators and results regularly • Reviewing the adequacy and effectiveness of risk management and internal control systems	Members of the risk policy committee need experience in the industry in which the company is active. However, the committee will likely benefit from having members with other areas of expertise such as risk management, finance, and operations. The committee should consist primarily of BoC members but the company may appoint professionals from outside of the company if needed.

Figure 21: Risk (Sub)Committee.
Source: IFC Indonesian Corporate Governance Manuel, (2018).

Committee (as explained in Figure 22) that identifies the main issues which the organization faces, the skill gap within the current board that needs to be addressed, and the key competencies which the board is looking for. In addition, this committee can also be involved in the self-evaluation of the board, ideally with the assistance of an experienced facilitator or reputable consultancy.

Another task beholden to the board is the board's self-evaluation. It is a proper process that looks at the performance of the board as a whole; it may focus on the role of the chairperson (or lead director in case of a one-tier board) by looking into the contribution to the development of strategies, approach to risk management architecture, the evaluation of the top executives, and the communication skills with stakeholders and shareholders or investors.

This corporate governance committee also evaluates each individual board member who constitutes the team by looking at the quality of the contribution made to the strategy and risk management, the relations with other board members and senior management, the communication skills in presenting views, creating trust and respect with individual performance and behaviour, and the contributions to activities outside the board meetings. It is also crucial that the members prove to possess the knowledge about the industry and the market, as well as a minimal understanding of corporate governance and financial reporting requirements. In addition, board processes may need to be evaluated in terms of effectiveness of agenda and decision-making, as well as the adequacy of board meetings in achieving the desired objectives related to strategy formulation, identification of major risks, succession planning,

Corporate Governance Committee	
Recommended for all companies (OJK CG Guidelines)	
Function	**Composition**
The corporate governance committee typically has the following responsibilities: • Assist the BoC in developing the company's corporate governance policies • Monitoring and reviewing the effectiveness of the company's corporate governance practices, including those related to environmental and social aspects.	Members of the committee should meet high integrity standards, enjoy the trust of all shareholders, and be knowledgeable on legal and ethical standards. The committee should consist primarily of BoC members, but the company may appoint professionals from outside of the company if needed. The corporate governance committee may be combined with the nomination and remuneration committee.

Figure 22: Corporate Governance (Sub)Committee.
Source: IFC Indonesian Corporate Governance Manuel, (2018).

disclosure policies, and the integrity of internal control. It is for that same reason that boards should be continuously trained through orientation programs and specific skill-set training.

If we agree that the supervisory but also the executive board functions as the stewards of the organization's assets, be it tangible or intangible, then one can expect the board to behave in such a manner as to create and capture value over a longer period. It may be good to repeat that a [supervisory] board should be independent in its decisions, adhering to the highest ethical standards that reflect integrity and trustworthiness – which is the basis for any leadership position – and that their ambition is to steer, to supervise, and to advise, never to take over or to replace the management. Unless in the very rare case of an extreme crisis caused or not fully addressed by the top management. The result of this kind of behaviour by a board can be seen in what we call 'setting the tone of the organizational culture', the climate at the organization exhibited by the behaviour of all its executives and employees following the lead of the board. *Organizational culture* can thus be described as the unwritten rules and values of what and how things happen in the organization. It goes without saying that mutual trust between the board and the management requires the acceptance of each duties and the internalization of the separation of executive and supervisory or control rights.

We argue that good corporate governance practices partially constitute the values of the organization and thus by extension the culture itself. That is also the reason that good corporate governance is more than the sum of the individuals and their values applied. Governance goes beyond mere compliance; it refers to a culture of integrity or responsibility, of accountability and respect, of fairness and transparency, and it secures the effectiveness of those principles embedded in the daily organizational culture. Corporate or organizational culture is a key in creating an atmosphere in which a set of desired behaviours flourish in the organization, whereby the tone is set at the board. Compliance without ethical values is almost like an oxymoron. Without integrity, boards would not properly function, whatever level of control and procedures. Earning the trust of other stakeholders and other colleagues is only possible by appropriate ethical behaviour and by professional acts that create value for stakeholders. The rest is pure academic. Without those values that guide ethical behaviour, corporate governance will be reduced to mere talk and interesting promised but mere high-flying principles on the wall. Organizations will need the right governance processes but also the right culture to succeed.

C) The *Right Information* that is Properly and Transparently Disclosed

Having the 'right' information to make informed decisions does not occur automatically. And as the agency problem of asymmetric information has thought us, members of the supervisory board have the right and the duty to take initiative to gather data and information that allows them to make decisions with proper knowledge and understanding of the risks involved.

Sharing relevant information constitute confidence in the way decisions are made at the board. Without this transparent disclosure of financial and non-financial information, it is hard to assess the quality of the board functioning. The need for the 'right information' also implies the right timing and the format of the information to be presented. Often the minimal format of this information sharing is imposed by the regulator. It is clear that the performance reports are critical inputs for both the board and the management. The quality of that disclosed information will partially determine the effectiveness of the board in steering and supervising the organization. It should not surprise us that the integrity of the information disclosed depends on the verifiability of the data as well as the comparability of the data with past data and with industry benchmarks. Performance reports should include the executives' projections and assessments of potential negative risks. Boards should be experts in managing uncertainty, by being able to distinguish the different forms of potential uncertainties and able to "foresee" or create a future that could be meaningful and lucrative for the organization. In that sense, the right information all boils down how that information is needed to make informed decisions, or how boards will obtain information that is useful or needed to enable them to properly prepare in the most knowledgeable manner for an uncertain but nonetheless promising future.

2.3 Fiduciary Duties in an Indonesian Context

In violation of any of two fiduciary duties of care and loyalty, the organization has enough sufficient reason to prosecute the member in question. Admittedly, it is very hard to prove that a supervisory board did not take an informed decision. But in case of an obvious violation of putting personal interests above those of the company can lead to real fines and or prison sentences. And we have ample cases, usually unethical behaviour by boards that clearly violated those duties: Enron, Parmalat, WorldCom, Wells Fargo Bank, We.com and many other well-known international cases. Our experience indicates – but research by Transparency International for instance has corroborated this intuitive feeling – that the list of unethical behaviour in Asia is long, very long indeed.

In Indonesia, the authorities and the private sector have made progress in strengthening the corporate governance framework since the Asian crisis of 1997 to better protect investors and depositors.[38] The recent global economic crisis (2008–2011) has also revealed some failing of supervisory activities of US and European boards. Successful companies assumedly have applied *"best"*[39] *[international] corporate governance practices.*[40] It should therefore be noted that PT Telkom for instance has a dual listing on both the Indonesian Stock Exchange and the Nasdaq in New York secondary exchange that enhances its reputation to institutional foreign and local investors and other relevant stakeholders. The reputational benefits to the board of Telkom for instance is directly connotated to the fact that the firm adheres to these very strict and enforced international best standards and practices.[41]

Under the Indonesian Company Law (ICL) – in line with these best practices, the duties of the executive *Board of Directors* are (A) to manage the company in the interest of the company, consistent with the objectives of the company, and (B) to represent the company both in and outside the courts of law. The duties of the non-executive *Board of Commissioners* are (1) to supervise the performance of the Board of Directors and policies made by the board, and (2) to provide advice to the Board of Directors. In addition, the supervisory board is also assumed (3) to secure "continuity" by ensuring a leadership pool to succeed the current top executives in due time.

As practitioners – Pak Tanri was then Minister of State Owned Enterprises and Peter was an advisor/consultant for IMF-IBRA (the Indonesian Bank Restructuring Agency or colloquially called the 'Bad Debt Bank' of Indonesia) – we strongly believe that more than half of the cases that led to non-performing loans at banks during the Asian crisis in 1997–2001 in Indonesia and in Southeast Asia in general was due to a lack of good corporate governance. More specifically, we have ample reason to prove that self-interest of some bank directors (both executives as non-executives) prevailed over the interests of the bank. These bankers were in the hoot with tycoons who obtained huge USD nominated loans for often "white elephant" projects such as golf courses, over-stretched real estate projects etc. We know for fact that the "guanxi" networks and relationships allowed bankers and tycoons to benefit often without proper due diligence. Worse, the due diligence was made after the agreement to formalistically comply with potential auditing purposes – completely undermining the reason for such analyses in the first place. In restructuring national debt, we saw what illegitimate behaviour – some would call it outright corruption – between bankers and those tycoons can ruin economies as the Asian flu of 1997–2001 has proven.

In all fairness, the recklessness of international Western bankers led to the Global Financial Crisis in 2008, similarly rooted in a lack of good risk oversight and peer-pressure induced speculation accompanied by individual greed. This speculation was often based on alleged triple-A rated debt, which in reality had become systemic risk securities infecting the global economy in 2008. What those professional investors completely ignored were those systemic risks. Just like the tycoons in Southeast Asia ignored the possibility of the "turkey story". It is not because the turkey has been fed by the farmer for 300 consecutive days, that this behaviour will continue for ever. Nobody did foresee that real estate prices in the USA that had risen for 25 consecutive years, could one day fall.[42] Everyone was surprised, and all these presumed risk-free collateralized debt obligations (CDOs) were suddenly worth less than a dollar for a dollar. In the same vein, tycoons did not take into account the possibility that the steady slightly depreciating local Asian currencies could completely lose their exchange value vis-à-vis the US dollar, as in the case of Indonesian Rupiah that lost more than 400% in less than 18 months (1997–1999). Boards' responsibility is to take prudent decisions and make sure that not all investments are put in one (USD nominated) debt basket.

Implementing these (supervisory) board objectives have been a serious challenge for most state-owned enterprises (SOEs) in Indonesia and elsewhere in Asia. "Consistency" nor optimizing financial performance seemed to have been an immediately "directive" or priority. Moreover, the continuous political influence and entrenchment made it hard for those SOEs to fully "professionally" function to compete.

Let us get back to the fiduciary duties of the non-executive (BoC) and executive (BoD) board to clarify this request for professionalism. Obviously, The Chair of the Board of Commissioners should understand the dynamics of these boards in order to lead them in a unified manner. Moreover, the non-executive board of commissioners should gain the respect from the executive directors for what they can contribute to the organization, not because of their legal power. Crucially, both executives and non-executive board members should function as an effective team aiming for the same purpose of creating value. For example, as former chairman of PT Telkom, Pak Tanri had no choice but to intervene when two opposing factions within the board of directors made proper governing and managing the company almost impossible. What followed was a paralysis of the executive board between the CEO and the deputy CEO, and at that point of crisis the chairman took the lead and in his consciousness – right or wrong – dismissed both because of the lack of team-playing, crucial in any firm in transition. The chair assumed the importance of team-work more crucial than the extraordinary functional talent of both quarrelling top executives.

Because of the paucity of public information, enforcement of contractual claims largely depends on the effectiveness and "quality" of those long term relationships, Southeast Asia will need to improve the effectiveness and efficiency of institutions that mediate between the economic and political actors through a better legal system, dramatically enhanced public and corporate governance and appropriately implemented values in business that accentuate and integrate its unique rich culture. We do not advocate to transplant a set of corporate governance features of often Anglo-Saxon origin, but we do believe that contextualizing "best" corporate governance principles as found in some of the best and thus most competitive firms will help Indonesian companies to gain *trust* from institutional investors and the business community and to become more effective in the process. Indonesian PT Telkom – despite the ongoing challenges and fierce competition – has proven that governance mechanisms can help to gain trust from both local and 'picky' foreign institutional and individual investors.

Consider the following Take Away Ideas of Chapter 3

---

1. The OECD principles of good corporate governance are based on the four principles: transparency, fairness, accountability and responsibility.
   We also claim that an organization is more than a nexus of legal contracts; it is also a nexus of relations which implies that a board needs to take into account the relevant stakeholders of the organization, as in customers, employees, suppliers and the community.

2. Both Western and Asian boards can become quite entrenched if members are not thinking independently, and align their decisions too much with the CEO or patriarch instead of focusing on the long-term interests of the organization itself.

3. Indonesian and other Asian boards need to make efforts to reduce potential conflicts of interests (between majority and minority shareholders), including the possibility of entrenchment potentially resulting in subtle 'expropriation' of assets away from the listed company (be it by the family or state majority owners).

Notes

1 How to define those kind of [personal] liabilities related in taking on the fiduciary duties at a board? Each commissioner will share personal liability for the company's losses if the commissioner concerned is at fault or negligent in performing the tasks to supervise and advise the BoD in good faith and with regard to the best interests of the company in accordance with its objectives and purposes. Where the BoC consists of two or more members, they will be jointly and severally liable for such losses, according to ICL (Indonesian Corporate Law), Article 114(3)(4). Board members may not be held liable for the losses if they can prove that (according to ICL, Article 114(5)):

- they have performed their duties in good faith and with prudence and in accordance with the company's interests, objectives, and purposes.
- they do not have any direct or indirect personal interest in the actions of the [executive] Board which caused such losses.
- they have given the [supervisory] Board advice to prevent the occurrence or continuity of such losses.

   Commissioners are not relieved from liability for actions and decisions made during their tenure after they have resigned from or are dismissed by the [supervisory] Board. On behalf of the company, shareholders representing at least one-tenth of the total number of shares with voting rights may sue members of the [supervisory] Board who cause losses to the company as a result of their fault or negligence in the district court, according to ICL, Article 114(6).

2 Corporate governance is a specialized domain within management studies. However, for a good overview, we refer to some influential authors within the mainstream corporate governance field: Bebchuk, L.; Cohen, A. & A. Ferrell, (2004), "What matter in corporate governance?", Working Paper Harvard Law School; Berle, A.A. & G.C. Means, (1932), *The modern corporation and the private property*, New York, Harcourt Brace; Bhagat, S. & B. Bolton, (2008), "Corporate Governance and Firm Performance", *Journal of Corporate Finance*, Vol. 14: 257–273; Charan, R., (2005), *Boards that deliver. Advancing corporate governance – from compliance to competitive advantage*, San Fransisco, Jossey Bass; Fama, E. & M. Jensen, (1983a), "Separation of ownership and control", *Journal of Law and Economics*, Vol. 26: 301–325; Jensen, M.C. & W.H. Meckling, (1976), Theory of the Firm: managerial behavior, agency costs and ownership structure, *Journal of Finance Economics*, Vol. 3: 305–360; La Porta, R., Lopez-De-Silanes, F. & A. Schleifer, A, (1999), "Corporate ownership around the world", *Journal of Finance,* 54(2), 471–517; Schleifer, A. & R. Vishny, (1997), "A survey of corporate governance", *Journal of Finance*, Vol.52: 737–783; and Zingales, L., (1998), *Corporate Governance. The New Palgrave Dictionary of Economics and Law*, London, MacMillan.

3 See IFC Indonesian Manuel for corporate governance. The following summarizes specific features that characterize Indonesia's corporate sector:

a. The role of state-owned enterprises: Over the last twenty years, Indonesia has converted a number of state-owned enterprises into partly privatized companies through public offerings and/or strategic alliances. Nevertheless, many important sectors in Indonesian economy remain either state monopolies or largely dominated by wholly state-owned enterprises, such as those in banking, electricity, mining, oil and gas, post and telecommunications, railway, and shipbuilding sectors. In numerous equitized state-owned enterprises, the state retains a majority interest of 51 percent, and exercises its control via the general shareholder meeting and by retaining the right to appoint commissioners and/or directors.

b. Concentrated ownership: Many companies in Indonesia start out as small private companies owned either by a single controlling shareholder, a family patriarch, or a small group of shareholders. Although many have expanded significantly, the controlling shareholders often have not changed. This concentrated ownership structure poses distinct challenges, such as how best to manage family conflicts; decide on succession; define ownership policies; strengthen strategic planning and other management functions; and broaden the membership of the BoC to include non-family, independent commissioners. Not being able to tackle these challenges effectively restricts the capacity of these businesses to attract the additional capital required for achieving full growth potential. Such insider dominance and weak protection of external shareholders/ investors have resulted in failed deals and the underdevelopment of the capital markets in Indonesia. A trend, albeit nascent, towards public offerings, and thus more dispersed ownership, has started. Whether these majority shareholders are truly willing to reduce or even exit their investments remains to be seen.

c. **Little separation of ownership and control:** Most controlling shareholders often occupy key positions at both the BoC and the BoD, although the ICL does not allow the same individual to serve concurrently as a commissioner and a director. Those companies that separate ownership and control often do so only on paper. Failure to separate ownership and control typically results in weak accountability and control structures (the majority/controlling shareholders oversee themselves in their function as commissioners and directors), abusive related party transactions, and poor information disclosure (insiders have access to all information and are unmotivated to disclose to outsiders or minority shareholders).
d. **Unwieldy holding structures:** Some major business groups, especially large state-owned enterprises, are set up in the form of parent companies that maintain control over their subsidiaries. While holding structures can serve legitimate purposes, cross-shareholdings and lack of transparency often lead to opaque ownership structures that can disadvantage minority shareholders. Poor or incomplete accounting records present another corporate governance issue that has yet to be tackled.
e. **Inexperienced corporate bodies:** Indonesia first introduced parts of the current concepts of the BoC and BoD in the ICL of 1995 and the Law on State-Owned Enterprises in 2003. However, these concepts were not taken seriously until recently, when companies began to draft detailed articles of association (AoA) or company charter that adhere to existing laws and regulations. In reality, it is still common for the BoD to attempt to bypass the supervisory mechanisms (such as the BoC) put in place by the AoA, and to limit direct contact with the controlling shareholder (to the extent they are not one and the same). The role of the BoC as well as its committees, the BoD, and corporate secretary in day-to-day company operations often remains unclear. Members of these bodies are supposed to be experienced and capable, but in reality they often lack awareness of their responsibilities and authoritiy, due to a historical lack of good practices in these areas. Lack of experience as well lack of independence in the field of corporate governance is a big obstacle for further economic development. Unfortunately, strong, vigilant, and independent corporate bodies remain a rarity.

4 See The Economist, January 22nd 2022: 67–68. This is not the first time that Unilever's board and its CEO has to deal with activist investors who wants the company to focus on profitability first and on prospective growth strategies – instead of allegedly losing time with nice sounding sustainability goals. The former CEO Paul Potman had to resist Kraft's raid on the company. The current CEO, Alan Jope finds himself in a similar position: how to improve the overall financial performance, without jeopardizing Unilever's well regarded sustainability goals. We will highlight this dilemma of "profit versus purpose" in chapter 5.

5 Badaracco, J.L., (2016), *Managing in the Gray. Timeless questions for resolving your toughest problems at work*, Cambridge MA, Harvard Business School Press.

6 Under this duty of care, non-executive directors or commissioners are deemed being responsible for exercising their rights. For that a commissioner of the supervisory board to be discharged he or she (1) should act honestly, on a fully informed basis, and in good faith, (2) use care and prudence to the maximum extent that may be expected of a good commissioner in a similar situation under similar circumstances, (3) not cause the company to act unlawfully, (4) regularly attend and actively participate in BoC meetings, (5) place matters on the agenda of BoC meetings and demand such meetings when necessary, (6) ensure that an effective and efficient system of internal control is in place, (7) ensure that the president director [or CEO] and the BoD provide adequate information to the BoC, so that its members are properly informed on corporate matters, and finally (8) exercise a reasonable amount of supervision over the BoD.

7 It is recommended by the Indonesian Corporate Law that:
- Commissioners should take steps to protect confidential information.
- Commissioners should not disclose information or use it for their own interests.

- Companies should set standards with respect to treatment of confidential information and set these out in internal regulations.
- Contracts between the company and commissioners stipulate the obligation of commissioners to not disclose confidential information for a period of ten years after they leave the company.
- To create an effective mechanism to prevent the unauthorized use of confidential information, the company should require commissioners to:
- Notify the BoC in writing of their intention to enter into transactions that involve securities of the company or its subsidiaries.
- Disclose information about previous transactions involving securities of the company in accordance with the procedures for disclosing material facts as specified by securities legislation.
- Upon their appointment, sign an agreement to comply with all legal requirements regarding the treatment of confidential information and non-disclosure of confidential information.

8 How to interpret "Conflicts of Interest" in Indonesia? See OJK Regulation No. 55/POJK.03/2016 on Implementation of Corporate Governance in Commercial Banks, Article 39. Examples of how a conflict of interest may arise include when a commissioner or his/her related person enters into a contractual relationship with a company, or holds commercial/financial interests in a way that can be reasonably expected to influence the commissioner's behavior contrary to the interests of the company Commissioners should refrain from actions that may potentially result in a conflict between their own interests and the interests of the company. They are also advised to refrain from voting in situations in which they have a personal interest in the matter in question. Commissioners should immediately inform and disclose to the BoC about any potential conflicts of interest. Such information must be disclosed at the first BoC meeting after the commissioner is aware of the conflict. For example, BoC members of banks are obliged to disclose their (a) ownership of shares which amount to 5% or more in any company, in or out of Indonesia; and (b) financial and family relations with other BoC and/or BoD members and/or controlling shareholders of the bank.

9 Legally, the duty of loyalty usually prohibits commissioners from (1) participating in a competing company, (2) entering into any transaction with the company without first disclosing the transaction and obtaining approval from the shareholders and the supervisory board, (3) using corporate property and facilities for personal needs, (4) disclosing non-public, confidential information to outsiders, and (5) using company information or business opportunities for private or personal profit or gain.

10 The ICL stipulates that BoC should not act as an assembly of individuals who represent various constituencies. Rather, as a company organ, the BoC must operate as a cohesive unit. While specific commissioners may be nominated or elected by certain shareholders (and sometimes contested by others), it is an important feature of the BoC's work that commissioners carry out their duties in an even-handed manner with respect to all shareholders. It is particularly important to establish this principle in a company whose ownership structure includes controlling shareholders that are able to select the majority of or in some cases all commissioners. In addition, commissioners and affiliated persons (for example, family, friends, and business partners) should not accept gifts from persons with a vested interest in decisions of the BoC, or accept any other direct or indirect benefits. An exception can be made for symbolic gifts that are given as a common courtesy or souvenirs that are given during official events. These exceptions should be described in internal regulations or other internal documents of the company.

11 People too often consider not seen risks as "black swans" or unknown unknowns, as quipped by the controversial but interesting author Nassim Taleb. See Taleb, N.N., (2005), *Fooled by Randomness. The hidden role of Chance in Life and in the Markets,* New York, Random House Trade Paperbacks; Taleb, N.N.,, (2007), *The Black Swan. The Impact of the Highly Improbable*, London, Allen Lane – Penguin; Taleb, N.N., (2012), *The Antifragile*, London; and Taleb, NN, (2018), *Skin in the Game. Hidden Asymmetries in daily life*, New York, Random House. Taleb for instance claims that the pandemic was not a black swan since it was known though admittedly not predictable. Hence

why some label the pandemic a "grey swan". Still unexpected but could have been prepared for since the dangers were known and prescribed by scientists.
12 Wucker, M., (2020), "Is your board risk-ready?", *Strategy + Business*, Summer, Issue 99.
13 De Haes, S.; Caluwe, L; Huygh, T. & A. Joshi, (2020), *Governing Digital Transformation. Guidance for Corporate Board Members*, Cham, Springer.
14 Managing the affairs of a company is a complex process. There is a risk that even when acting reasonably and in good faith, the BoC may make decisions that prove to be adverse to the company's interests. Companies should allow their commissioners to protect themselves from, or at least limit the liability for, losses incurred while they fulfill their duties. Such mechanisms may include: (1) a liability insurance; (2) provisions in the company charter and/or internal regulations that indemnify commissioners against claims, litigation expenses, and liabilities in certain circumstances . Companies may wish to obtain liability insurance for commissioners to cover the risk that their actions might result in losses to the company or third parties. Liability insurance for commissioners allows companies to use civil law remedies more productively, and the protections that such insurance offer may help companies to attract competent commissioners. In addition, companies may reimburse a commissioner for expenses incurred in defending a claim related to his/her role as a [supervisory] Board member, if he or she acted: honestly, in good faith, in the best interest of the company, and in compliance with law and regulations, the AoA, and internal regulations.
15 Lovallo, D. & O. Sibony, (2006), "Distortions and Deceptions in Strategic Decisions", *McKinsey Quarterly*, April, Vol. 1: 18–29; and Lovallo, D. & O. Sibony, (2010), "The case of Behavioral Strategy", *McKinsey Quarterly*, March: 30–343.
16 Tinsley, C., Dillon, R. & P. Madsen, (2011), "How to avoid catastrophe", *Harvard Business Review,* April: 90–97.
17 Nonaka, I. & H. Takeuchi, (2019), *The Wise Company. How companies create continuous innovation*, Oxford, Oxford University Press.
18 For more details on this distinction, we refer to the forthcoming book: Verhezen, P., *Wising up. Responsible Leadership competing in era of Artificial Intelligence* (in 2022).
19 Charan, R., Carey, D. & M. Useem, (2014), *Boards that Lead. When to take charge, when to partner, and when to stay out the way*, Cambridge (MA), Harvard Business Review Press.
20 This is a revised update and summary of our paper, see Verhezen, P. & T. Abeng, (2020), "Boards that Govern and Lead", *Strategic Review*, Vol. 10(2): 42–57.
21 Verhezen, P.; Chambers, P. & S. De Haes, (2018), "Cyber-threats: Facing the Faceless", *Strategic Review*, Vol. 8(2): 24–40.
22 *Ibidem.*
23 To effectively enforce provisions that regulate the liability of commissioners, it is recommended that the company keep detailed minutes (and possibly verbatim reports) of BoC meetings to determine who voted for a certain decision and who can be held liable (to the extent the court considers such factors). In addition, the company should:
– Encourage commissioners to perform their duties in a proper way
– Take measures to terminate the authority of commissioners who are responsible for inflicting losses
– Hold commissioners responsible when they do not fulfill their obligations to the company.
24 De Smet, A.; Lund, F.; Weiss, L. & s. Nimocks, (2021), "Boards and decision-making", *McKinsey & Company*, April. Why do disciplined boards outperform their peers with this huge difference in performance? Better performance depends on the quality of the debate. One of the hallmarks of high quality debate at boards is their diversity of perceptions. Having someone functioning as the devil's advocate on strategies is a proven method to create different and more options that likely improves decision-making. Moreover, bringing in experts for additional information to handle specific domains of uncertainties also helps. But having a voice on the table does not mean to have a

vote. That distinction needs to be daftly handled by the chair. Ongoing discussions without any final decisions= is detrimental to the organization. Again, the chair's ability to steer the board to make informed and good decisions – especially for big bets, high consequence decisions that are not made frequently. A second type of agenda items is where you need to approve usual assessments related to bylaws, regulations and mainstream governance topics. Taking swift decisions here, will free up time for discussion and guidance – especially for high existential impact events.

25 *Ibidem.*

26 There is a huge literature on the biases of decision-makers and specifically group-thinking. One of the major initial research has been done by Kahneman and his colleagues: Kahneman, D. & A. Tversky, (1979), "Prospect Theory: An Analysis of Decision Under Risk", *Econometrica*, Vol. 47 (2): 263–291; Kahneman,. D., (2011a), *Thinking, Fast and Slow*, London, Penguin-Pearson; Kahneman, D., (2011b), *"Beware the inside view"*, McKinsey Quarterly, November; Kahneman, D. & D. Lovallo, (1993), "Timid Choices and Bold Forecasts: A Cognitive Perspective on Risk Taking", *Management Science*, Vol. 39(1): 17–31; Kahneman, D. & G. Klein (an interview), (2010), "Strategic decisions: When can you trust your gut?", *McKinsey Quarterly*, March; Kahneman, D.; Lovallo, D. & O. Sibony, (2011), *"Before You Make That Big Decision"*, Harvard Business Review, June: 50–60; Kahneman, D.; Rosenfield, A.M.; Gandhi, L. & T. Blaser, (2016), *"Noise. Inconsistent Decision-making"*, Harvard Business Review, October: 38–46; and finally his most recent work Kahneman, D.; Sibony, O. & C.R. Sunstein, (2021), *Noise. A Flaw in Human Judgment*, London, William Collins.

27 See Argüden, Y., (2009: 22), *Boardroom Secrets. Corporate Governance for Quality in Life*, Hamsphire, Palgrave Macmillan., and Heath, C. & D. Heath, (2013), *Decisive. How to make better decisions*, London, Randomhouse. Groupthinking is often the result of falling into the trap when (1) not considering an adequate number of alternatives, (2) not evaluating all of the dimensions of the alternatives, (3) not being properly informed as to the risks and costs of each alternative, and finally (4) not giving enough attention to plans regarding implementation.

28 Verhezen, P. & G. Martin, (2018), "Corporate Governance & Ethical Behavior affecting Performance: Propositions and Peculiarities at Indonesian Firms within its Institutional context", *Melbourne Business School Working Paper, financed by IFC World Bank*.

29 How to define the notion of Independence? International best practice classifies different categories of commissioners according to their degree of involvement in a company's corporate affairs. In Indonesia, the ICL provides that commissioners fall within two main categories: independent commissioners (*komisaris independen*) and delegated or representative commissioners (*komisaris utusan*). Independent commissioners must have no affiliation to the company. Delegated commissioners, on the other hand, may include shareholders and/or individuals who are affiliated with members of the BoC or BoD. An independent commissioner shall be appointed by a shareholders' resolution from among the parties not affiliated with the ultimate shareholders and other BoC and/or BoD members. The BoC nominates delegated commissioners by way of a BoC resolution. Many Indonesian public companies are controlled by a single majority shareholder, or a group of shareholders, that is well informed of the company's affairs. The remaining ownership is often widely dispersed. Many of these minority shareholders lack the resources and information to effectively monitor management or defend themselves against potential abuse by the majority. ISn these types of companies, independent commissioners play an especially vital role. Independent commissioners should make up at least 30 percent of the BoC of a listed company in Indonesia. Indonesia's Corporate Governance Code provides that the number of independent commissioners should ensure that the control mechanism runs effectively and in accordance with laws and regulations.

30 See Verhezen, P., *Wising up. Responsible Leadership in an era of Artificial Intelligence*. Forthcoming.

31 We like to note that women hold only 13.7 percent executive directors roles in FTSE100.

32 Because we are staunch defenders of meritocracy and performance, we would defend the position to have more diversification on a board, including the importance of more experienced women on the board. We doubt that a 40% quota imposing women on the board, as is the case in Scandinavia and other European countries, is a good solution. It is a form of positive discrimination that over a longer term may not be in the best interest of the organization. Women have proven to be great CEOs and board members, often superior to men. But selecting someone based on gender or race – instead of experience and expertise – does not bode well in our humble opinion.

33 A good start to deepen the understanding of decision-making, are the following authors: Lovallo, D. & O. Sibony, (2006), "Distortions and Deceptions in Strategic Decisions", *McKinsey Quarterly*, April, Vol. 1: 18–29; Sibony, O., (2019), *You're about to make a Terrible Mistake! How Biases distort decision-making – and what we can do to fight them*, New York; Boston; London, Little-Brown Spark; Klein, G, (1998), *Sources of Power: How People Make Decisions*, Cambridge MA, MIT Press; Klein, G., (2003), *The Power of Intuition. How to use your gut feelings to make better decisions at work*, New York, Currency Paperback; Klein, G. (2009). *Strengths and shadows: Searching for the keys to adaptive decision-making*, Cambridge MA, MIT Press; Klein, G., (2014), *Seeing what others don't. The remarkable ways we gain Insights*, London; Boston, Nicolas Brealy Publishing; Kahneman, D. & A. Tversky, (1979), "Prospect Theory: An Analysis of Decision Under Risk", *Econometrica*, Vol. 47(2): 263–291; Kahneman,. D., (2011a), *Thinking, Fast and Slow*, London, Penguin-Pearson; Kahneman, D., (2011b), *"Beware the inside view"*, McKinsey Quarterly, November; Kahneman, D. & D. Lovallo, (1993), "Timid Choices and Bold Forecasts: A Cognitive Perspective on Risk Taking", *Management Science*, Vol. 39(1): 17–31; Kahneman, D. & G. Klein (an interview), (2010), "Strategic decisions: When can you trust your gut?", *McKinsey Quarterly*, March; Kahneman, D.; Lovallo, D. & O. Sibony, (2011), *"Before You Make That Big Decision"*, Harvard Business Review, June: 50–60; Kahneman, D.; Rosenfield, A.M.; Gandhi, L. & T. Blaser, (2016), *"Noise. Inconsistent Decision-making"*, Harvard Business Review, October: 38–46; and Kahneman, D.; Sibony, O. & C.R. Sunstein, (2021), *Noise. A Flaw in Human Judgment*, London, William Collins.

34 See Leblanc, R. & J. Gillies, (2005), *Inside the Boardroom. How boards really work and the coming revolution in corporate governance*, Ontario, John Wiley & Sons Canada. In aligning executive directors and commissioner competencies with behavioural expected characteristics and the important corporate strategy remains a quite challenging job. In many ways, selecting a new director in relation to the strategy of the organization is one of the important and difficult tasks of a nominating committee. A harsh reality may be imposed on a board – which may prefer "not to rock the boat", and whose objective may be status-quo – demanding a impactful transformation for instance. Each contextual situation may require different types of leaders. For instance, a consensus-builder is best suited for long-term, less difficult strategic change, corresponding to what is labelled cooperative strategies. However, a challenger-type will obviously initiate difficult strategic changes, whereas a change agent will be needed for dealing with complex, longer-term strategic change. At the other hand, a counsellor is someone who involves personal contact and negotiation (in for instance short-term, less difficult strategic change). A care-taker chair or conformist will not upset the current status quo. So shareholders need to define the context first before determining what is needed at the board.

35 See Badaracco, J.L., (2013), *The Good Struggle. Responsible Leadership in an Unforgiving World*, Cambridge MA, Harvard Bus School Press; and Badaracco, J.L., (2016), *Managing in the Gray. Timeless questions for resolving your toughest problems at work*, Cambridge MA, Harvard Business School Press. And especially Peter's vast research on the topic of corruption-guanxi-gift practices in business: Verhezen, P. (2008), "Guanxi: Networks or nepotism?" in Zsolnai, L. (Ed.), *Europe-Asia dialogue on business spirituality*, Antwerp; Apeldoorn, Garant, 89–106; Verhezen, P., (2009), Gifts, Corruption and Philanthropy. The ambiguity of gift practices in business, Oxford; Bern, Peter Lang Publishing; Verhezen, P., (2010), "Giving voice to a culture of silence: from a culture of compliance to a culture of integrity", *Journal of Business Ethics*, Vol. 96(2): 187–206; Verhezen, P., (2015), "Fear, Regret or Trust? Transparency to control or transparency to empower", *International Finance Corporation*

(World Bank) Paper, No 38, Washington; and Verhezen, P., (2018), "Is Indonesia serious about corporate governance?" *Strategic Review*, Vol. 8(3): 48–59.

36 In Indonesia, it is called KPK, the relatively powerful anti-corruption agency that was perceived as quite independent in pursuing potential criminals, till some of that power was recently curbed by the parliament.

37 Mere fear is often a bad guide and those who live in fear for possible prosecution should not be at that board to start with, because most often than not, they have something to hide. Top managers show a confident humility and are basically honest. In such a case, there is nothing to fear from prosecuting regulators or judicial officials. Unless those public officials are corrupt themselves, which makes any fair game almost impossible.

38 In 2006, Bank Indonesia introduced rules for corporate governance in banks. The Code of Good Corporate Governance (CGCG), first adopted in 1999, was amended in 2006, and sector specific codes were issued for the banking and insurance sectors. In 2007 a new company law was adopted that introduced explicit duties for board members of listed companies at IDX. The Ministry of State Owned Enterprises has also carried out significant corporate governance reform in the state owned enterprise sector.

39 Earlier in this 3rd chapter we have argued for the adjective "good" instead of "best" because the latter assumes to have achieved the final stage which we don't think is the case; it is always a work-in-process. However, in this particular instance, we will follow the usually used expression "best practices".

40 It can be assumed that these successful companies have diligently incorporated and integrated (1) the protection of basic shareholder rights, (2) the prohibition of insider trading, (3) disclosure of board and top managers interests and adherence to international disclosure standards, (4) a respect for the legal rights of main stakeholders of the company while acting responsibly within a wider community context, (5) an independent audit committee that regularly meets, (6) the norm that all shareholders should be treated fairly by the board, (7) the expected disclosure of capital structures that enabled certain shareholders to obtain disproportionate control, (8) providing good access to information by the board members to allow fair and timely dissemination of information to all relevant parties involved, and (9) nominating the best top executive team for the job to be fairly remunerated according to their performance.

41 Although by law PT Telkom has two separated boards, they started to function as one board under the chairmanship of Tanri Abeng aiming at the same ultimate goal to continuously create value for its shareholders and stakeholders.

42 We refer to the three only economists (Shiller, Rajan and Roubini) who did "foresee" – or predict – this international "global financial crisis" of 2007–2011. They both have written a very good summary on this crisis that almost demolished the whole international financial system, precluded by UK Premier Golden Brown who called in G8 to ship in to secure the financial system. See Nobel Price winner Shiller, Robert, (2008), *The Subprime Solution. How Today's Global Financial Crisis Happened, and What to Do about it*, Princeton; Oxford, Princeton University Press; and Shiller, R.J., (2012), *Finance and the Good Society*, Oxford; Princeton, Princeton University Press. We also highly recommend Rajan, R.G., (2010), *Fault Lines. How Hidden Fractures Still Threaten the World Economy*, New Jersey, Princeton Univ Press, and Roubini, N. & S. Mihn, (2010), *Crisis Economics. A crash course in the future of finance*, London, Penguin.

Chapter 4
Two-Tier Boards Versus Single-Tier Boards
Applying Governance Principles in different
(Legal and Cultural) Contexts

> Culture eats strategy for breakfast.
>
> Peter Drucker

> The world we have made, as a result of the thinking we have done thus far, creates problems we cannot solve at the same level of thinking at which we created them.
>
> Albert Einstein

The generic principles behind good corporate governance may be clear. But what about applying these general principles in a specific jurisdiction like Indonesia or Thailand? By now, we may clearly grasp the meaning behind the major fiduciary duties of the board, and how they are translated in three main functions of the board: (1) steering and advising on the future strategy, (2) monitoring and supervising the performance of the top executives and the organization in general, and (3) finally safeguarding leadership continuity by securing a proper leadership succession.

This chapter zooms in on governance structures that has caused some organizational confusion among quite some board members both inside as well as outside Indonesia. Understanding a dual-tier versus a monistic single-tier structure, as well as the special "power-structures" at state owned enterprises (or SOEs) is crucial for anyone investing in Indonesian (or other Asian) firms. These State owned enterprises always have had a special function in most Asian economies with access to vast natural and human resources, but also the enormous political stake those huge national (if not nationalistic) organizations can have.

China is a clear example where enormous corporate but also economic and even socio-political power is concentrated in these huge state owned national enterprises. But so is Indonesia with over 140 state owned enterprises, constituting more than half of Indonesia's annual gross domestic product. They play a key role in a range of critical industries – such as electricity, pharmaceuticals, air navigation services and air transportation, food distribution and logistics, gas-& oil, banking, telecommunications among others. Or take the example of national sovereign funds, like Temasek in Singapore that functions as a superstructural foreign investment vehicle with local investments, as in Singapore Airlines for instance, but also investments in other countries like in the Indonesian Telkomsel, a subsidiary of state-owned enterprise Telkom. Similar situations exist in the other ASEAN countries with crucial strategic state-owned enterprises, though the private sector is gaining in importance. Because of the differences in interpretation of what is beneficial in business, a clear answer of what and how any organization should best function remains very contextual, dependent on the socio-historical and legal background of the country in which those organizations are established.

Hence why we feel the importance to highlight the very specific feature of a dual-tier board structure one finds in a number of countries – as in Germany, the Netherlands, Scandinavian countries like Finland, Indonesia, China, among others. Some European countries like Belgium, France and Italy have the option to choose between a monistic or dualistic board structure. Most Anglo-American jurisdictions and those which inherited the common law system have a one-tier board structure.

Without honing in on specific socio-historical features of a specific country, we felt it important to highlight how a double-tier board structure in Indonesia substantially differs from a single-board structure in Singapore, Hong Kong and Malaysia. A similar monistic single-tier structure under common law prevails in the USA and UK where the traditional biggest international institutional investors are incorporated. What are the benefits and weaknesses of those double- and single-tier board structures? The practical experience of some Indonesian cases will be elaborated, more specifically the struggling state carrier Garuda, or the state owned telecommunication company, Telkom, and the huge gas- and oil state company, Pertamina. Let us get started.

1 Single-Tier Boards Versus Double-Tier Boards

Governance is much more than compliance. Good corporate governance is a question of creating a conducive culture and a climate to apply these best principles, which can be considered the foundation of [organizational] trust. Boards need to create trustworthy relationships, providing guidance and oversight to the directors and management in order to ensure that the company creates value on a sustainable basis while protecting the interests of all stakeholders.

Shareholders appoint the board members. Despite the different legal structure of a board in different countries, the underlying governance principles and the objectives remain the same across borders. Concretely, it means that any board should aim (1) to **supervise or monitor** the performances of the top executives to secure that performance objectives are met and the oversight of the organization in general– including to sign off and to be discharged on audit reports; (2) to **coach and assist** the executive management team to strategize the potential business opportunities and to pursue risks within agreed risk appetite borders; and finally (3) to prepare and **develop [new] leaders** for an orderly **leadership succession** in the future. Indeed, this final word of caution refers to the increasing pressure on shareholders and boards in any jurisdiction to find the right professional management talent and right team to steer and to run the enterprise – either private, public or state. The roles of a board should be properly defined and the duties of each of the directors well understood and specified as explained in the previous two chapters. And yes, the board composition and committees' structure should be clarified and codified in the articles of association or the constitutional charter of the organization. Finally, the board's working procedures and functioning should be clearly expressed and documented, whereas specific envisaged board practices should be spelled out in the notules or even in the constitution of the company.

That begs the question whether these different governance practices and structures will converge over time. We do not think so, especially in the short term. The legal historical context predetermines the legal implementation of corporate governance. Indonesia has inherited the dual-tier board structure from its colonial master, and will likely continue to develop corporate law and corporate governance specifically along its own historical legal context.

There is a huge distinction between the functioning of a board that follows a double-tier board structure with two separated boards, and a single unified board structure, a characteristic for most boards in the USA, UK and Australia, and other Anglo-Saxon legal jurisdictions. In addition, the ways boardrooms behave in state owned enterprises can be distinctively different from public listed corporations (multinationals or family controlled ones). The principles of good corporate governance may be common to all firms, but the specific translation remains unique. Proper incentives for a board and its management should be implemented in order them to pursue objectives that are in line with the interests of the company and its shareholders.

One of the major challenges for any board – whatever the structure – is to minimize the potential *entrenchment* of a board[1] and *mismanagement* or to avoid the lack of professionalism (and expertise) at the board level. Corporate governance plays an important role in protecting investors from preventable risks and from possible expropriation of corporate assets by a too powerful executive team or by rent-seeking majority shareholders at the expense of minority investors. Executives make decisions on a daily basis that are supposed to serve the organization. Regularly those decisions may better the executives at the expense of other parties related to the firm: those costs are known as *agency costs* which find its roots in the separation of ownership and top management. A system of check and balances – the basis of corporate governance – is assumed to lessen those agency costs by controlling and monitoring top management. But also to guarantee proper decision-making within the board, following the stipulated procedures and processes, especially allowing minority shareholders (and their respective board members' representatives) to be heard and where appropriate to impact the decisions to be made. It is important that the interest of the organization prevails, and not just the majority shareholder's interest.

Under the *dualistic or two-tier board structure*, the supervisory board of commissioners' main task is to *monitor and oversee* the performance of the (executive) board of directors and to safeguard the continuity of the organization, aiming to ensure effective management and its succession with the aim to act in the best interest of the company's long term goals. But these non-executive directors or commissioners also provide valuable advice and mentoring to top management. In this *advisory capacity*, the supervisory board pays attention to guide top management's decision that aims to balance risk versus reward. The board is a governing body elected to represent the interest of shareholders and the company at large. Interpreting this in an Indonesian context, we believe that Boards should not just supervise and govern the organization, but under certain circumstances should also take a *lead*.[2] When a crisis hits the organization, usually, the chair steps in the limelight to quell speculation and to govern the organization with transparent and candid communication.[3]

Governance systems are influenced by the number of stakeholders: the owners of the firm, its managers, creditors, labour unions, customers, suppliers, investment analysts, the media, and regulators and all those who could significantly affect [the value of] the company. Unfortunately, those stakeholders who deserve the attention of the supervisory board are hardly heard or considered in the boardroom. In practice, non-executive directors spend most of their time on supervising audit reports as well as on determining the executive compensation according to monitored performances. In addition, quite some time is used to make sure that management activities are performed according to and compliant to existing regulatory norms. Unfortunately, in general the board spends much less time on advising management on strategic planning for instance, as in preparing to create and capture value, making competition less "relevant", or, in preparing for crucial leadership succession. Let us get started to explain what we mean by ensuring a more effective "boardroom" functioning.

1.1 Principles of One-Tier Versus Double-Tier Boards

Although a substantial portion of Asian companies in terms of assets are SOEs, quite a number of listed companies are owned by families or are local listed subsidiaries of reputable international companies. Interesting is the comparison of governance in "family" business in the USA-UK versus Europe with the latter being much more similar to the Asian context. Admittedly, there is a trend to professionalize governance and top leadership to secure a "common investment language". Having said this, we still see a lot of idiosyncratic characteristics, unique to Asia, *in casu* an Indonesian context. Not just from

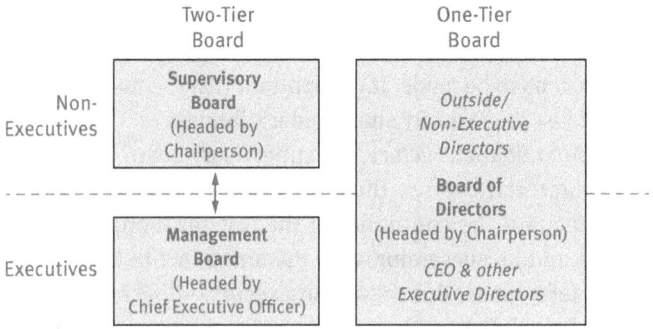

Figure 23: Structure dual-tier versus single-tier boards.

a regulatory perspective (that admittedly is not our focus in this book) but also from an "owner" and organizational perspective. A company like Indofood within the Salim group, or Smart within Sinar Mas or Siloam hospitals with the Lippo group – owned by "Indonesian conglomerates" – is very differently governed in comparison with Telkom or Pertamina. We explain why, and whether a converging trend in governing these listed organizations can be expected or not in the not too distant future.

What does make dual-tier boards so special and distinctive from single-tier boards? The major difference is that dual-tier boards have legally engrained a supervisory board in the board structure of an organization, whereas single-tier boards do not have such a separated supervisory board. Both systems have advantages and disadvantages: a dual-tier board has proper supervisory structures in place to monitor the performance of the executive boards members and limit the power of the top executive if deemed appropriate.

The visualization of power structures of a dual-tier under Indonesian corporate legislation in Figures 24 and 25 suggests that shareholders appoint a board – both a supervisory and executive board – during an annual general meeting of shareholders (GMS). The two-structured boards each have a particular function to fulfil.

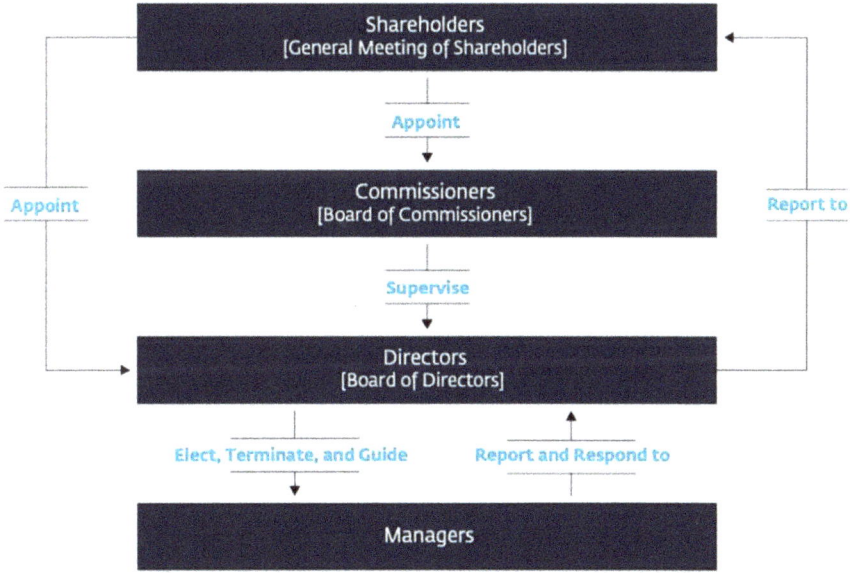

Figure 24: Corporate governance structure in Indonesia.
Source: IFC, 2018, *Indonesian Manuel for corporate governance*

The dual tier board stipulates that the supervisory board monitors and supervises the executive board, but withholds from mingling or micro-managing the executive board. The supervisory board looks after the implementation of the good corporate governance principles, and advises the executive board where deemed necessary and appropriate, and organizes the general meeting of shareholders.

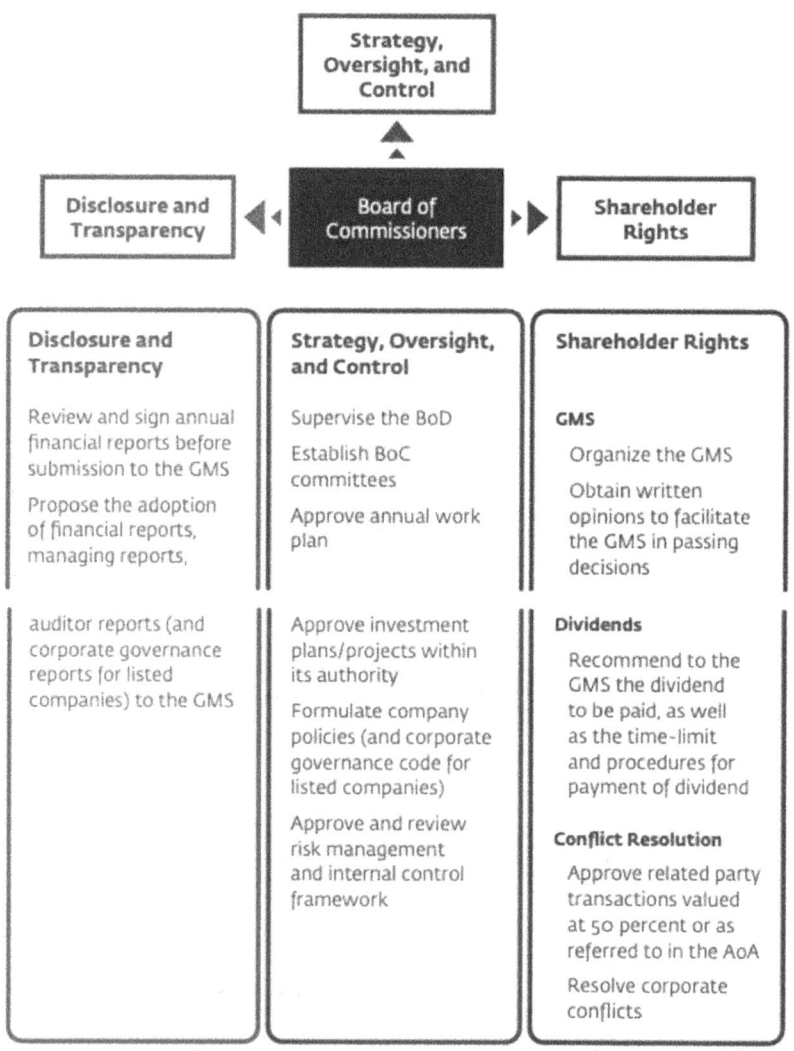

Figure 25: Authority of the Supervisory Board (BoC).
Source: IFC, *Indonesian Manuel for corporate governance*, (2018: 156–157)

It is the board of commissioners (constituting the supervisory board) who is appointed by the shareholders to overlook and supervise the performance and the interests of the organization and thus of the shareholders.

Single-tier boards – as visualized in Figure 23 – are usually more "unified" in making more swift strategic decisions to adapt to changed market conditions, and the CEO can be quite powerful. The side-effect of such powerful boards and its executive leaders can result in taking advantage of asymmetric information – constituting the traditional agency challenge. Even the Chair can be quite hands-on under those single-tier structures – and very powerful with situations where more than 65 percent of the US-based corporations combine the two functions of Chair and CEO. Leading a company requires a lot of dedication and commitment. If properly handled, dual-tier boards can leverage their natural advantage of proper governance and supervision, while also using the "natural [Indonesian] culture" of "*unified in diversity*" which allows the two distinctive boards to "team up" in a more cooperative and empowering manner by jointly focusing on main risks and major strategic decisions to steer towards a more competitive and productive organization.

These best governance practices are applicable to both public and private listed companies, but with substantial differences in terms of mandatory listing requirements by the respective regulators. Is it not indicative that some Western firms have recently stated to de-list from the capital market[4]? This de-listing is mainly to avoid "short-termism" of relentless investment analysts [working for big institutional investors]. It allows the owners of these privately taken delisted companies to be more "flexible" and or to prepare for the future by ensuring long-term investments, that occasionally may "jeopardize" some short term profit-taking. That is exactly how most family businesses across national borders have always run and governed their operations and investments. The ever quarterly pressure of the US capital market has made governing an organization quite challenging. That continuous capital market pressure may be slightly less prevailing in an Asian context.

State-owned enterprises face another and more fundamental challenge: even though state owned enterprises may be temporary "protected" through regulation or a captive market by the state by their mighty owners, there is no guarantee that such model will last. The risk of complacency and non-competitiveness as result of its given monopolistic power is real and may potentially wipe out considerable capital market gains or even lead to virtual non-solvency.

Similarly, private non-listed companies have no choice but to remain competitive and stay on their toes for any potential technological or competitive disruption. Ask traditional taxi companies in Indonesia, Thailand, Malaysia and Vietnam with the arrival of Grab and Gojek, or Didi in China. Or remind traditional retailers in Indonesia how the ongoing merger of Gojek and Tokopedia into GoTo – and other Asian e-commerce and fintech companies – is affecting their more traditional business model. Boards inevitably need to react or better pro-act in order to survive this continuous 'evolutionary competitive' onslaught.

Allow us to reiterate the fiduciary duties of a dual-tier board: once the decision on the direction of the strategy is jointly discussed and prepared by the supervisory (BoC) and executive board (BoD), the executive board is responsible and accountable for its execution. Nonetheless, the supervisory board[5] [BoC] will **overlook** the performance of the executive board **and supervise** the BoD's execution, but won't and shouldn't be involved in the actual *execution* of the strategy (which is the BoD's task). One of the authors was asked as chair by the "minister-owner" to "intervene" in the executive management "to make the needed change happening". However, getting involved in the executive board would have overstepped the fiduciary duty of a supervisory board.[6] Only in crisis, a chair should take the "front" seat if deemed appropriate. The chair and supervisory board are assumed to steer and facilitate the [demanded] change, not to execute or "make" the change itself. A subtle but important distinction. Hence why we believe that the supervisory board is expected to closely control the functioning of the [executive] board, but should refrain from getting too much involved: "nose in, but hands out" should be the slogan for the Board of Commissioners, as visualised in Figure 26.

Figure 26: Duties of the supervisory versus executive board.

While a board needs to actively participate in strategy and be well informed about the activities of the company, it needs to refrain from interfering with day to day management. There is also the danger, with so much focus on codes and other definitions of good corporate behavior, that boards fall victim to form rather than substance. If time is spent only to meet the letter of the law, if due diligence committees and advisors hold sway, there is a definite risk that the real issues behind the corporation's governance becomes obscured. Even more important, if the focus on governance processes leads the board to be slow or more risk adverse in making decisions in the light of incomplete information, it is not clear that the company or shareholders will benefit. Business is never about a 'sure thing', bold moves are never without risk. If a board's focus on process overcomes its willingness to take risk, shareholders will not be better off. In the end, the board is responsible not merely for conformance to the code, but for the performance of the company.

More specifically, we believe that a supervisory board should "institutionalize" some form of entrepreneurial innovation or *managerial entrepreneurship* to improve the performance of the firm in the process, which the executive board will need to "execute". Both the supervisory and executive boards need to strike a balance.

1.2 Advantages and Disadvantages of Both Board Structures

Does corporate governance improve performances of companies? Facts seem to suggest that well-governed corporations outfox their competitors. Two-tier systems seem to have an alleged natural structural advantage of supervision and monitoring. The subsequent question then begs whether a dual-tier corporate governance system outperforms a single-tier board? The answer is more ambiguous. As mentioned above, Anglo-Saxon governance structures (like in the USA, UK and Australia) have what is known a single-tier unilateral board structure whereas countries with a civic law background such as Indonesia have often implemented a dual-tier board structure. Does it mean that an Indonesian corporation such as PT Telkom has the potential to outperform Telstra or Vodafone? Not quite. It is true that dual-tier boards have some potentially powerful advantages in terms of oversight and in preventing particular risks to occur.

Single-tier boards (in the USA) have sometimes been described as "managerial capitalism" with extremely powerful top executives (CEOs) who combine this executive top position with the chairman position of the firm.[7] The main advantage of such combined function is that strategies are better communicated and executed under such unilateral structure. However, the main disadvantage is that with a unified Chairman-CEO[8] position, there is potentially less strong oversight, which can be compensated by the appointment of a strong Lead Director. Such single-tier boards do not have the inherent built-in oversight mechanisms that dual-tier boards have. Moreover, it has been more and more agreed that the function of chairman requires different capabilities than that of the CEO. The by now well regarded Cadbury report (1992) in the UK therefore has started to clearly distinguish these two functions as "a best practice". The result is that in the UK most boards feel compelled to follow this "best" recommend practice of splitting the CEO and Chair function, and "if not" followed, the regulator now expects them "to explain" why not.

Strengths 1-Tier Board	Strengths 2-Tier Board
1. Speedy, fast and swift decisions where necessary 2. Flexibility 3. United towards the outside world	1. Good supervision 2. Clear distinction between monitoring function and execution function 3. Assumed more accountability and potentially less entrenchment

Weaknesses 1-Tier Board	Weaknesses 2-Tier Board
1. Less clear supervision: who controls the CEO (especially if CEO also combines the Chair title as in >60% in USA)? 2. More potential entrenchment and a possible bigger Agency problem	1. Slower and unclear decision making 2. Less flexible and sometimes ineffective 3. Cumbersome decision-making process 4. Often not unified 5. More complex board dynamics 6. Often paper boards

Figure 27: Advantages and Disadvantages of Single- versus Dual-tier boards.

The USA firms do not really follow this practice of splitting the function of CEO and Chair because of some obvious advantages of swift and unified power to react to changes if deemed needed.

There are obvious pros and cons for both structures – visualised in figure 27. The major advantage of a dual-tier board is the structurally stronger supervision role over the executive board, whereas the single-tier board can easier take unified and faster decisions. There are each other flip-side of this opposing legal structure.

Clearly dual-tier boards have the advantage to reduce the power of managers and bring the power back to the board who supposedly represents the shareholders. However, in an Asian context, one cannot ignore the presence of informal corporate governance mechanisms and powerful owners behind the scene. Family members or their loyal lieutenants are likely to be in charge of management, alluding to the importance of aligned insiders who may make or break corporate governance in those companies. Despite the imposed dual-tier board structure under Indonesian law, the informal and formal powers of the main blockholding shareholder, be it a family or the state, often override the advantage of the inherent monitoring function of the board of commissioners.

In other words, the issue in Asia is not so much that top management has too much power (as in US firms that may result in a traditional agency problem), but that major shareholders may override the board decision or even occasionally attempt to [illegally] expropriate valuable assets away from the listed corporation at the expense of minority shareholders (usually institutional or individual investors who are not related to the main family shareholders or state owned enterprise).

The tension of formal corporate governance implementation and informal governance practices could be substantial. Formal (often rightfully perceived as "Western") governance is based on an *arm's length system* that strictly endorses transparency, accountability and responsibility to reduce agency problems, whereas an informal *relationship-based system* that prevails in Indonesia (and Asia in general) is often seen as the main currency for any exchange. Such leaning on an informal attitude of governance will need to be steered to a manageable balancing act that integrates both globally acceptable "best" corporate governance practices aligned to a specific Asian "relationship-oriented" context.[9] Such a balance will evoke the importance of transparency and disclosed information, as it will emphasize the importance of protecting all shareholders based on the principle of fairness, accountability and responsibility. A board and its management can still integrate those traditional governance values with a unique system of relationship building. A similar tension can be found in China where one needs to find a delicate balance between the loyalty as institutionalized by the hierarchical Confucian values,[10] and professionalization of management practices based on meritocracy and economic efficiency. The culture of state owned enterprises tend to be even more hierarchical where loyalty and seniority prevail over efficiency and merit. An extremely difficult balancing exercise to succeed in a state owned enterprise context which is much less flexible or adaptable than a family conglomerate, or a privately held enterprise.

2 How to Initiate Dual-Tier Boards to Collaborate more Closely?

Although Indonesia has inherited a dual-tier board structure, we believe that taking advantage of a "combined" approach, may suit Indonesian firms and their boards well. We believe that boards in Indonesia and other jurisdictions with similar board structures need to combine the strengths of one- and two-tier boards. At the end of the day, the supervisory and executive board functions as a team, and therefore complementation and collaboration is not a luxury but a necessity. Figure 28 summarizes the complementary function of the supervisory board (BoC) and the executive board (BoD).

As a former policy maker, and practitioner, Dr. Abeng has always maintained the argument to combine both structures in a pragmatic manner to optimize board functioning as visualized hereunder. As a former Chair at Pertamina and Telkom, and current chair at the state owned enterprise Bio Farma, he attempted to push through this "idea of combined strengthening" and reform at those state owned firms, with admittedly mixed results.

We are both convinced that the advantage of a *de iure* dual-tier board structure where the supervisory board supervises and advises the executive board should function as a *de facto* single-tier unified board in which the two boards

- BoC pr supervisory board steers the organization and should not set corporate strategy on its own, but:
  ↳ BoD should formulate corporate strategy
  ↳ BoC should question, challenge & approve the strategy
  ↳ BoD & Management Team should then take ownership over and implement strategy
  ↳ BoC and BoD take ownership of the result

- BoD or executive board then runs and manages the company by delegated authority–supported by Management Team. Yet:
  ↳ Has autonomy, independence & real authority;
  ↳ Takes initiatives & deploys resources to purse objectives;
  ↳ Is justified in expecting rewards (though under Indonesian practices, the rewards for SOEs is strictly regulated and "limited", but when taking into account the special perks that member of boards at state-owned enterprises can be quite significant, and exceed the total package of members of privately held firms).

- In light of this authority, the 'Board' (BoC + BoD) has a set of duties. Notably:
  ↳ The duty of care (e.g. to provide accurate & timely reports)
  ↳ The duty of loyalty (e.g. to avoid conflicts of interests)
  ↳ The duty of prudence (e.g. to run the firm within the agreed risk appetite boundaries)

Figure 28: How to foster collaboration at two-tier boards?.

collaborate as two dancing partners, as modelled in Figure 29. Let us have a closer look at three giant Indonesian state owned enterprises in the field of aviation, telecom and gas-& oil.

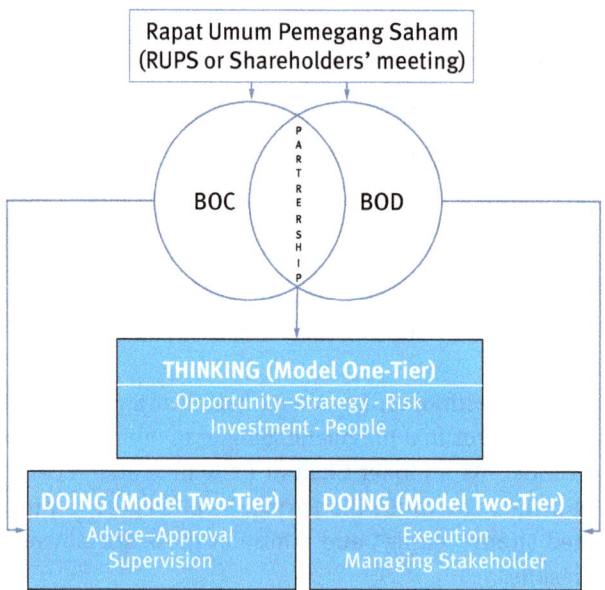

Figure 29: Combining dual- & single-tier board structure.
Source: Model prepared and applied by Tanri Abeng

2.1 The National Carrier Garuda: From being saved to Doom again

L'histoire se repète – history repeats itself, or rather history rhymes. Since 1993 the national carrier Garuda has been grossly over-debted. At the same time, the monopoly of Garuda ended in 1999, when President Soeharto was forced to resign, under pressure by social unrest and IMF stringent conditions of lending money to Indonesia at the beginning of the Asian crisis in 1997–1998.

When the national carrier Garuda was on the verse of bankruptcy in 1998, the then minister of state-owned enterprises, Tanri Abeng, brought in Roby Djohan, an experienced banker, to turn Garuda around, and this transformation continued under the subsequent CEO. Garuda, was hardly worth one dollar in 1999. It was estimated to be worth more than USD 1 billion within two years of the restructuring, under the guidance of CEO Abdul Gani. For that short period in which Garuda underwent a transformation to be run as a competitive company – and not a bloated fiefdom of some inefficient patrons -. it started to make [small] profits again for a couple of years till 2003.

What has happened since 2005? Garuda has been burdened under massive debts since it started to make losses in 2004 and 2005. However, the board fell short in being transparent to its stakeholders and even shorter in doing something about this declining capital base to absorb external potential shocks. Despite this debt-burden, Garuda continued to improve its operational competitiveness. The improvement of overall performance allowed the board to take advantage of this new gained reputation to get Garuda listed on the stock exchange in February 2011, with an IPO price of IDR 750 per share.

The accumulated efforts paid off when in 2012 Garuda was named the Best International Airline, outmaneuvering that year other very reputable airlines like Singapore Airlines, Emirates, JAL and Cathay Pacific – all quite notorious for their superb client oriented service. That same year, Skytrax, named Garuda as the best regional airline in Asia. Admittedly, that Skytrax award became a game changer for Garuda, its employees and customers. It brought trust back to the company. Not surprisingly, the CEO Emir Satar was awarded "Person of the year" (in 2010) by Orient Aviation. This all signals that Garuda was getting back on track, which boosted the morale and consequently the productivity of the employees at Garuda, emulating in a five star-ranking – the highest possible – by Skytrax in 2015.

But not long thereafter, the situation started to deteriorate when Garuda's stock decreased from a 2015 high of >IDR 700 to IDR 220 per share when the trading of the stock was halted mid 2021; mainly due to failing to pay back the principal debt. What did cause this downfall? How is it possible that an organization that came close to the brink of failure in 1998 was transformed into a trusted company worth more than USD 1,4 billion in 2000, accumulating to a five star status and an IPO in 2011, reaching a market capitalization of USD 1.6 billion. A decade later in 2021, Garuda is technically bankrupt (again), worth minus USD 2,3 billion, and even close to

USD 3 billion in the negative, anno 2022. Between September 2021 and the subsequent months, Garuda was losing USD 100 million per month, not even able to cover the variable costs of the airline.

As a state-owned enterprise protected by the government, Garuda did not have the DNA in its culture to relentlessly seek improvement of performance, and to really push for economic and management efficiency. In fact, it only managed it twice, under the duo-leadership of Tanri Abeng – Roby Djohan when Garuda lost its monopolistic power and was forced to drastically restructure its debt, subsequently taken over by Abdul Gani to complete the restructuring of the airline, and again under the helm of Emir Satar who proved that a transformed Garuda could compete with the best in class. Unfortunately, those efforts did not last and were eroded by weaker management that followed.

There are likely numerous reasons to explain the downfall of Garuda. We see three major causes of Garuda's demise: (1) a board that did not have the vision or ability to properly execute a visionary strategy, and was unable to collaborate as a team and to address the challenges in time. And being driven by too much pride to keep some unprofitable routes to the West instead of focusing on efficiency as could be expected by well paid professionals. (2) A [supervisory] board that did not intervene to correct or question at least the unusual and obsessive high rental costs for some of those planes as well as the excessive purchasing price of some of the new aircrafts. And yes, (3) the aviation crisis in 2020 as result of the covid pandemic did not help either. Underlying the first two reasons is the almost continuous political intervention by powerful political elite and ministers over those years between 2003 and 2021, leading to regular changes at the board which made long term planning and execution under such short tenures at BoD and BoC extremely difficult and unlikely.

The fact that the supervisory and executive board were not able to partner together to assess the situation and to understand the ramifications of an increasing massive debt, nor were able to evaluate and or to mitigate some of those related financial risks, partially explain the cause of Garuda's unfortunate situation. Did the supervisory board (BoC) not have the alertness to see that there were serious obstacles in front of them that could (and did) derail the carrier? What we really suspect is that the supervisory board did not intervene in time or take a lead to halt inappropriate behaviour at the executive and management level, nor was able to slash uneconomic [international] routes or push for a strategy that could work – major fiduciary duties on behalf of the supervisory and executive boards. Nor was Garuda able to enhance a fruitful and effective collaboration based on genuine trust among the board members to address these internal and external challenges.

Garuda's *de iure* dual-tier board was never able to function as a *de facto* single-tier partnership board that was expected to be unified in spirit as expressed in Figure 29. In-fighting at Garuda's board has been rive for years. Without strong leadership, one may have the most beautiful plans on paper, nothing will be executed if there is not enough trust at the board to really jointly address the life-threatening issues at stake. Instead, it seems that the board was hiding behind opaque decision-making and tick-the-box conformity cosmetics, without really turning the ship around. Worse, there is strong indication of inappropriate if not unethical behaviour at the board level that definitely further undermined the trust in the organization.

The last appointed board was put in charge to save a sinking ship. That requires a strong expert crisis management team. Unfortunately, it was not business as usual anymore where a state-owned enterprise can rely on a cash-rich government to bail them out. Countries face an economic crisis now, and Garuda rides a perfect storm, likely aggravated by previous mismanagement. This uncertainty and instability, not exactly features that Garuda's board has proven to be good at to deal with. Any crisis is always hard, but not impossible to raise from as a real garuda bird would. History teaches us lessons, and fortunately a case like Japan Airlines a decade ago may render us hopeful, provided that the Boardroom is effectively functioning as a real team and has the expertise in house to prepare for a brighter future.

2.2 The "Telkom" Case in Indonesia: A Unified Board that makes the Right Decisions

The dual-tier boards in Indonesia have the inherent advantage of having a legal built-in structure in place that allows the 'commissioners' or non-executive directors to supervise and monitor the top executive management team at *arm's length*.[11] However, the board of commissioners of PT Telkom for instance took a much more active role to generate agility. Indeed, the idea behind this closer than usual collaboration under this two-tier structure in securing a highly performing team. And we should keep in mind that this Indonesian state owned telecommunication company is listed at the Indonesian Stock Exchange with a secondary listing on the New York Stock Exchange. The former chair at Telkom made sure that both the supervisory board and the executive team were fully in sync with respect to important strategic decisions they jointly made that determined the future of the organization.

As can be expected from any properly governed company, PT Telkom institutionalized two main committees at the board of commissioners' level: an audit & risk committee and a nomination & remuneration committee. These subcommittees at Telkom did more than just signing off on the proposals of the executive board. For instance, the chairman of the board, Pak Tanri, made sure that the sub-committee of investment – a kind of Risk Committee – would scrutinize any investment above Rp 100 billion and then prepare a final assessment for the complete board to be approved in a plenum session. Although some may have criticized that this process slows down the overall decision process, the facts at PT Telkom proved the opposite. Admittedly, the decision on a particular investment above Rp 100 billion (or about USD 7.1 million) to be jointly discussed by both the executive board (BoD) and the supervisory board (BoC) took at least a few days more to reach a consensus. However, at the end this consensus-building-as-one-unified-team was faster by avoiding any administrative and stalling tactics in the execution or roll out once a unified investment decision has been approved upon. In some instances, it was even the BoC of PT Telkom who urged the BoD to speed up the decision and execution process. In other words, the non-executive board members play an important advisory and "jointly thinking" role to enhance the consensus building – taking a little more time at the beginning but gaining time thereafter – as a joint unified team as suggested in Figure 29.

That the reputable Singaporean Sovereign Fund, Temasek through SingTel, has been a substantial but still minority co-owner with 35 percent stockholding in PT Telkomsel (Telkom's mobile phone subsidiary). That participation has likely sped up the professionalization and adherence to "best" corporate governance practices. The stringent listing requirements of PT Telkom being listed on NYSE likely contributed as well.

It is well known that the chair of a State Owned Enterprise can be quite powerful in pushing for choices in first and even second strategic layer appointments. Under Tanri Abeng's chairmanship, the nomination committee installed a governance mechanism that emphasized the evaluation of any candidate for a strategic position, to be introduced by the executive board. The joint team-work at the board to vet a new potential top officer invigorated the executive team's coherence, closely supervised by the non-executives board members. However, this desired coherence in the team functions two ways. When a previous CEO of PT Telkom was about to leave the company, he tried to appoint about 20 close associates of him in strategic positions. By installing an institutionalized dual system of suggestion (by Bod) and evaluation by the Nomination Committee, one eliminates personal favouritism and enhances the professionalization of the board. Once the Nomination Committee had assessed and agreed on the potential candidate, in about 99 percent of the time the board of non-executives at PT Telkom approved the candidate, while avoiding nepotistic tendencies.

Secondly, the non-executive directors or commissioners provide valuable advice and mentoring to top management. In this *advisory capacity*, the board pays attention to guide top management's decision that balance risk and reward, whereas in its *oversight capacity*, the board aims to monitor management and ensure that it is acting in the best interest of the company's long term goals. Telkom's board of commissioners got involved in the planning and strategy and collaborated with the board of directors as one unified board, attempting to reach consensus on a committed strategy. Once agreed, the executives got on with implementing the agreed plan whereas the non-executives continued to closely monitor the progress by the executive directors.

A *de facto* 'unified' board is a governing body elected to represent the interest of shareholders and the company at large. At PT Telkom for instance, there was an occasion where two highly performing professionals of the top team – the CEO and Deputy CEO – were not collaborating with each other anymore, undermining the goals of the firm. After numerous advice and trials and despite their outstanding respective individual professional skill sets, the Chairman and his board of commissioners finally decided to dismiss both this President Director (CEO) and Vice-President Director (CFO) with the argument that this clash was undermining the efficiency of the functioning of the boards as a real team. And that is what boards and management should be all about: creating good functioning teams that effectively and efficiently execute decisions to optimize the interests of the organization and thus its owners – usually summarized as a return on the investment as in profitability. This particular case of PT Telkom indicates that a separated supervisory Board of Commissioners was able to effectively monitor top management because there was less entrenchment with top management than what is often the case with a *de iure* unitary board.

A dual-tier board structure may show some distinctive competitive advantage in terms of "control of remuneration", and in having a check and balance of risk management, and finally making sure that a clear mandate for "succession planning" is under way. But despite the enormous governance progress PT Telkom made since the Asian crisis of 1997, it still has a journey ahead to improve its overall governance and to enhance its global competitiveness.

PT Telkom focused on a number of important governance issues trying to answer both (a) governance feature and (b) governance function related questions.[12] Moreover, Telkom has made other attempts to professionalize the board, answering (1) whether the *organizational design* should be decentralized or centralized in structure, (2) how the *organizational culture* encourages cooperation, and how risk-taking is encouraged, tolerated, or discouraged; and finally (3) to assess the *personality of the CEO* in terms of leadership style and individual's ethical standards. As long as both boards can enrich each other in a professional way by jointly planning, discussing and approving major strategic decisions, aware of the "people and risk challenges and opportunities", PT Telkom will hopefully become even better at fulfilling its organizational objective of sustainable growth.

2.3 PT Pertamina in Indonesia: An Attempt to Reform in spite of Patronage

At PT Telkom, the chair of the supervisory board did involve the executive board to assess, analyze, and debate major risks that could affect certain major investment decisions. Well-functioning teams with aligned minds can achieve more than superb individual expertise, and an entrepreneurial open mindset taking risks allows firms to create new business opportunities. Indeed, as explained above, any investment that strategically would affect PT Telkom was jointly decided by the two boards, guaranteeing to be on the same page, unifying the two distinctive boards, and empowering both to fulfil their fiduciary duties of care, loyalty and prudence to make the right decisions that benefited the organization. Unfortunately, a similar fiat and performance was not exactly repeated or achieved at PT Pertamina.

A) An Entrenched Board with a Particular Mindset

A number of factors may have contributed to a difficult "turn-around" of a huge company like Pertamina, among which (a) a lack of consistency with having three different CEOs appointed, and the replacement of 18 board members at the "discretion" of the minister of state-owned enterprises over a period of only five years (2014–2019), making it extremely difficult to create a cohesive and empowered team, (b) Pertamina being torn by too many different and sometimes opposing vested [political] interests, (c) having the unfortunate reputation of long term engrained corruption and nepotism (known as "KKN" in Indonesia) in the operations and even at board level, and finally (d) confronted with strong local fiefdoms that were hard to break up. Internally, it seemed that the organizational culture was not really attuned to an open mindset to create new value for new potential customers. The replacement of those board members created discontinuity in executing the strategy, and on top of it, it caused confusion and inconsistency. Not exactly an ingredient to make it a winner. A different entrepreneurial and more professional efficient mindset is needed.[13] Was there also the idea to secure a strong status-quo, backed up by a nationalistic parliament?

Although boards may have the ultimate legal power in any organization, boards do not necessarily have the monopoly of truth, and will need to induce "managerial entrepreneurship" throughout the organization, learning from a number of international cases such as for instance *Polaroid* (the now defunct inventor of instant pictures), IBM ("the elephant that learned to dance") or *Bridgewater* (a very successful international investment company, handling over USD 170 billion in investments for governments, pension funds, universities and charities). It is a challenge for any big corporation to remain agile enough to adapt to new challenges. A huge library can be filled with the literature that attempts to explain this need for ambidexterity to remain competitive, in any industry, be in the automotive, mining or technology field.

How can the chairman assure that the supervisory board (BoC) *collaborates* with the executive board (BoD) to ensure optimization of organizational value creation and preservation, while at the same time walking that fine line of supervisor/collaborator securing the necessary *check and balances*? We all have heard of stories where friends or acquaintances are appointed at boards to "look after" the interests of their respective patrons who put them on that board. Such practices often result to blatant nepotism or even corruption where the interest of the particular boss or party will prevail over the generic interest of the organization.

How can boards avoid unnecessary and often harmful political intervention in appointments of board members at State Owned Enterprises? At PT Telkom, proper and very strict governance procedures were in place to guarantee proper adherence to predetermined rules and not becoming too dependent on the whim of [too] powerful and politicized owners. Unfortunately, at PT Pertamina – fully owned by the state and without any formal pressure by international and local market players – such strict predetermined and market induced procedures do not apply. Value creation and an open managerial mindset is likely not the first characteristic on the table when appointing non-executive and executive board members. The result is that Pertamina has been run since its inception as the fiefdom of the powerful Indonesian political elite.

Moreover, to change a board, Pertamina's owner does not have to argue at an extraordinary shareholder meeting why there is a need to change the board; the minister of State Owned Enterprises just calls in the relevant parties and single-handedly change the chair, CEO or the whole board according to his or her discretion. Consequently, the philosophy among Pertamina's board is securing status-quo and pleasing the [vested interested of] politicians and or the minister in charge, to secure a full term tenure at least. The yardstick used at state owned enterprises to appoint board members are somehow somewhat "unclear". Do political power relations and "nationalistic" feelings prevail over economic efficiency? Hard to tell in such an ambiguous context. But politics do matter, indeed. Obviously, a similar debate on governance takes place between more "democratic" institutions versus more "authoritarian" regimes, both having pros and cons.

From a corporate governance perspective, the supervisory board and the owners of these state owned enterprises should stay out of the operations and non-strategic decisions which is the executive board's responsibility. And obviously, the owners (i.e. the minister in charge of state owned enterprises) and the supervisory board (BoC) should stay clear from mingling with fields for which they have given a delegated authority to the executive board (BoD) and its management team.

B) A Confusing Corporate Governance Structure

However, there is an additional complication to secure good governance due to the specific holding structure at Pertamina and some other state owned enterprises. The idea behind this idiosyncratic holding and subholding structure at state owned enterprises in Indonesia is the result of trying to make those enterprises more effective and agile. Prior to 1998, Indonesia had about 159 state owned enterprises spread over 17 ministries. Today, we have roughly 140 state owned firms in Indonesia, under the control of one ministry of state owned enterprises. The ownership power was taken away from those 17 different ministries in 1998 because of the establishment of a new ministry of state-owned enterprises in Indonesia that now "supervises" those state firms. Not coincidentally, this transition occurred with the take-over of presidential power of long serving Soeharto by his then vice-President, Prof. dr. Habibie. There was a need to organize and simplify the task of the newly created ministry of state owned enterprises in 1998: hence why the initiation of twelve holding structures in which the state gave power and authority at the holding level to steer these organizations at the sub-holding level. The role of boards at the holding level –

empowered by the minister of state owned enterprises – was ideally (1) to delegate, (2) to develop the needed managerial competencies, and (3) to be accountable for the assets at the holding company to their shareholders. Concretely, it meant that the board at the holding level was assumed to authorize or delegate some of their power to the sub-holding or operational level to optimize the use of capital and human innovative expertise in generating cash flow. It was assumed that a competent supervisory and executive board at the holding level had the authority and competency to be able to select a board at the sub-holding operational level, while creating a managerial talent pool for those operational sub-holdings, and making sure that the sub-holding firms were also accountability for their performance. In other words, the holding replaced the "function" of the minister and the shareholders, whose boards now would be able to approve strategy and allocate the necessary financial and human capital resources to those [sub-holding entities] who needed it to generate operating profit.

Currently, the Ministry of State Owned Enterprises in Indonesia "manages" and oversees about fourteen holding firms and about twenty stand-alone state owned enterprises, among which PT Telkom, PT PLN (the national electricity company) and PT Mandiri (the biggest bank in Indonesia). These 20 state owned holdings operates independently and may have invested in stand-alone subsidiaries. In those twenty cases, there is no legal or structured governance confusion whatsoever.

Unfortunately, in the other fourteen holding cases, confusion rives. Ideally, having learned from this experience, Dr. Tanri suggests that the appointments and restructuring of boards at the State Owned Enterprises should be managed independently by a body or institute – "badan" – overseen by an independent minister in charge. But again, even such independent body may create additional overlapping, or worse, outright confusion in terms of authority and decision power. At the end, it all boils down whether a board is sufficiently professional and competitive to perform the assumed fiduciary duties as anywhere else in the world. And when a board of a holding proves not to be ready for the task, the minister – as the legal representative of the ultimate shareholder – needs to immediately replace or restructure. Similarly, at the operating level, the sub-holding supervisory and executive board need to be accountable for the performance of their sub-holding company, to be supervised by the "super" holding boards, not the minister.

By allowing some authority and decision-making power at the sub-holding or operational level, the holding company intended to secure the potential of talented managers at the sub-holding level to pursue certain strategic directions to perform and generate above average cash flow. In other words, the actual cash flow is generated at the sub-holding operational level, "supervised" and controlled by the holding company. At this moment, the Indonesian ministry of state owned enterprises roughly oversees about fourteen holding companies which do not operate themselves but they do own "subsidiary" sub-holding operating firms. These fourteen state holding entities can be found in a number of strategic "industries" like mining, fertilizer, gas and oil, bio-pharma, cement and a couple of others crucial national treasures – almost all related to raw materials which remains the major export revenues and cash flow generator for Indonesia. Allow us to raise the thought that too much dependency on raw materials – also a potential curse – may need to be diversified into more added value business activities.

It is at the holding level that the ultimate investment decisions and strategic direction are made and approved, whereas the actual operational decisions are always made at the sub-holding level. In other words, the actual growth is derived and materialized at the sub-holding level, but the assets and people are legally "held" at the holding level. Structurally, an additional but also artificial "wall" has been installed between the strategic investment decisions at the holding level (with in itself a dual-tier board) and the operating cash-flow generating sub-holding level (also with a two-tier board structure). Indeed, the actual performance of people resides at the sub-holding level whereas they are "owned" by the holding – creating huge confusion between the actual "duty" of the BoD at the holding company, and the BoD at the sub-holding company. The same structure then is repeated at the respective supervisory board, both at the holding and sub-holding level. Confusing, indeed. There is an overlapping of authority that makes clear direction quite uncomfortable in case of possible disagreement.

In fact, the executive directors and management at the sub-holding operating organization does not legally own the assets it uses to create growth in revenues, profit and cash flow. And what makes it even more "inefficient" is that in reality, all holding and sub-holding boards report directly to the minister of state owned enterprises in charge of these state owned assets. However, that doubles the work of the central power and undermines the authority of the boards, definitely at the holding level, but to a certain degree also for the supervisory boards at the sub-holding who not just report to the holding board but also to the minister. A double (shall we say overlapping) reporting structure that may not exactly incite good functioning or optimal efficiency. Indeed, the current (new) holding structure at Pertamina complicates the matter in steering the organization by having a holding structure overviewing the presumed independent six sub-holdings, each with their own supervisory and executive board at the sub-holding level. Almost re-doing or repeating the job of the board at the holding.

C) A Dual-Tier Board Structure of SOEs at the Holding and Sub-holding / Subsidiary Level

Somehow, one could argue that the supervisory board (BoC) mainly is assumed to think through the strategy, to reflect upon the future of the organization, seeking opportunities and avoiding threats, whereas the executive board (BoD) is expected to deliver, to do or to execute the envisioned strategy and objectives. And for that, proper governance procedures and processes at a board helps to fulfil these expected [fiduciary] obligations as visualized for Pertamina in Figures 30 and 31.

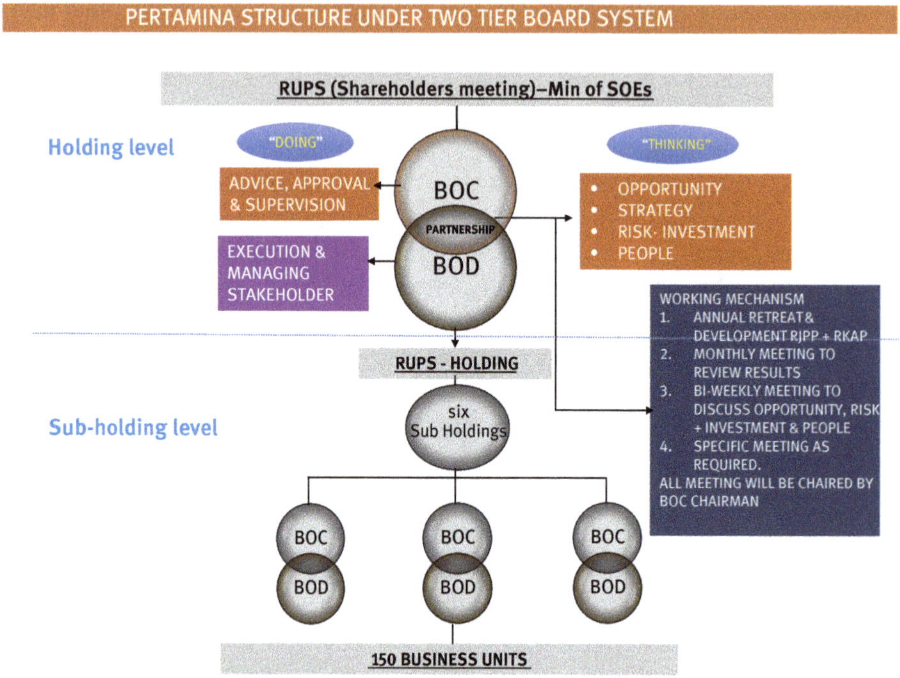

Figure 30: Board structure at Pertamina.
Source: prepared by Tanri Abeng for board training at Pertamina, 2021

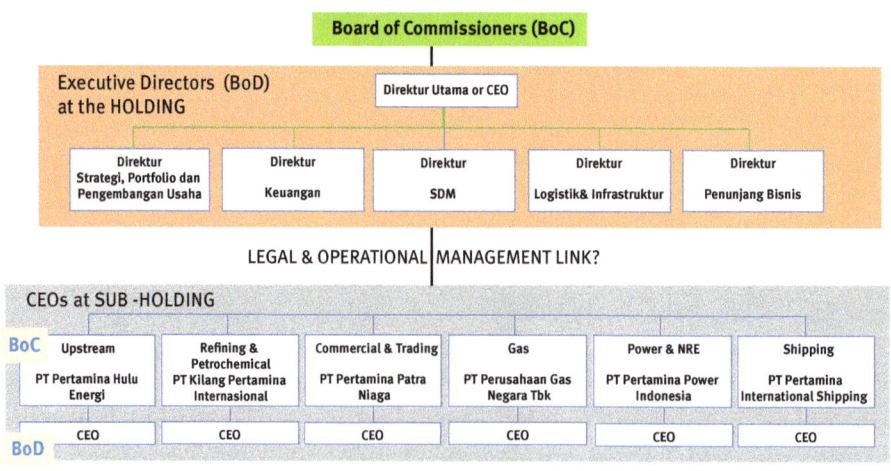

Figure 31: New Holding structure of Pertamina.
Source: prepared by Tanri Abeng for board training at Pertamina, 2021

The question begs what the exact function is of the holding executive board when dealing with the executive board of the gas sub-holding for instance. Despite the efforts by the Minister of SOEs to make Pertamina more efficient, and to ensure proper control and monitoring, Pak Tanri is far from convinced. The new holding structure may bloat the hierarchical reporting responsibilities and in the process undermine the objective of more efficiency. Indeed, the executive director of logistics and infrastructure at the holding level may have a strong opinion about how the executive director of refining should execute his or her ideas. But the current structure is extremely unhelpful to make Pertamina more efficient in the long term. Structures and mechanisms are supposed to help efficiency, not to burden them.

Running a huge complex corporation like Pertamina has always been a real challenge, even for the most experienced. The Pertamina holding-subholding structure rather complicates than simplifies the governance and management responsibilities and authority. How to reduce this apparent inefficient or convoluted structure? Above the usual difficult strategic and operational decisions a board and executives have to make, they face (a) bureaucratic processes that are not always straightforward, (b) occasional political intervention putting heavy pressure on the board, and (c) the continuous challenge to safeguard having the right team and talent at the holding level, but also at the operating sub-holding or subsidiaries level.

Today, the remuneration at Indonesian state owned enterprises is competitive with the private sector. Indeed, the biggest challenge remains to find and install the right team for the supervisory board and especially for the executive board at the holding level but also at sub-holding level. Any responsible owner or policy maker is aware of the enormous impact an experienced executive and executive board can have to steer complex organizations. Installing the right [executive] team is crucial. An experienced top executive, proven his or her abilities to outperform industry averages, can eventually move into a non-executive chair position. Finding the right people and the right team for the executive board at the holding level who can be trusted to appoint the right team for the sub-holding level – supervised by an experienced supervisory board-team – is crucial to make any sensible amendment to increase governance efficiency.

Relatively speaking, Malaysian Petronas has been performing better[14] because the firm has been a stand-alone company reporting directly to the prime minister. In other words, much less political intervention, and focused on using the available assets to optimize profitability without concerns of divided authorities and responsibilities, under the supervision of a single-tier board. Petronas - being a stand-alone corporation (in contrast to Pertamina) with some investments in subsidiaries - is structured in a much more straightforward manner and consequently more competitive. Moreover, in additional of the complex structures, it should be noted that Pertamina has never developed new upstream products over the last 25 years, hardly invested in refinery which pushed them instead to import those products, and finally, did not really fulfil their fiduciary duty to create and sustain a worthy talent pool, despite having established a corporate university. There is definitely a concern for talented leadership and a continuity of good accountable and responsible leadership within SOEs.

D) A Potential "Premortem" Exercise

Obviously, a complicated legal structure – holding and subholding – without clear authority delineation does not contribute to focus on economic efficiency. Despite the initial good intentions of power delegation, it seems that in reality the opposite took place: numerous fiefdoms at different levels who all try to protect their turf and power which in itself is not clearly defined. You add the challenge of establishing a performing unified team between the supervisory and executive board, and you can imagine that governing and running a USD 54 billion company like Pertamina is quite demanding.

So one of the first exercises, or as a thought experiment at least, we would suggest the full board to go through the following counter-intuitive question or "premortem" thought exercise[15]: "how to kill the old Pertamina-culture encumbered by vested political and personal interest and entrenchment" that may be able to help the board to engage in increased accountability while at the same time avoid group-thinking and to become better "managerial entrepreneurs" for the company. A daunting and almost impossible task for many, as all consultants and academics are well aware of: organizational culture is the software of an organization which "eats every other challenge for breakfast".

Running and steering a huge company is always difficult, and taking charge of a corporation like PT Pertamina is even more daunting. Pak Tanri graciously admits that he did not fully succeed either during this term as Chair of PT Pertamina to put all the *right people* at the right place. Regrettably, making the old mighty a more lean and functioning organization remains nothing but a dream today. His successor may want to focus on this unfinished task of developing the right professionals for leadership positions within PT Pertamina to secure appropriate succession within the firm and withstand unproductive political interventions and to safeguard the competitive survival of the firm.

Today, the organization features 30 executive board of directors at the subholding level (6 subholdings at Pertamina) and similar amount of commissioners who are often political appointment; not exactly the example of a nimble board. It somehow seems to reflect the ultimate representative of the Indonesian state, president Jokowi's current rather bloated cabinet, that attempts to accommodate the numerous political interests. Maybe it is part of the culture to pacify all interests in a "unified manner"?

The former Jakarta governor Basuki "Ahok" Tjahaja Purnama – someone who would dare to ruffle feathers with the establishment – was appointed as the chairman of Pertamina in 2019. His mandate is to further reduce the entrenchment challenges that has characterized Pertamina for so many years, which is only possible if there is enough political will to reform. Maybe making Pertamina *run like* a publicly listed owned company according to best corporate governance practices and procedures may be a good start? And yes, we are mindful that [the owners of] PT Pertamina may not chose to go through an IPO process; we nonetheless believe that applying good corporate governance practices and professionally running the firm accordingly would hugely benefit all stakeholders involved over a longer term.

The culture in state owned enterprises is still monopolistic culture. What should be the culture at Pertamina? We practically define culture as the sum of the behaviour of all people, reflecting the implementation of coherence in values. Organizational culture – the coherent behaviour of the employees and management alike that is based on integrity and trust – could definitely can strengthen state owned enterprises, because the culture "directs" the people into one desired direction. The current minister, Erik Thohrir uses the label "*Akhlak*" to describe his intention to impose a more professional and ethical culture in those state firms. The notion '*Akhlak*' refers to core values, integrity, trust and agility in the firm. In a context of concentrated ownership, one owner, with enormous responsibilities and power in the hands of the board members, both non-executive and executive directors, properly governing such a huge organization (both at the holding as at the operational subsidiary level) remains a daunting task. Time will tell wether the attempted restructurings will bear any concrete fruit, as in a more lean and efficiently run organization.

2.4 Concluding Remarks on the Dual-Tier Board Structure

The Indonesian law stipulates that the BoC is responsible for supervising management policies, overseeing management of both the company and the company's business operations, and advising the BoD on its management duties.[16] Indeed, the BoC's primary role is to supervise rather than manage.[17]

The Indonesian Corporate Law (ICL) and the Corporate Governance Code require limited liability companies in Indonesia to adopt a two-tier board system, comprising the BoC and BoD. Each of these bodies possess distinct responsibilities, as set under the ICL and other regulations. Companies may set out details and/or additional responsibilities in their articles of association or the constitution of the firm beyond these mere legal requirements. Nevertheless, both the BoC and BoD are responsible for maintaining the company's long-term sustainability. Accordingly, the BoC and BoD must share a mutual perspective of the company's vision, mission, and values. An effective, professional, and independent BoC is essential for good corporate governance. In Indonesia, the BoC is the corporate organ that is responsible for overseeing and advising the BoD as well as ensuring that the company implements good corporate governance practices, and guaranteeing continuity in leadership. The Corporate Governance Code prohibits the BoC from participating in making any operational decisions. While the BoC cannot change the economic environment in which a company operates, its role in providing strategic oversight and control over management can have a positive influence on the company's performance.

The BoC's activities may go entirely unnoticed when an economy is strong, share prices are rising, and everything appears to be going well. On the other hand, when things go badly, the importance of the BoC becomes clear.

Companies should observe the following principles when establishing a BoC. The composition of the BoC should enable it to act independently and to make decisions efficiently: (1) BoC members must be professionals who possess the integrity and capability to enable them to properly carry out their functions. (2) The BoC's oversight and advisory functions include acts related to prevention of breaches of national law and internal company regulations concerning corporate governance, improving compliance with these requirements, and temporary suspension of BoD members when deemed necessary in the interests of the company. Despite the close resemblance of the interpretation of good corporate governance practices that Indonesia and the regulator have taken over, we still do not see a converging trend of one solution for all. Yes, it has become obvious that those generic good corporate governance practices based on the OECD principles have been almost universally accepted by most regulators across borders, the interpretation of them remains very contextual giving a unique idiosyncratic character to each country.

As a matter of rule of thumb, we suggest to follow the suggested procedures in Figure 32 to establish or to improve an effective supervisory board: specifying the fiduciary duties, authorities and responsibilities; deciding on the structure, subcommittees and size of the board; identifying the specific skill sets and competencies needed to fill the positions at the two-tier board; making sure that the right team is selected for the board; and after acceptance, inducing the new board members to their respective responsibilities at the board while continuing to prepare future leaders. Boards should be regularly evaluated and trained – like any executive and organization is expected to continue to learn. Only learning organizations will survive the fierce international competition.

From the analyzed cases, we dare to conclude that the main tasks of a [supervisory] board to steer, advise and develop a talent pool remains a huge challenge. However, weak(er) national governance structures may put corporations in such countries at a comparative disadvantage. *Having the right people and the right team in place, with appropriate governance processes and procedures based on the right information that is transparently disclosed to the shareholders* therefore becomes even more crucial to stand out. In any country, super-performers outmanoeuver their industry peers with significant margins.[18] However, underperformers are equally worth our attention, especially if these firms – often state owned enterprises – concern national "asset treasurers" that deserve better. Those state owned firms need to wake up, and their boards are in urgent need to be professionalized. Political appointments at those boards refrain them from choosing the "right team", undermining economic efficiency. We strongly advise to curb this political over-entrenchment in order to enable those "national treasures" to emerge as proper companies that stand on their own competitive feet. True in any country.

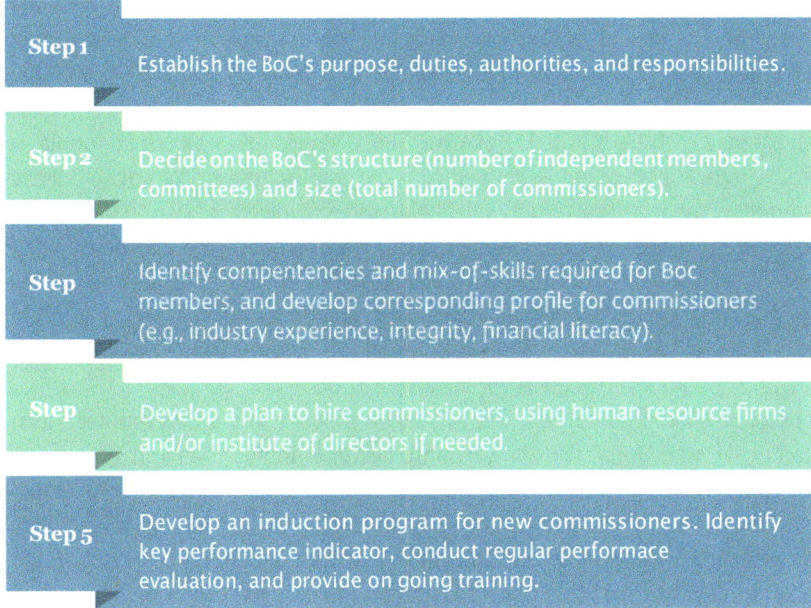

Figure 32: Five steps to develop an effective Board of Commissioners.
Source: IFC World Bank: Indonesia Corporate Governance Manuel, (2018), 2nd Edition: 153

In the case of Pertamina, Garuda and Telkom, we are convinced that the two following factors should be given priority: (1) **openness** and *transparency in decision-making,* and (2) to install and agree on **objectives** that are specific for which one can *be accounted for,* reducing the burdensome silo-mentality that prevails at many boards of SOEs. It also means that the chairman who chairs the board meetings **collaborate** with the executive board by finding a subtle balance in advising, coaching but also supervising on important decisions like strategy. The supervisory board should be involved with the selection of the CEO and should be responsible to set the tone on the top in terms of ethical integrity of all its board members. The supervisory board should also take charge of modus operandi of the board functioning and the professional competence of all its board members. Moreover, the supervisory board should partner with the executive board and the owners on the risk appetite, the development of a talent pool, and install a culture of decisiveness, and on potential mergers and acquisitions and its subsequent resource allocation.

We strongly believe that one cannot serve two masters. Then, how to determine the accountability of the board members of state owned enterprises? Should they serve their political masters as we often see today, or should we expected a board to be fully accounted to the objectives of the organization they represent and serve? Foremost and above all, the board should professionally focus on the organization's objectives that should take priority over political interests. However, the objective to run an state owned enterprises as effective and efficiently as possible, does not necessarily mean that there is only one financial objective to be pursued – as in a mainstream Anglo-Saxon context to "maximize" profitability or shareholder value [only]. It is quite possible that the dual-tier boards of a state owned enterprise will adhere to a "stakeholder" model with different stakes to be fulfilled. However, those stakes and objectives should be transparently, clearly and properly defined to avoid any fuzziness. Too much "discretion" and entrenchment by powerful political elite to be involved in boards' functioning should be avoided for the sake of a more open and transparent communication. The organizational (and thus not political) objectives of a state owned enterprise should be clearly defined, assessed and analyzed. They may include employment of Indonesian staff, or stable energy provision security for instance within particular benchmarks, next to financial and operational objectives for instance.

Big companies like Pertamina face the danger of being so big that innovative entrepreneurship or managerial entrepreneurship becomes impossible, and governance is reduced to mere compliance of some rules and regulations. Boards can do much more and can help to induce innovation – the necessary oxygen for any company – by giving the example on how to avoid group-thinking or status-quo and how to improve decision-making. Just sticking to the status quo and the average will not be a solution anymore. The nation state, the employees and the board have a duty to optimize the opportunities of SOEs and use their vast resources more professionally and optimally in a transparent manner underpinned by proper levels of integrity. At the same time, the non-executive and executive board of any SOE should minimize threatening risks or to avoid making regrettable decisions that would continue to undermine the competitiveness of their organization. Organizations deserve better. The nation's vast resources are at stake and should not be spoiled for political misguided short term objectives.

Consider the following Take Away Ideas of Chapter 4:

---

1. Dual-tier boards have the advantage of structurally being more stringent on supervision of the executive board, but likely less flexible in taking joint decisions – based on consensus. Whereas single-tier boards have the advantage of being fast in decision-making and being more flexible. However there is structurally less strong supervision, though a lead-director assumes the supervisory role on a powerful CEO under a single-tier board system.

2. Whatever the board structure – single or dual tier board structure – a board has particular functions to fulfil, as in steering, advising and supervising top executives. Under the dual-tier structure, as in Indonesia, a supervisory board is focusing on this monitoring functionality to secure that top executives fulfil their fiduciary duties of care, loyalty and prudence to optimize long term profitability of the firm. Indonesian family owned businesses do not face classical agency problems, but rather the potential conflict of interest between securing family interests (with a majority stake in the company) at the expense of minority shareholders. In state-owned enterprises, a chair or CEO can be very powerful and take advantage of that position, though at the end the CEO's and Chair's position remains in the hands of the minister representing the state.

3. The Indonesian cases of the state-owned enterprises Garuda, Telkom and Pertamina, it is clear that the board need to learn to collaborate more as a team, and not being hung up to the created title at the respective board. Both the supervisory and executive board – "the board" of an organization in a dual-tier structure – will need to find ways to combine their strength and jointly steer the organization as a unified team, embracing real business opportunities outperforming their peers and reducing the risks.

Notes

1 Corporate governance was catapulted to the forefront after the catastrophic collapse of Enron in the United States. Indeed, this collapse drew attention to corporate governance and management of the board of directors. On May 7, 2002, the United States Senate concluded the following with respect to the role of the Board in Enron's collapse and bankruptcy:
- Fiduciary failure: Enron's Board failed to safeguard shareholders and contributed to the collapse of the seventh largest public company in the United States.
- Lack of independence: Financial ties between the company and certain board members compromised the independence of the Board.
- Conflicts of interest: Despite clear conflicts of interest, the Board approved an unprecedented arrangement allowing Enron's Chief Financial Officer to establish and operate private equity funds that transacted business with Enron and profited at Enron's expense.
- Excessive compensation: The Board approved excessive compensation for company executives, failed to monitor the cumulative cash drain caused by Enron's annual bonus and performance unit plans given in FY 2000, and failed to monitor or halt a company-financed, multi-million dollar personal credit line.
- High-risk accounting: The Board knowingly allowed Enron to engage in high-risk accounting practices.
- Extensive undisclosed off-the-books activity: The Board knowingly allowed the company to conduct billions of dollars in off-the-books activity to make its financial condition appear healthier than it was, and failed to ensure adequate public disclosure of material liabilities that contributed to the company's collapse.

2 Charan, R., Carey, D. & M. Useem, (2014), *Boards that Lead. When to take charge, when to partner, and when to stay out the way*, Cambridge (MA), Harvard Business Review Press.

3 See Verhezen, P., (2015), *The Vulnerability of Corporate Reputation. Leadership for Sustainable Long-term Value*, Berkshire, Palgrave Pivot Publishing: http://www.palgrave.com/us/book/9781137547354.

The exemplary of proper crisis and communication management has been former CEO Burke during the Tylenol crisis at Johnson & Johnson in the 1980s where ethics and candid honest communication trumped any form of usual corporate spinning and even corporate legal justification and legal management. The CEO went beyond the legal minimum requirements to ensure the trust of his clientele.

4 Since peaking at around 6,500 to 7,000 enterprises sometime in the mid-to-late 1990s, depending on your data source, the number of companies publicly listed on U.S. exchanges has steadily declined. In 2016, according to Credit Suisse, that number got down to around 3,600. That trend is especially today, closer to 6,000 companies trade on the NYSE and Nasdaq. That trend is especially alarming when you consider the performance of the U.S. market compared with the rest of the

world. U.S. large-cap stocks have consistently outperformed their international counterparts for the last decade – and the COVID-19 pandemic has only widened that gap. Indeed, it is quite interesting that over just four-five decades, we have only half of the number of corporations on the NYSE in New York today, the biggest and most liquid capital market in the world. Partially, this halving of the corporations publicly listed – today only about 2400 US companies and 500 international companies are found on the stock exchange in New York, compared to more than 6500 in the 70s-90s – is due to a consolidation process of bigger corporations absorbing, acquiring smaller competitors and companies, partially because some companies like Kodak for instance filing for chapter 11 (a unique way under US corporate law to escape creditors and avoid straight bankruptcy) or going under, and thirdly, partially because some companies go "back private" giving them more flexibility without too much regulatory and listing requirements. Private funds and hedge funds seem to become more attractive for investors these days.

Allow us to note a clear distinction between the NYSE and the younger Nasdaq. The NYSE and Nasdaq exchanges are worth a collective $32 trillion in market capitalization, making up a sizable portion of the global equities market anno 2021. The NYSE has over 2,400 companies. It's also home to many of the big "blue chip" companies that have existed for decades, like Walmart, Exxon Mobil, or General Electric. This is partly because the exchange has existed since 1792. Meanwhile, the Nasdaq has more companies than the NYSE, but has a wider spectrum in terms of the size of companies. Of course, the exchange is known for having the large tech-focused companies like Facebook, Google, and Amazon, but there are many smaller listings on the Nasdaq as well. In total, there are over 3,800 companies listed on the Nasdaq. The Nasdaq is seen as a place for growth-oriented tech stocks. It was where the action was in the Dotcom boom and bust, and it's the place where the world's largest tech stocks are listed today.

5 Key issues every BoC should closely monitor include the following: the company's overall performance, especially in comparison to its competitors and industry peers; the BoD's compliance with law and internal procedures, including on corporate governance, risk management and internal control, and ethics; the BoD's performance, both at the team and individual levels; implementation of the company's strategy; and relations with key stakeholders, including the company's shareholders, as well as employees, suppliers, and customers. The BoC typically also has the authority to approve internal documents related to dividend policy, information policy, ethical standards, control and supervision of the BoD and company management, risk management, audits of the financial and business activity of the company, and policy on the corporate secretary. Listed companies in Indonesia must make public disclosure of the company's corporate governance practices at the annual GMS. The BoC should prepare the corporate governance report and submit this to the annual GMS. The corporate governance report should detail all essential elements of the company's corporate governance policies and practices. The BoC must disclose the extent to which the company complies with the CG Code and explain any discrepancy from these requirements. Finally, the BoC should also use the corporate governance report to make suggestions for improving the company's corporate governance practices.

6 It is as if asking the well-regarded Zidane – former successful player and now former coach of Real Madrid – to get on the pitch for his Real Madrid team which would likely not be considered as appropriate either: as coach and supervisor (though he himself used to be a top player for the same club) Zidane is assessing, selecting, monitoring and steering his team to remain a world class winning champion. The execution of Zidane's strategy and tactics is entirely up to the team itself. Both have a clear defined and interdependent role to play to succeed.

7 Even as the market moves toward "institutional capitalism", these investment funds by huge institutions like BlackRock, Vanguard Asset Management, State Street Global Advisors, have remained quitter "passive" investors over the last couple of decades. Lately, however, some of them have started to react more "actively" – becoming 'activist investors' trying to improve topics within

the corporate governance agenda, and often to improve or even replace top management and the board itself to secure better corporate governance at the company. Admittedly, some US-based investment funds (like the infamous KKR fund) have been perceived as acting more like "barbarians at the gate" to influence the aimed firm to change track, to change strategy, and or to cut the assets in pieces to materialize short term profit. Sometimes they succeed, sometimes they fail. This is a specific issue within corporate governance (M&A) that plays less of a role in Indonesia and other Asian countries, mainly because of the firm control by the family or state and to a much lesser extent because of a less financial less sophisticated capital market in those Asian countries.

8   Under Indonesian corporate governance law, the Chair is labelled the '*commisaris utama*' or "General Commissioner", and the CEO is known as '*direktor utama*' or "president director".

9   Li, J.S.,(2003), "Relation-based versus rules-based governance: An explanation of the East Asian miracle and Asian crisis", *Review of International Economics*, 11(4), 651–662.

10   See Confucius, *The Analects*, London, Penguin.

11   A dual-tier board structure as practiced in Indonesia seems to have an inherent advantage of effectively imposing a supervisory structure upon top management, which is in line with the main controlling and monitoring functions of boards within the prevailing *Agency Theory*. Moreover, the German banks for instance – having a similar dual tier supervisory board structure as Indonesia – seem to have relatively wavered the current financial global crisis more effectively because of their relatively different and separate corporate governance structures in comparison with the Anglo-Saxon (banking) environment with its single tier governance structure. Excessive risk taking in those German institutions was effectively constrained by a kind of prudence, exercised by these dual-tier boards. We believe that formal corporate governance mechanisms that emphasize the importance of "independent" non-executive directors have contributed to a more open and transparent business environment that is able to reduce management entrenchment.

12   Indeed, one should shift from verifying which governance features are in place to one that evaluates the success of various functions of good corporate governance.

1. CEO Succession:
   a. Does the company have a CEO succession plan in place?
   b. Is the CEO succession plan operational? Have qualified international and external candidates been identified? Does the company engage in ongoing talent development to support long-term succession needs?
2. Risk Management:
   a. Is risk management a responsibility of the full board or non-executive directors, the audit committee, or a dedicated risk committee?
   b. Do the board [of non-executive directors] and management understand how the various operational and financial activities of the firm work together to achieve the corporate strategy? Have they determined what events might cause one or more of these activities to fail? Have these risks been properly mitigated?
3. Executive Compensation:
   a. What is the total compensation paid to the CEO? How does this compare to the compensation paid to other named executive officers?
   b. How is the compensation package expected to attract, retain, and motivate qualified executive talent? Does it provide appropriate incentive to achieve the goals set forth in the business model? What is the relationship between large changes in the company stock price and the overall wealth of the CEO (and or Chairman)? Does this properly encourage short- and long-term performance without excessive risk?.

13   See Dweck, C.S., (2006), *Mindset: the new psychology of success*, New York, Random House.

14   We see a possible causal correlation between accountability and openness, between well governing boards and improved innovative entrepreneurship within the company. How else to explain

why the USD 32 billion Malaysian *Petronas* – with assets of about USD 145 billion and roughly with a revenue stream of above USD 26 billion in 2020 but a loss of USD 4.9 billion in comparison with a profit of USD 11.39 in 2019 has been outperforming its Indonesian neighbouring competitor for many years. Pertamina – with much more complex if not debilitating structures – with assets worth USD 54 billion in 2019, made USD 2.5 billion in 2019, reduced to USD 1,05 billion profit on USD 41.47 billion revenues in 2020. Lately, Pertamina has benefited a little from the relatively current high oil prices, but the firm should not be seen as an example of super-efficiency or performance. Over a longer period, relatively speaking, Petronas has been outperforming Pertamina – partially due to the less complicated structure, less political intervention and focused on economic performance. The simpler structure of Petronas is characterized by being part of Kasana, the holding company above Petronas, that is an investment holding under the Malaysian Ministry of Finance.

15 The term "premortem" has been introduced by psychologist Dr. Gary Klein. See Klein, G. (2009). *Strengths and shadows: Searching for the keys to adaptive decision-making*, Cambridge MA, MIT Press; and especially Klein, G., (2014), *Seeing what others don't. The remarkable ways we gain Insights*, London; Boston, Nicolas Brealy Publishing.

16 The Indonesian Corporate Law (Article 116–118) requires the BoC to take minutes of BoC meetings and keep copies of these minutes; report shareholdings held by BoC members or their families in the company or other companies; report to the annual shareholders' meeting on the performance of its supervisory duties during each financial year; approve or assist the BoD in performing certain legal actions as conferred to the BoC by the AoA (the BoC may only act within the scope of authority provided under the AoA); perform management activities in specific situations as provided in the ICL for a specified time, when the AoA or a GMS resolution confers authority to do so. As a rule, the BoC has the authority to decide on all issues that do not fall under the authority of the GMS and/or other corporate bodies. To avoid ambiguity over the division of powers between the GMS, BoC, and BoD, any additional responsibilities the AoA grants to the BoC should correspond with the typical function of the BoC.

17 The constitution of the firm may also assign additional powers to the BoC to meet the company's needs. The articles of association (AoA) or the constitution of a limited liability company will typically stipulate the general duties of the BoC, as follows: supervise the company's management (the BoD); perform any duty specifically provided for by the AoA, prevailing laws and regulations, or general annual shareholders' resolutions; perform its duties, authority, and responsibilities in accordance with the company's articles of association and shareholders' resolutions; act in the interests of the company and be accountable to the shareholders; supervise, review, and approve the implementation of the company's work plan and annual budget prepared and submitted by the BoD; assess the BoD's periodic report and, at any time, provide a response on the performance of the company and report the implementation of its duties to shareholders in a timely manner; follow the development of the company's activities. In the event of corporate distress, the BoC must report to the shareholders as soon as possible and provide advice on steps that may be taken for recovery; propose candidates for appointment as the external auditor to the shareholders' meeting; and examine, review, and sign the annual report prepared by the BoD.

18 Bradley, C.; Hirt, M. & S. Smit, (2018), *Strategy beyond the Hockey Stick. People, Probabilities, and big moves to beat the odds*, New York, Wiley & Sons – McKinsey & Company.

Chapter 5
Accountable and Responsible Leadership
From Shareholder Primacy to Organizational Sustainable Value

> Value or Profit is a false choice. Exceptional financial performance reflects value creation.
> Oberholzer-Gee, (2021: 19)

> The crucial difference between human cognition and that of other species is the ability to participate with others in collaborative activities with shared goals and intentions.
> Tomasello (2005)

We cannot deny that many market prices are wildly out of whack, completely ignoring negative externalities. It seems that firms are rewriting the rules of the game in ways that maximize their own profits while simultaneously distorting that market.[1] Some speak of uncontrolled free markets,[2] characterized by concentrated power in the hands of a few – which goes against the idea of building a "just and sustainable world" as formulated by the seventeen UN sustainable development goals.[3]

That we need to change is now clear – not just for Western firms but to any firm that wants to operate more sustainably. And although West-European firms may take a lead in the search for more sustainable products and services, all organizations will need to embrace this new thinking to be able to sustain over a longer period. The incredible shift towards hybrid or electric cards in the automotive industry is obvious, initially led by Tesla in the USA, but now taking front stage in almost all European, Japanese and South Korean car manufacturers. China is also getting on board with the electrification of their automobile sector, more than two in five cars sold in China today are electrified.

We may envision a "reimagined capitalism".[4] The question is *how*, and what exactly does this means.

1 From Maximizing Shareholder Value to "Sharing" Created Value

Boards are not just accountable to their capital providing *stock-holders*, but have an equally significant responsibility toward engaged *stake-holders* of the organization. Governance is a way to translate this organizational accountability and responsibility into concrete and often [partially] procedural decision-making that prepares the organization for a promising future. However, we often see that investments initiatives that impact the socio-ecological context suffer from poor governance. This lack of good governance practices highlights the importance to secure better and wiser decision-making. A well-governed transformation must satisfy different *stake-

holders across an organization and be agile enough to accommodate multiple types of initiatives, while ensuring enough robust predictability (with the use of artificial intelligence) to achieve strategic alignment and efficiency. At the same time, organizations and its leadership need to show grit[5] and resilience when unforeseen adversity or crisis hit the organization. How do we translate this into concrete decision-making?

One could argue that shareholder value is a managerial or board's choice.[6] But not the only possible one allegedly stipulated by the law. As a matter of legal fact, boards control the organization, not the shareholders though the latter has the legal power to dismiss or retain the board at the Annual Shareholder meeting.[7] Hence why it could be argued against mainstream liberal economic theorists that "Shareholder primacy ideology is inconsistent with both corporate law, and [. . .] with empirical evidence.[8]"

All depends on what perspective the board will take. Western organizations are been considered more transactional whereas Asian companies are more inclined to see the importance of long-term relationships.[9] At the heart of Asian ethics and business in general is defining the role of the organization and its leadership in their interdependent relationship with those in power, the "Mandarins". But Asian managers must equally envisage strategies that are helpful to govern and control the organization in a world that continuously changes. This emphasis on relationships is an element that may help organizations to address the challenges we face and will affect us over a longer period, beyond mere focus on transactions that boards expect to result in short-term profitability. To become more effective, boards should find that balance between short-term exploitation of assets that drive transactions, and a longer-term perspective that likely involves treasuring and developing relationships and investment in innovative technologies.

1.1 Firms are both a *Nexus of Contracts* and a *Nexus of Relationships*

From a board's perspective, compliance with existing rules is necessary. Boards' duties also imply to assess how to interpret the *duty of care* and *loyalty* as new technologies, changing trends and evolving community standards become more prevalent. Steering the organization, providing oversight and coaching top management and leadership development can be described as the board's fiduciary duty.

Whether we are smart or wise depends on the way we organize ourselves.[10] Interestingly, organizations are often perceived as **a nexus of contractual agreements** that determine to a high extent how their members will react to each other and to outsiders. If indeed, we would adhere to mainstream liberal market economics where organizations are considered as owned by the shareholders, all decision-making in firms is in function of optimizing the net return on the investment.[11] However, if we would opt for a slightly broader definition of corporate governance, then fiduciary duties of care and loyalty to the firm can be translated as optimizing share-holders' value and those – employees and suppliers – that are directly involved in creating value for the organization while taking care of relevant stakeholders' concerns – such as customers and communities, and often the regulator – who can affect the firm's reputation.[12] In that sense, we interpret the organization as *a nexus of relationships* that optimize the value of the organization. Admittedly, the notion of *relationships* is a more encompassing notion than a more stringent contractual agreement, but relations also inherent to why and how humans cooperate and collaborate within groups.[13]

For instance, the incoming CEO of Amazon, Andy Jasy – who is best known for creating Amazon's colossal profitable cloud computing business unit – is replacing one of the world's most recognizable businessman, Jeff Bezos, founder of Amazon and to some the embodiment of capitalism's excesses (*anno* 2021). The new CEO is going to have to put way more energy into Amazon's relationships with society in general and government in particular as rules and regulations are expected to change tech companies. In particular, Amazon's board and the new CEO may hope to improve Amazon's reputation as an employer of 1.3 million people, that crucially remains quite "challenging", if not deplorable. Having installed an independent chair is a first step to amend the relationships with (potential) unions, Amazon's disgrundled employees, and regulators across the world.

How to outperform the average? Focus on value creation based on trust, not just on mere profitability. Profit will almost logically follow.[14] Performance is achieved by creation of value to customers, employees and suppliers that likely results in higher profitability. Organizations that seek to create better value for customers – through the use of AI or more sustainable products – will increase their willingness to pay. Similarly, when firms offer more attractive work for their employees, their engagement, their job satisfaction increases, and the relative willingness to sell at a particular price by the employee – or his/her remuneration – decreases (relatively speaking). And likely the productivity will increase.[15] Any awarded firm that has the reputation to "the best place to work" knows that value in terms of higher productivity and lower employee turnover. And if your firm finds ways to reduce the supplier's cost of working with your firm, it will be able to capture part of that value because the supplier's willingness to sell will decrease and favour to collaborate with your firm. For instance, IKEA's trusted relational network with its preferred suppliers has resulted in sustainable competitive advantages. This value-based thinking could also be extended to other stake-holders like the community. Organizations that establish trustworthy relationships and "share" some of that created value with the community in which they operate will benefit from it. Please ask some of the mining companies in distant places on islands in Indonesia or Philippines, and you'll find out the enormous efforts that companies need to take to create trust within the affected communities. Newmont Indonesia invested heavily in basic infrastructure like roads, schools and hospitals – which should be the responsibility of the government – in remote places like Sumbawa, partially out of self-interest. However, Rio Tinto, for example, spoiled some of its previously gained social capital through proper stakeholder management by blowing up an archeologically important but also sacred mountain for the abroginal community in West Australia in 2020, for extracting iron ore. It caused a public uproar in Australia that ultimately led to the dismissal of its CEO and pressure to replace the governing chairman.

Focusing more on the relations instead of the contractual agreements between the different stakeholders will likely contribute to *sustainable* or *shared value* creation. Companies must earn a profit, but it is also true that only those organizations that make some contribution to society – and not demolish it in one form or another – will survive. Ultimately, society and its judicial system only permits companies who contribute to society. Companies create value and benefits for customers, employees, and their partners – be it suppliers or distributors. The company will capture some of that value where profit becomes a result of and not the ultimate objective of good and effective business leadership.

We finally may move from a paradigm of *profitability maximization* to *optimizing and sharing created value*. Profit maximization has been the prevailing adage of most boards and business schools training those potential future members. Today, creating shared or sustainable value is now more and more acknowledged. Stakeholders' benefits have become part of business attention, and the organization's *wising up act*[16] may result in *sharing* some of the economic value that is created, making the organization [more] acceptable by society and, therefore, sustain its economic sustainability.

Paradoxically, optimizing economic value may not be a mathematical one-dimensional maximization challenge, but usually involves harmonizing and balancing the interests of a number of engaged stakeholders. Even opposing interests are not necessarily a choice between either. *Paradoxal leadership* can turn the "Power of And"[17] into motion. It would mean that such an exercise attempts to reconcile purpose and values with the major objective of making money and profit. Strategic thinker and philosopher Darden Business School Professor Ed Freeman is a staunch believer that taking the stakes of those involved in the organization seriously can release an unbound energy that enhances the traditional organizational flywheel focus on profitability. "Stake-brokers" are highly engaged and informed individuals who strongly believe that organizations need to "build skills of relationship repair and resilience[18]". A creating-value-for-stakeholders mindset[19] transcends the potential conflict between the different stakeholders. One could easily argue that in the long term, it is impossible to optimize profitability by emphasizing just the providers of capital and ignoring all the others. Serving all stakeholder groups in one way or another – and not necessarily with equal weight – requires a committed form of paradoxal leadership. The board is charged with serving the best interests of the corporation and its shareholders – including long-term shareholders, diversified shareholders and pro-social and pro-ecological shareholders. All depends on how we define shareholders: expanding our understanding of the nature of 'the shareholder' would benefit both legitimate investors[20] as well as concerned parties with a stake in the organization.

The strategist thinkers, Harvard Professor Michael Porter and activist Michael Kramer have popularized the notion of *corporate shared value*,[21] in which both the business and society benefits. Instead of emphasizing the tensions between business objectives often translated in maximizing profitability versus societal objectives as expressed in the well-being and welfare of its citizens, this model focuses on the *interdependencies* of both business and society. Creating value in the context of a liveable planet and a healthy thriving society is desirable. Hence why creating sustainable or **"shared" value** equals building such a liveable planet and society, and doing the right thing while also creating a profitable business, as in simultaneously reducing risk, cutting costs, and meeting the demands for increasingly "sustainable products". Creating shared value is quite sensible because the executives' mindset is focused on the interdependencies [of relations] between business and society, and not only on the unavoidable differences and tensions between them. We are convinced that taking care of your primary stake-holders – i.e. customers, employees and suppliers – will allow companies to thrive and possibly result in [above average or at least a fair] return on invested capital for the investors or owners. But 'sharing' this created value with concerned stake-holders will strengthen this virtuous cycle of trust, ultimately benefiting capital-providers or stock-holders. To convince the providers of capital to engage in a more enlightened form of capitalism, one will need additional and new audible and replicable metrics that capture costs and benefits of addressing environmental and social challenges. Such new measurements would also allow investors to understand the benefits of creating shared value, colloquially labelled ESG criteria as in environmental, societal and governance.

Business can only thrive within a healthy broader societal context, and vice versa. A community only thrives with meaningful businesses that creates material wealth and prosperity. Similarly, smart leaders are expected to create products and services that result in *at par* or above industry average return on investments. **'Sharing' created value** aligns the longer term stockholders' profitability objectives with the stakeholders' demands and concerns. And if one links this values-based approach with network effects, a leveraging flywheel amplifies the efforts. Network effects reinforce the importance of connectivity and 'relations'. Networks create a positive feedback loop: the more passengers Uber, Lyft or DiDi, Grab or Gojek can attract, the more drivers will join, which in turn, attracts more passengers. Call it the "network" effect.[22] Many of the leading tech companies rely on network effects to drive up the willingness to pay (from the customer). Networks are affected and determined by trust. Indeed, trust is the major glue in any economy – something Adam Smith already knew.[23]

1.2 Re-interpreting Fiduciary Duties aligned with Enlightened Ownership

When talking about contractual agreements it is necessary to distinguish possession from ownership. The latter is a cooperative and thus relational arrangement among individuals in a society who agree to respect one another's property. Possession is a relation between a person and a thing, the object, whereas ownership is a cooperative relation between persons with respect to a thing or object. And although its nature may differ across cultures, in all societies the division of resources is accompanied by some norms and rules that establish private ownership. For instance the shareholders' stock ownership implicitly requires agreement on norms and rules to be followed and implemented. Although research has shown that shareholders' [equal] stock ownership is better protected under a common law system than under civic law,[24] it is equally true that a lot depends on how children and young adults are educated to deal with their relation vis-à-vis property. The sense of private property in some community-oriented cultures (such as most Asian communities) is much more restricted – in which resources and potential "individual" property are shared – in comparison with more expansive interpreting individualistic capitalist cultures.[25]

The fiduciary duty of directors is often misinterpreted as "shareholder primacy" – putting shareholders first to assure short term profitability. The paradigm of shareholder value is partially linked to some influential scholars like Nobel laureate Milton Friedman from Chicago University and quite a number of his colleagues in the finance department at the Chicago Booth School who had immense influence on President Reagan's and Prime Minister Thather's policy making in the US and UK respectively. Similarly, Harvard Business School professor Michael Jensen's seminal papers on shareholder value and stock options[26] had also a significant impact on boards and their governance decision-making. Jensen's influential thoughts stood by the shareholder value but amended it with a nod to a form of enlightened stakeholder theory. These scholarly work is crucial in understanding the tension in this paradigm battle and ongoing shift. Today, the obvious focus is shifting to a longer term sustainable value creation aligned with societal expectations (and pressure) to respect ecological and socio-ethical boundaries.

This long term or sustainable value[27] is only "real" when a new *Zeitgeist* takes charge by assuming that the current externalities should be effectively taken into account (as the market does for any information incorporated into the stockprice). In other words, shareholders may indeed be the residual claimants after all the other debt holders are paid by the organization. What is left is indeed net income that can be either distributed as dividend to the shareholder or being retained in the organization for future investment. The point we like to make is that most of these [most often negative non-priced] externalities are harming certain stakeholders, especially the environment. Till recently, nobody spoke about the harmful effects of these organizational activities. If we would take the literal legal position that shareholders are indeed paid out the residual after all others with a stake are accounted for, then likely the real profit of mainstream economies and their organizations would be much smaller. It is not too difficult to comprehend why powerful lobbying groups of industries and organizations have undertaken all possible efforts to limit legal actions against such negative externalities which are currently not properly priced or accounted for. Because of the changing context where it is acknowledged now that climate change and pollution have initiated an undeniably vicious circle, people, politicians, activists and stakeholders have swayed policy makers, politicians and parliaments to sign off on the Paris Climate Agreement for instance. Executives and boards have woken up and are changing track by embracing the potential of new production processes and a more circular economy with plenty of business opportunities. Business leaders have not much choice if they wish to stay competitive.

Whatever the policies and strategies by organizations, public good problems like clean air and fresh water is a challenge to us all. The prevailing shareholders' value primacy can easily result in an investors indirect "Tragedy of the Commons"[28] in which nobody cares for the organization's long-term health or whether or not these organizations cause negative externalities that may prove to be bad business or bad strategy for investors collectively or over a longer period. Call it a real wicked problem.

Organizations will need to learn to cooperate more – probably with some 'assistance' or benevolent nudging from the governmental regulators. In the global mining industry for instance, child labour and human rights violations are unfortunately not the exception. And often, companies are tempted to free ride unnoticed when they can. Till now, self-regulation has been the usual solution, but has proven to be fragile. Most likely, the private sector is part of a more holistic reality in which institutions and government will need to be "upgraded" as well. Most likely, a more balanced equilibrium is desired in which the power of the market and purpose-driven corporations may need to be supervised by the power of inclusive institutions and a fair government.[29]

Purpose provides the emotional fuel that allows vision and mission to be implemented in organizations. Each company will need to think this through and decide how to best express their own unique purpose or how to incorporate core values in their value proposition. Crucial for our argument is the idea that business is basically the practical knowledge and wisdom to know *how relationships work* and how these relationships can strengthen an organization. Research makes it clear that engaged employees in the business significantly increase the overall productivity. How will we use artificial intelligence to strengthen and not to undermine this productivity of engaged employees. Similarly, how will Apple for instance continue to communicate with loyal customers who are anxious to know today how one of the most valuable companies on the planet deals with suppliers and its workers in that supply chain. Today, any misconduct by any of the suppliers in emerging economies (such as China) also reflects on Apple or any other global brand.

What is so different today, compared to two-three decades ago? An awareness about the need for more collaboration and thus relationship-building to resolve some of the pressing ecological and socio-relational sustainability challenges has seeped in at the boards of organizations. The *wising up* at Boards sees this debate around *creating* and *sharing value* in first instance as a way to innovate, more precisely as an *architectural innovation*.[30] The organizational system's architecture deepens and changes the relationships between the components of the system without changing the components themselves. Because this kind of architectural innovation is quite invisible, it is hard to react to this kind of innovation. Probably, clearly articulating an organization's purpose that strengthens the "emotional relations" beyond profit maximization may be key for preparing such stealth architectural innovation.

In vain, General Motors, for instance, attempted numerous times to copy Toyota's manufacturing processes like "just-in-time" inventory systems in their new factories in the early 1980s. They got a good understanding of the continuous innovation processes of the Japanese, but they omitted the thought that Toyota's advantage lay in its relationship with its employees. Instead, GM focused on the tangible changes to the production process, overseeing the real relational component that constituted the architectural advantage of Toyota. That trust between the organization and the employees – its real flourishing human capital – functioned as the glue of the invisible trusting relations at Toyota factories in the 1980s. Goals were discussed and a common consensus was reached through an invisible [bottom-up as well as top-down] communication process across multiple levels within Toyota. This 'tacit' Toyota approach was completely different from GM's traditional command- and control management style, partially explaining why GM never was able to match Toyota's competitiveness. Mainly because GM didn't incorporate Toyota's rather architectural innovation, its "invisible" strong relationship with stakeholders.

The trust and legitimacy of business leaders has been under scrutiny lately. It's unlikely that the thorny problems and dilemmas of business can be formalized in a codex or in mere algorithms. The answers lie elsewhere.[31] We need not just *competent* leaders who understand their industry and operations, but we also need *smart* leaders who are aware of their biases and errors, and are innovative enough to sustain the firm's competitive advantage. These *smart* leaders will "exploit" the current core assets and continue to "explore" new innovative processes and products. But above all we now need *wise* leaders. Indeed, should not every organization wish to have wise leaders who understand to make reasonable ánd responsible decisions, treasuring both the visible core assets and resources and the invisible strong relations with all those who have a real stake in the firm. Be it employees, suppliers, customers, community or investors. That is why the traditional fiduciary duties of care, loyalty and prudence need to be reinterpreted and re-contextualized, and aligned with enlightened ownership. You can call this reinterpretation an act of "wising up" at the board and top leadership level.

Some even dare to speak of a new phase in the capitalist system, from institutional capitalism to *stakeholder capitalism*,[32] arguing that business ecosystems evolve and stakeholders start to play an increasingly scrutinizing role. Social media allows to track and "measure" companies who publicly take a stance to defend or protect stakeholders. Not speaking out may be already enough for certain activists to name or shame those organizations for lacking commitment or for falling short of expectations. Such radical transparency is brutal. Second, it seems that there is a growing evidence that companies with a long-term view outperform their peers in terms of earnings, revenues, investment and job growth, though we appeal to be careful for too hasty or inconclusive statements. Yet, we do assume that serving stakeholders is an ethical good that can also be a source of competitive advantage. And when enlightened boards of organizations decide to go green, they still need to make money or face the economic reality of becoming defunct. To win within "stakeholder capitalism", a few principles may be worth mentioning: (1) for stakeholder engagement to become real, commitments start at the top; one needs to get the board on board since they decide on long-term interests of the company, and they sets and govern strategy; (2) organizations with a clear stakeholder ethos should commit to putting their principes into practice by publishing concrete, achievable and measurable goals, especially in relation to the broader environment; (3) a company's sense of responsibility must go beyond its direct operations and include the social and environmental impact on suppliers and employees. Organizations need to work with suppliers to build capacities and skills; (4) recognizing how goods and products affect customers, organizations should take action to reduce these negative conmsequences. In other words, organizations may opt to serve consumers' long-term needs; and (5) employees should be treated with respect and dignity; the organization that invest in their future, will likely benefit in the long term, by being more attractive to possible hires, and inspiring greater loyalty and productivity among those they already employ.[33]

2 From *Stock-holding* Primacy to *Stake-holding* Engagement, resulting in ESG Impact

Competent smart decision-making in business is allegedly assumed to effectively and efficiently contribute to capital allocation that optimizes the profitability among other financial objectives. Those decisions may not help to preserve cultural or ecological equilibria, or worse they may occur at a great expense for a number of stakeholders. Trends are changing though. For instance, shareholder value maximization may be "smart" in the short term, but is often a misguided fiduciary objective to claim to be the only goal of business.[34] *Wising up* is a profound reaction against this short-termism and [speculative] equity-holding primacy. Wise decision-making is meant to take full accountability and responsibility for the firm's activities. Such attitude goes against the traditional myth that shareholder returns should be maximized even if that is at the expense of ethical and ecological concerns. And wasn't it Nobel laureate winner Milton Friedman who famously stated in 1972 that the only fiduciary duty of managers is to make money for their shareholders. It became the paradigm of neo-classical economics and business.

However, a fundamental interdependent relationship between those who are directly engaged with the organization needs to be restored. Half a century later after Friedman's popularized argumentation for share-holders' primacy, it is now widely agreeable that business leaders' decisions are aimed at deriving economic benefits but also stimulate their own social capital[35] by taking into consideration socio-ethical and ecological relations and or constraints. Admittedly, like in any transition from one theoretical paradigm to another,[36] tensions, ambiguities and paradoxes will accumulate, and time is needed to make that transition in the most effective and peaceful manner.

2.1 Stake-holder Engagement

Since our focus is not just compliance to particular organizational objectives of profitability maximization, but to create sustainable organizational value, understanding those evolving *relations* (with society, environment and those who have a stake in the organization) are crucial for the survival of the organization. The abundant literature about *social capital* or networks[37] over the last couple of decades has clearly proven the importance of these relationships. There are founded on trust in organizations and trust generated between organizations and the society at large. Similarly, an increasing amount of academic research proves that organizations embedded in an ecological system cannot and should not ignore the *natural capital*[38] that they have taken for granted till now. The relationship between the organization and its broader socio-environmental eco-system have been ignored for too long. Despite some persistent scepticism among a few about the climate change research,[39] it has become obvious that industries and individual (over)consumption alike have increased the chance of irreversible damage to our planet. Hence why natural and social capital should be part of our decision-making variables. Fortunately, we can learn from companies like Unilever for instance whose 'purpose-led sustainable living brands' were growing 69 percent faster than the rest of the business, contributing to 75 percent of the company's growth in 2019.[40]

Shareholders recognize that the integration of ecological, social-ethical and governance (ESG) factors into business practices is undisputable key to managing risk and to create long-term value. Research by INSEAD Business Ethics professor Craig Smith and his colleagues suggest that an increasing number of board members recognise that their sustainability responsibilities have changed, and that they need to ensure they are equipped with the knowledge and people to better meet these obligations.[41] Although this majority of global boards acknowledge that their organizations need to incorporate sustainability into their business practices, only half have the right information and measures in place to assess and evaluate their progress on sustainability. Similarly, family business embraces the digital and sustainability challenge if they see immediate business opportunities in terms of new green products or more cost effective processes with less waste and pollution. In a recent survey, only a minority of 37 percent of family business, however, have an articulated an explicit sustainability strategy. This sustainability, expressed in the acronym ESG, gets a much wider resonance today and is expected to play an important role in business in the future. About 20 percent of these global boards struggle to see how sustainability fits into their firm's strategy. Only 17 percent of boards have a dedicated Sustainability Committee. And despite the urgency, it will become harder to act appropriately beyond "low-hanging" ESG fruit such as minimizing carbon emissions. It is possible that "market-led actions" may not suffice any longer.

Starting dialogues with the communities in which these firms operate is highly recommendable. Unilever's "Sustainability Living Plan" sees this corporate sustainability obligation extended beyond a fiscal responsibility to shareholders; it forms part of the company's purpose to sustain the company's success and the longevity of the planet.[42] Even counting on (supra)governmental regulations to provide a fair playing field in the (international) market, may be seen to realize much needed adaptation to a new reality. The contribution of organizations to steer the conduct of business sustainably would be a good start for a "joint" solution of current socioecological challenges.

The stake-holders are "embedded" agents, in relationship with the organization. Omitting them – as mainstream shareholder theory does – potentially undermines not only social capital or *guanxi*, but over a longer period the goal to optimize profitability itself. But is also true that according to a recent survey by Accenture and UN Global Compact an overwhelmking majority of 82 percent of corporate executives believe that govenments have failed to give clear guidelines or directives on a framework to implement ecological sustainability goals. Ecological pledges are promising but not enough to have a real impact on the planet's boundaries. We need action now, both from corporations – concrete short and long term ESG objectives – as well as from governments – imposing a carbon tax for instance – and civil society.

2.2 ESG-Reporting and ESG-Impact

Does absolute CO_2 emission of all aggregate firms still grow? Yes. And that is troublesome. Clever accounting and ESG reports[43] and PR may give a feeling that corporate leaders and politicians taking real action whereas it rather may be (un)intentional "greenwashing"[44] to cover up for the ongoing fetish of continuous eternal growth without any qualification to it. Admittedly, as long as there are no firm ESG standards that can objectively verified and or falsified, greenwashing and white-washing will continue to occur.

The public mood is shifting though. Indeed, the mindset of many people is changing. Courts seem to follow in some instances like in the Netherlands and Belgium in May-June 2021. Under mainstream free liberal market theory, companies were not paying the market price for the public good services our planet is offering[45] – clean air and water for instance, and abundance of nature and fertility of our soil. It was silently accepted that firms could pursue any activity as long as they minimally complied with the prevailing rule of law. The real costs of non-calculating the natural capital and its services distort the market by externalizing those to other [future] groups. Not exactly "forward thinking". Today, these non-financial objectives have swiftly become quite a primary concern of organizations in this volatile, uncertain, complex and ambiguous (VUCA) context. In many European jurisdictions non-financial objectives have now become part of the overall performance criteria of boards and top management. It is true though that the measurement of ESG is not yet *at par* with the mature and well established accounting metrics that finds its culmination in clear and mathematical measurements and reporting that eloquently maximize net income or profitability of the organization.

Quite indicative was the 2018 annual shareholders' letter of Larry Fink, the CEO of US-based BlackRock – the world's largest financial asset fund managing USD 9 trillion in worth – clearly stating that "society is demanding that companies, both public and private, serve a social purpose. To prosper over time, every company must not only deliver financial performance, but also show how it makes a positive contribution to society. Companies must benefit all of their stakeholders, including shareholders, employees, customers, and the communities in which they operate."[46] Quite a different and unusual tone compared to most US-based CEOs of financial institutions who for a very long time would have argued that accountability to everyone means accountability to no one. Unfortunately, BlackRock's own considerable CO_2 footprint is not really translated in actively pushing boards to pursue more actively ESG measurements, according to a few commentators such as climate activist and billionaire Christopher Hohn.[47] Is this presumed mental shift – presumably adhering to ESG metrics and impact – of this powerful and influential CEO merely cynical PR relationship-building? Or can we expect something more substantial in terms of socio-ecological pressure from this powerful financial elite on the boards of many organizations? And let us not forget either that asset owners (or investors) may be focused on the long term, asset managers of funds may not be. Institutional investors in the USA and the UK held more than 65 percent of the outstanding public corporate equity (in 2017). Although the investors may look for long term return, their investment managers might well prefer short-term returns and taking gains from churning that are linked to their compensation packages, partially explaining that persistent dichotomy between investors' long term perspective and their managers' short term view.

The global [Western] institutional context in which firms operate is changing into a new reality that is less forgiving. External stake-holders like customers, governments, and communities, but also employees and investors who have "internal stakes" in the organization, have expressed concerns over neglected socio-ecological and governance aspects. Firms remain accountable and responsible for both financial and non-financial performance. Boardrooms and MBA programs are "programmed" to maximize profitability of the firm. It is seen as an evident truth in business. Other goals than aiming to optimize shareholders' net return on investment was till recently seen by managers and employees as betraying their fiduciary duty of care and loyalty, but also a fast way of losing their job. Many business observers consider global challenges such as climate change and rising inequality and malfunctioning of institutions as external risks. These should be left to governments to deal with though organizations may attempt to circumvent these external risks. In seems that shareholders and their private for-profit organizations have created an institutional context in which public goods are not their obligation. Today, this mainstream economic paradigm is under scrutiny and may be changing: without good government policies and proper public governance, free capitalist markets will collapse under its own self-destructing behaviour. Be it by degrading its own environment in which it operates or by contributing to an asocial and unethical disengagement which would disfranchise and alienate the most ardent stakeholder. A good functioning public sector with fair governance needs a wealth-creating innovative private sector, and vice versa.[48] The economic and political institutions are meant to be inclusive and interdependent to remain sustainable.[49]

Some argue that ESG is a necessary cost to do business. Their boards adhere to a "tick-the-box" exercise to minimally comply or pay a carbon tax or carbon credit purchases for continuing to pollute.[50] It is also true that quite a number of boards and their CEOs perceive this new institutional context as "asking the impossible" from their organizations. Admittedly, running a business today is much more demanding and complex than just a decade or two ago. But the trend is clear: social and environmental issues[51] – partially caused by these same organizations – cannot be "externalized" for free anymore. Hence why today, nearly a third of the world's financial assets are managed with some kind of sustainability criterion.

For instance, the German chemical giant BASF has embraced a more circular economy since 2014 with emphasizing to recycling waste and reducing its CO_2 footprint. The integrated principle-based BASF sustainability report shows how the different management processes are interdependent. An IIRC approach[52] in combination with industry specific standards that reflects the *triple line reporting* encompasses economic profit, ecological impact and respect for social-ethical behaviour. The integrated IIRC and SASB reporting – indicating the material impact for each specific industry – zeroes in on the financial impact of sustainable performance.[53] Materiality is here interpreted as capturing aspects in non-financial performance that have a significant impact on profitability. The disclose on materiality impact of non-financial objectives drive capital allocation which drives the outcome. BASF looks at four major influencing 'material' sectors that they integrate with their strategy and financial management: environment, human capital, business model & innovation, and leadership & innovation. For the top executives of BASF,[54] ESG contributes to value creation and constitutes for a considerable portion of their remuneration bonus. The energy efficiency and resource efficiency as result of this ESG focus, results to considerable cost savings at the organization. By accelerating the innovation process to create more sustainable products, BASF increases its overall sales. By emphasizing the relational aspect as in building capacity in their supply chain, BASF's supplier relations have become a stabilizing competitive force, especially during crises where disruption is kept to a minimal. Having performed well on the ESG criteria and by having them communicated openly, it allowed BASF to get easier access to capital. These cases indicate that investors may penalize those firms who remain silent about their emissions per sale, which urges big companies like BASF to disclose ESG information transparently. Disclosing something bad is better than saying nothing. In other words, not disclosing ESG information carries a cost for big cap firms. Moreover, in 2020, BASF got their first green bonds from debt investors, while their [blockholding] equity investors have clearly expressed a long term orientation. Not surprisingly, BASF is now featured on a number of quite visible and reputable sustainability indices that function as flywheel for more investment.

The overall scrutinizing eyes of regulators and communities are much less forgiving these days, compared with two or three decades ago. Reporting non-financial objectives does not turn corporate multinationals into corporate compassionate stewards or exemplary corporate citizens. But organizations need to start somewhere and being part of a process to reduce the negative impact is a good begin. BASF and so many other multinationals are aware that their longer term legitimacy[55] is at stake if they don't take action today.

These new non-financial measurements focus on the stakeholder relationships rather than the traditional contractual agreement perspective. However, ESG criteria carry the reputation of being less precise, and thus less enforceable. Undoubtedly, the traditional financial accounting professionalization had more than 250 years to mature, whereas the socio-ecological accounting standards are rather new and still evolving.[56] When the Business Roundtable – a forum of powerful American CEOs – opted to promote an economy that "serves all stakeholders: customers, employees, suppliers, communities and shareholders", the institutional investors immediate reacted by emphasizing the importance of long-term shareholder value, being accountable to the company owners while respectful to stakeholders.[57] This enlightened form of shareholder value sounds acceptable, would it not be for often being a cover up hiding the ruthlessness of organizations zealously maximizing quarterly profits at the expense of other goals. Can we embrace a pro-social purpose beyond profit maximization and take responsibility for the health of the natural and social systems on which organizations rely? Do firms have a duty to pursue the maximum possible profit, even if doing so they almost certainly cause significant negative consequences for their customers, their employees, or society at large? Is it possible to reconcile profit optimization with ESG standards? Responsible behaviour carries a moral obligation, if not a fiduciary duty. Despite people often claim that business ethics is an oxymoron, research has shown that "doing good can be good business".[58]

However, business is even more sensitive to real cost increases than beautiful narrative stories about sustainability. Making a company environmentally greener should not be at the expense of profitability according to many financial analysts. For instance, Mr. Faber recently lost his job as CEO of Danone after activist shareholders voiced their displeasure with the firm's financial underperformance, strategy and governance in comparison with Nestlé, one of its main competitors. It seems to indicate that COEs need to mindful about the potential short term trade-off between profitability and sustainability. A recent study confirms that CEOs of big visible multinationals who enact greener and more sustainable policies are significantly more likely to get accounted for and being fired for poorer short term financial performance than CEOs who do not.[59] Thus was indeed the fate bestowed on Mr. Faber at Danone and Mr. Polman at Uniliver who were booted out as CEO by activist investors who were not satisfied with financial profitability expectations.

Though research has not proven to be 100 percent conclusive, it seems that in many cases the "return on responsible behaviour" can be quite significant in financial terms. Actual performance indicators of the last two years at the Bank of America for instance clearly shows that social factors such as providing health care and safety policies added "alpha" during the first quarter of 2020 bear market.[60] In other words, relative superior alpha returns were created when social issues[61] were part of the firm's strategy. Alpha returns in the investments at the Bank of America correlated with increased attention for human policies as shared in the Human Capital Reports of companies. Equally revealing was the fact that more alpha returns were created among small cap firms who embraced ESG in comparison with big cap firms. This is likely due to the greater ESG disclosure among bigger multinationals which are under increased pressure to disclosure, and the stock price of this big caps has likely already factored in this information. Smaller companies, however, benefit relatively more from ESG disclosures, indicating that investors value this information which may have been previously unknown to them.

This new perception around organizational responsibility start to put pressure on the organization and their stock-holders. For instance, early May 2021, almost 89 percent of the stock-holders of Royal Dutch Shell, the oil company, backed up the management plan to reach net zero carbon emissions by 2050. Prior to the 2021 annual shareholders' meeting, the company had come under pressure from green activists who claim that Shell does not go far enough, whereas other investors say that Shell's strategy lacks the focus of some of the American oil giants who remain centred on oil and gas.[62] It means that the board has no choice but to carefully balance those different opinions among the different investors or the capital providers.[63] Independently of this shareholders' activism, in a landmark climate case around same period, a Dutch court ordered Shell to cut their direct CO_2 emissions by 45 percent by 2030. This extraordinary legal ruling on ESG in Europe may be a wake-up call for the whole gas- and oil industry. Obviously in some countries like the Netherlands, the court enforcing regulations trump the traditional organizational self-regulation. Mainstream consensus among organizations and governments in most jurisdictions gave boards the discretionary power to pursue [or not] a more ecologically savvy strategy that would optimize the shareholder value. In the USA, two non-executive directors from a small environmentally minded hedge fund with the support from Blackrock were elected to the board of the gas- and oil giant ExxonMobil. It can be easily interpreted as a victory by activist investors to urge oil firms to embrace non-financial objectives to be translated in improved ESG reporting.

In our experience it is obvious that the younger generation of family businesses hold the key to a more embedded ESG approach. We have seen first-hand that in companies like the SinarMas conglomerate group in Indonesia for instance where the second generation owners of this palm oil and paper pulp (besides real estate and financial services) conglomerate fiercely battled with Greenpeace and other green activists in the 1990s and 2000s. An uncontrolled palm oil production in Indonesia and Malaysia has become an environmental disaster in process. Its continuous deforestation undermines the balance of our ecological system. Today, the third generation of the SinarMas family owners now collaborates with these same green activists to ensure a more "green" future, with less likely reputational damage. They are making efforts to limit the CO_2 footprint of their huge and very profitable palm oil division in line with the expectations of the new more conscious and more demanding younger generation. International standards like the RSPO have also played a levelling influence.[64]

ING bank, for instance, got reprimanded by NGOs because the credit-provider did not take into account this RSPO certification of proper management practices at Belgian based Socfin company's palmoil plantations in Indonesia. In contrast, Sipef, an Antwerp family with palm oil plantations in Indonesia emphasizes that their production process is according to the RSPO certification for which it got credited by NGOs and financiers alike. A lot depends on perception though, not necessarily based on clear measurable and comparable metrics. But actively trying to control the organization's narrative around genuine ESG positive impact related activities by the firm definitely helps.

The pressure is mounting. For instance, the Swiss firm Nestlé the largest food company and maker of KitKat, Maggi noodles and Nescafé, had to acknowledge that more of 60 percent of its mainstream food and drinks products did not meet a "recognized definition of health", this in contrast to the French firm Danone who has made health its strategic focus. Unfortunately, quite a number of Nestlé's products will never be healthy no matter how much renovation it will undertake to make them more sustainable. As long as customers are willing to pay for Nestlé's products, it may survive. However, a clear trend forward to healthy food is underway. That is exactly the strategy the French group Danone has undertaken.[65] This trend seems to extend to other regions as well: the Indonesian conglomerate Indofood, for instance, is collaborating with local universities making efforts to improve the nutritional and health content of their popular noodle products like IndoMie.

Our life is both societal embedded in a broader eco-system as it is becoming more digital than ever.[66] Without acknowledging the fact that organizations are embedded in a bigger relational holistic eco-system, leadership may churn out (unsustainable) products or services that could result in some short-term gains, but likely fail over a longer period. Some even argue – and they are not waiting for the European Green Deal – that those who do not embrace "green" by 2030, won't survive. Moreover, without digital technology, leadership won't succeed in any new project today. One needs both digital innovation and the acknowledgement of (inter)dependent relations within this eco-system to remain relevant today. Companies trying to sustain their competitive advantage are currently investing in greener and more circular products, as well as embracing a digital transformation, especially through artificial intelligence and big data analytics to support that transformation. For instance, data-driven offshore windmills in the North Sea off the Belgian coast produce green energy that is currently competing with traditional sources of energy like nuclear energy. Without the use of this data and its algorithms, the company would be less competitive to generate green energy. A nice example of how digitization and sustainability can be complementary strategic forces.

Today, both authors work at educational institutions, that train boards and executives. In the past, our focus was on driving competitiveness. Now it is about responsible management. This book has tried to show that one can do both. Being compassionate and socio-ecologically savvy without financial performance won't last. Nor will cut-throat financial profit maximization be economically sustainable if at the expense of anything else. We need to establish some balance that rebuilds trust. For our customers to trust us, but also our capital provides, our suppliers, and employees. Today, we need to add the community in the equation in which organizations operate. Their socio-ecological concerns are valid and should be heard at least, and possibly be embedded in the strategy of the firm. Savvy effective leaders figure out how to synethesize and integrate the sustainability mindset while enhancing a positive net present value for their investment projects.

Can we determine how those potential future leaders are taking "wiser" more intelligent and responsible decisions[67]? Let us attempt to give a provisionary answer in the next chapter.

Consider the following Take Away Ideas of Chapter 5:

1. The myth of stock-holders' primacy: does the board – as the custodians of the organization – only acknowledge the providers of capital? Or do they take the concerns of other stakeholders seriously as well? The authors claim that profit is a byproduct – but a necessary one – of creating value for customers, employees and other partners (be it suppliers or distributors), not a supreme goal. Shareholders' primacy at the expense of other stakeholders and society is scrutinized and criticised today. Other goals like ecological and social-ethical goals have become mainstream.

2. Disclosing ESG information often results in a number of [strategic] advantages and even premium returns from investors.
   Impact investing – a form of ESG-driven investing – has proven to create superior return on investments. The Bank of America recently analysed alpha returns in their portfolio of US firms that emphasized social and health initiatives during the recent Covid 19 pandemic.

3. Most stake-holders, employees, customers, investors, and government agencies, increasingly ask for more sustainable products and services. The shareholders primacy [myth] is giving way to a more balanced stewardship approach of business. However, during the annual board meetings, blockholding shareholders' "representatives" still make the ultimate decisions, by appointing the members on the legally powerful board. No change there. The motivations and reasons behind these decisions, are slightly changing though, taking ESG variables much more seriously in 50% of the cases, and growing.

Notes

1 Henderson, R., (2020), *Reimaging Capitalism in a World on Fire*, New York, Public Affairs-Hachette Publications: p19–20. The main criticism here against the shareholder value paradigm is that this model has gone "off the rails because 1) externalities are hardly priced in the market price charged to the end consumer, 2) many people are not in the position to have genuine freedom of opportunity in the labour market that is skewed against many of them who do not have a [STEM] degree, and 3) firms engage with lobby groups where possible to fix the rules of the game in their own favour, especially the big cash rich companies (lately AI tech companies)."
2 We refer to Harvard Professor Rebecca Henderson's recommendable last book, *Reimaging Capitalism*, (2020). In addition, we like to refer to the very critical analysis about capitalism by Jason Hickel, (2021), *Less is more. How degrowth will save the world*. He assesses how capitalism causes an ecological breakdown and how to revamp our violent current economic system.
3 See www.un.org/sustainabledevelopment/sustainable-development-goals/.
4 *Reimaging Capitalism* is indeed the title of Professor Henderson latest book (2020).
5 Duckworth, A.,(2017), *Grit. Why passion and resilience are the secrets to success*, London, Vermillion.
6 Stout, L.A. (2013), The Shareholder Myth", *Cornell Law Faculty Publications*, Paper 771.
7 The annual shareholders' meeting is translated as "RUPS" (Rapat Umum Pamegan Saham) in Indonesia.
8 Stout, L.A. (2012:46), *The Shareholder Value Myth. How putting shareholders first harms investors, corporations, and the public*, San Francisco, Berrett-Koehler Publications.

9 We like to highlight that the traditional Chinese scholars would see the universe as one big correlative network, wherein everything is linked to everything or, at least, wherein each element of that network requires the presence of another or the other to be able to fully function. Whether Confucius or Menzius, relationships are been perceived as crucial for the proper functioning of any organism or organization, or state and family. And in quite a number of Southeast Asian countries, successful businesses are being led by tycoons, more often than not by people of Chinese origin.

10 See forthcoming book, Verhezen, P., (2022), *Wising up. Responsible Leadership competing in an era of Artificial Intelligence.*

11 Within the **corporate governance** debate, we describe this mainstream model as the *Shareholder theory* or *Agency theory* where all agent, i.e. managers and employees contractually working for a firm or principal have the fiduciary duty of care, loyalty and prudence to optimise the objectives of the firm. See Jensen, M.C. & W.H. Meckling, (1976), Theory of the Firm: managerial behavior, agency costs and ownership structure, *Journal of Finance Economics*, Vol. 3: 305–360; Jensen, M.C.,(1986), "Agency cost of free cash flow, corporate finance, and takeovers", *American Economic Review*, 76, 323–329; Jensen, M.C., (2002), "Value maximization, stakeholder theory, and the corporate objective function", *Business Ethics Quarterly*, 12(2), 235–256; Bebchuk, L.; Cohen, A. & A. Ferrell, (2009), "What matters in corporate governance", *Review of Financial Studies*, Vol. 22: 783–827;Bhagat, S. & B. Bolton, (2008), "Corporate Governance and Firm Performance", *Journal of Corporate Finance*, Vol. 14: 257–273; Claessens, S.; Djankov, S.; Fan, JPH. & LHP. Lang, (2002), "Disentangling the incentive and entrenchment effects of large shareholders", *Journal of Finance*, Vol. 57: 2741-2771; Claessens, S.; Djankov, S.; Fan, JPH. & LHP. Lang, (2002), "Disentangling the incentive and entrenchment effects of large shareholders", *Journal of Finance*, Vol. 57: 2741-2771; Fama, E., (1980), "Agency problems and the theory of the firm", *Journal of Political Economy*, Vol. 88: 288–307; Fama, E. & M. Jensen, (1983a), "Separation of ownership and control", *Journal of Law and Economics*, Vol. 26: 301–325; Fama, E. & M. Jensen, (1983b), "Agency problems and residual claims", *Journal of Law and Economics*, Vol. 26: 327–349; La Porta, R., Lopez-De-Silanes, F. Schleifer, A.& R. Vishny, (2000), "Investor protection and corporate governance", *Journal of Financial Economics*, 58, 3–27; Mallin,, C., (2004), *Corporate Governance*, Oxford, Oxford University Press; Morck, R.; Schleifer, A. & R. Vishny, (1998), "Management ownership and market valuation: an empirical analysis", *Journal Finance Economics*, Vol. 20: 293–316; Schleifer, A. & R. Vishny, (1997), "A survey of corporate governance", *Journal of Finance*, Vol.52: 737–783; Zingales, L., (1998), *Corporate Governance. The New Palgrave Dictionary of Economics and Law*, London, MacMillan.

12 The **stakeholder and stewardship governance model** claims that the responsibility of fulfilling objectives is not just serving the shareholders' rights – i.e. the last claimants after everyone else's rights have been fulfilled – but also taking into account the objectives of other important players involved in the organization, such as employees, communities, customers, and even government and society at large. Obviously, trying to optimize the different and sometimes seemingly opposing objectives at the same time is almost impossible as Jensen has argued convincingly (2020). Nonetheless, not just the shareholders have a stake in the firm; many more have invested time and effort in the organization: they even have a professional relationship with the firm. One cannot overlook these other stakes without damaging the reputation or even the long survival of the organization. In fact, within governance, one could easily argue that once you have entered the firm as a board member for instance, your duty is to that organization and not to the individual investor's group you may feel to represent. See Freeman, E et al (Eds), 2010, *Stakeholder Theory*, Cambridge Univ Press; Freeman, E.; Martin, K.E. & B.L. Parmar, (2020), *The Power of AND. Responsible Business without Trade-offs*, New Yiork, Columbia University Press; Badaracco, J.L., (2016), *Managing in the Gray. Timeless questions for resolving your toughest problems at work*, Cambridge MA, Harvard Business School Press; Charan, R., (2005), *Boards that deliver. Advancing corporate governance – from compliance to competitive advantage*, San Fransisco, Jossey Bass; Clarke,

Thomas, (2007), *International Corporate Governance. A comparative Approach*, London; New York, Routledge; Granovetter, M., (1985), "Economic action and social structure: the problem of embeddedness", *American Journal of Sociology*, Viol. 91(3): 481–510; Granovetter, M., (1995), "Coase revisited: Business groups in the Modern Economy", *Industrial and Corporate Change*, No.4: 93–130; Macey, J.R., (2008), *Corporate Governance. Promises Kept, Promises Broken*, New Jersey, Princeton University Press; Macey, J.R. (2013), The death of Corporate Reputation, *How Integrity has been destroyed on Wall Street*, New Jersey, Pearson Education FT Press; Mobius, M. (2003). "Corporate governance", in Cornelius, P.K. & Kogut, B. *Corporate governance and capital flows in a global economy*, New York, Oxford University Press, 401–412; Rezaee, Z., (2007). *Corporate governance post-Sarbanes-Oxley:Regulations, requirements, and integrated processes*, Hoboken, NJ, John Wiley & Sons; Rezaee, Z. (2009), *Corporate governance and ethics*. Hoboken, NJ: John Wiley & Sons, and Verhezen, P. & Morse, P. (2009), "Consensus on global corporate governance principles?" *Journal of International Business Ethics*, July, 2(1): 84–101.

13 People forming an organization usually collaborate in very effective manners. Thus group-minded attitudes have been analysed in many research projects. Interestingly, humans have that inherent ability to collaborate with fellow humans: it is part of their evolutionary process. From three to five years of age, young children become ever more group-minded as their capacities for collective intentionality mature. Human children are born into a nexus of relationships guided by social norms exhorting them to behave in certain ways and not in others. From early life, children confirm to social norms as articulated and enforced by adults. This bonding within the same culture comes naturally; it is part of being human. See Tomasello, M., (2019), *Becoming Human. A Theory of Ontogeny*, Cambridge MA, Belknap Press of Harvard. Similarly, we argue that organizations are an extension of this "group-mindedness" with clear "social" or organizational intentionality embedded in those organizational structures.

14 Oberholzer-Gee, F., (2021b), *Better, Simpler Strategy. A value-based guide to exceptional performance*, Cambridge MA, Harvard Business Review Press.

15 See Oberholzer-Gee, F., (2021a), "Eliminate Strategic Overload. How to select fewer initiatives with greater impact", *Harvard Business Review*, May-June: 89–97.

16 See Verhezen, P., (2022), *Wising up*. Forthcoming publication.

17 Freeman. R.E.; Martin, K.E. & B.L. Parmar, (2020: 69), *The Power of And. Responsible Business without Trade-Offs*, New York, Columbia Business School Publishing. Ed Freeman explained me during some dinners in Melbourne when we both were teaching at the Melbourne Business School that stakeholders have a crucial stake in organizations, and that one could organize a "stakemarket" as there exists a market for shares. For Freeman – the initiator and promotor of stakeholder theory – a broader definition of stakeholder captures "the idea that if a group or individual can affect a business, then the executives must take that group into consideration in thinking about how to create value. Put another way, a stakeholder is any group or individual who can affect or be affected by the realization of an organization's purpose". I would argue that any group or individual that can affect the reputation of an organization needs to be taken seriously by any board.

18 Freeman. R.E.; Martin, K.E. & B.L. Parmar, (2020: 216), o.c.

19 The former CEO of Medtronic Company, and now adjunct professor at the Harvard Business School, Bill George believes that serving all stakeholders is the best way to produce long term results that also guarantees a growing and prosperous company. See George, B., (2004), *Authentic Leadership*, San Fransisco, Jossey-Bass: 102–104.

20 According to financial theory, short term speculators – short sellers for instance – and very short term equity traders – are legally also considered shareholders. Those "vultures" have a "cleaning" function to fulfil in financial markets. Some advocate their crucial existence to make the market more efficient and effective (for instance Prof. Vermaelen from Insead, or Prof. Macey from

Yale; see Macey, J.R., (2013), *The Death of Corporate Reputation. How Integrity has been destroyed on Wall Street*, New Jersey, Pearson Education FT Press).

21 Porter, M.E. & M. Kramer, (2006), "Strategy and Society: The Link between Competitive Advantage and Corporate Social Responsibility", *Harvard Business Review*, December: 78–93; and Porter, M. & M. Kramer, (2011), "Creating Corporate Shared Value", *Harvard Business Review*, Jan-Febr: 62–77.

22 See Libert, B; Beck, M & J. Wind, (2016), *The Network Imperative. How to survive and grow in the Age of Digital Business Models*, Cambridge MA, Harvard Business Review Press, and Gupta, S., (2018), *Driving Digital Strategy. A guide to reimagining your business*, Boston MA, Harvard Business School Press.

23 Besides Adam Smith's famous "The Wealth of Nations" (1776), that is seen as the first scholarly work on a capitalist economy driven by self-interest and an "invisible hand", it was his other work on "The Theory of Moral Sentiments" (1759) that initiated the idea of empathy as the glue for any economic transaction.

24 See the fundamental research on **shareholders' rights** in distinctive legal jurisdictions by La Porta, R., Lopez-De-Silanes, F. & A. Schleifer, A, (1999), "Corporate ownership around the wor ld", *Journal of Finance*, 54(2), 471–517; La Porta, R., Lopez-De-Silanes, F. Schleifer, A.& R. Vishny, (2000), "Investor protection and corporate governance", *Journal of Financial Economics*, 58, 3–27; and La Porta, R., Lopez-De-Silanes, F. Schleifer, A.& R. Vishny, (2002), "Investor protection and corporate valuation", *Journal of Finance*, Vol. 57; 1147–1170. Also this governance research has hugely contributed to a better understanding of the differences in equity treatment in different jurisdictions: Morck, R.; Schleifer, A. & R. Vishny, (1998), "Management ownership and market valuation: an empirical analysis", *Journal Finance Economics*, Vol. 20: 293-316; and Morck, R. & B. Yeung, (2004), "Corporate Governance and Family Control", *Global Corporate Governance Forum – World Bank, Discussion Paper no 1*; and Claessens, S.; Djankov, S. & L.H.P. Lang, (2000), "The separation of ownership and control in East Asian Corporations", *Journal of Financial Economics*, Vol.58: 81–112; Claessens, S.; Djankov, S.; Fan, JPH. & LHP. Lang, (2002), "Disentangling the incentive and entrenchment effects of large shareholders", *Journal of Finance*, Vol. 57: 2741–2771; and finally Claessens, S. & B.B. Yurtoglu, (2013), "Corporate Governance in emerging markets: A survey", *Emerging Markets Review*, Vol. 15: 1–33.

25 Tomasello, M., (2019), *Becoming Human. A Theory of Ontogeny*, Cambridge MA, Belknap Press of Harvard.

26 See Jensen, M.C.,(2002), "Value maximization, stakeholder theory, and the corporate objective function", *Business Ethics Quarterly*, 12(2), 235–256.

27 *Ibidem*, p17. According to his Harvard professor, the competitive advantage of any firm does not exceed 5 to 10 years. In that sense, "long-term" value advantage is a very relative concept. See also Columbia Business School professor Rita Gunter-McGrath, R., (2013), *The end of competitive advantage. How to keep your strategy moving as fast as your business*, Cambridge MA, Harvard Business Review Press. However, (continuous or disruptive) innovation successfully initiated by the firm can prolong this competitive advantage.

28 See the original paper by G. Hardin, (1968), "The Tragedy of Commons", *Science*, Vol 162 (3859): 1243–1248.

29 Fairness is to be debated in political economy or political philosophy. In a nutshell, we trust that *liberal social democracies* may be the best option we have till proven differently. This debate is beyond the scope of this essay. See other related work on fairness: Scanlon, T.M., (1999), *What we owe to each other*, Cambridge MA, Harvard University Press.

30 Henderson, (2020: 70–72), *o.c.*. She argues that "architectural knowledge – the knowledge of how the components fit together – becomes embedded in the structure, in the incentives, in the information processing capability of the organization, where it becomes effectively invisible, making it very difficult to change". Professor Henderson sees the creation of shared value as an act of imagination, may I add, moral imagination. Incremental and disruptive innovation has been well researched. However, architectural innovation is more difficult to assess because most of the time it is invisible, and embedded in the organizational culture, even as part of the mainstream paradigm. For instance, one could argue that Kodak was brought down by the lack of architectural innovation, rather than the often quoted disruptive innovation of digital cameras. This disruptive innovation was tough to counter despite the fact that Kodak master this new innovative digital technology. This disruptive was also very visible. But what was not visible, was Kodak's strong adherence to a certain organizational culture of making superb photographs. That cameras became a component of telephones instead of stand-alone professional machines was difficult to imagine for Kodak engineers. The same story goes for the Black Berry mobile phone sets that did not want to accept that small portable smart computers – the iPhones to start with – took over the telephone capabilities that has made them so competitive and strong. Because architectural innovation is so difficult to see, it is consequently hard to respond to such changes.

31 See 2016: https://www.amrop.com/wise-decision-making-sustainable-performance.

32 Hunt, V.; Simpson, B. & Y. Yamada, (2020), "The case for stakeholder capitalism", *McKinsey & Company*, November.

33 *Ibidem*. Companies that embrace the idea of stakeholder capitalism may have to deal with backlash. Short-term oriented investors may believe their returns are suffering. Employees could be irritated if they believe their expectations are not being met. Competitors will be happy to jump on any bad news. Making stakeholder capitalism work, then, is a matter of striking a delicate balance among competing priorities. Real progress will take time.

34 Stout, L.A. (2013), "The Shareholder Myth", *Cornell Law Faculty Publications*, Paper 771.

35 Aoki, M., (2010), *Corporations in Evolving Diversity. Cognition, Governance and Institutions*, New York, Oxford University Press Inc.

36 See the philosophers of science, Kuhn, Lakatos, Agassi, and Popper who clearly explained how scientific paradigms shift from one to another theoretical framework. Imre Lakatos clearly has shown how paradigms shifts. His book Proofs of Refutations: the Logic of Mathematical Discovery was published after his death. In 1960, he was appointed to a position in the London School of Economics (LSE), where he wrote on the philosophy of mathematics and the philosophy of science. The LSE philosophy of science department at that time included Karl Popper, Joseph Agassi and J. O.-Wisdom. It was Agassi who first introduced Lakatos to Popper under the rubric of his applying a fallibilist methodology of conjectures and refutations to mathematics in his Cambridge PhD thesis. With co-editor Alan Musgrave, he edited the often cited *Criticism and the Growth of Knowledge*, the *Proceedings* of the International Colloquium in the Philosophy of Science, London, 1965. Published in 1970, the 1965 Colloquium included well-known speakers delivering papers in response to Thomas Kuhn's *The Structure of Scientific Revolutions*.

37 see Granovetter; Putnam, R; Coleman; and Verhezen.

38 We refer to the 610p **Dasgupta Review** that analyzes the different components of "nature as capital and not just as an invisible asset": A group of 43 scientists answered the question about their (subjective) assessments of the likelihood that under global climate change there will be major "restructuring of the Atlantic circulation, the Greenland/West Atlantic Ice Sheets, the Amazon rainforest, and El Niño-Southern Oscillation (ENSO). The authors arrived at a conservative lower bound for the probability, 16%, that at least one of the events would occur for a rise in mean global temperature of 2–4 °C above the mean temperature in the year 2100, and a probability of 56% for a rise of over 4 °C. In an interesting and important paper, Cai et al. (2016) have constructed a stochastic integrated-assessment model to convert the subjective probabilities reported in Kriegler et al. (2009) for arriving at corresponding estimates of 'hazard rates'; that is, probability rates that Earth's climate system will be at a tipping point conditional on it not having reached the point until

then. The authors have deployed the numbers on perhaps the most sanguine of global climate models, the DICE model constructed by Nordhaus (1994), to find that the social cost of carbon is far higher than the US$20–40 per tonne of carbon dioxide implied by DICE, as high as US$200 per tonne. The social cost of carbon is the loss in social well-being from a marginal increase in carbon emission. The existence of tipping points (worse, a cascade of tipping points) lying in wait raises the cost of carbon, meaning that it raises the cost of inaction. Consider then an ecosystem from which goods and services are being drawn in excess of its regenerative rate. It is known that the ecosystem will tip over and collapse if it is continued to be overused, but the state of the ecosystem at which collapse will occur is not known. So long as the ecosystem has not suffered from a regime shift, decision-makers has two options: (a) stick with business-as-usual (i.e. the status quo); or (b) change course of action. Imagine now that DM is able to forecast the impact on the economy if the ecosystem tips over. That forecast will itself be uncertain, but we may assume decision-makers is able to summarise that future in terms of expected social well-being. We assume, reasonably, that if the ecosystem was to suffer from the regime shift, expected social well-being under decision maker's forecast would be lower than it would be under either of the options (a) and (b). For vividness we imagine that the regime shift would be a catastrophe."

39 See Dasgupte Report, 2021. Among the many serious academic scepticists is Lomborg (2001) who is the most widely cited among authors in recent years to have expressed scepticism of the environmentalist's concerns. "Vigorous endorsement of the book by *The Economist* newspaper helped to foster public scepticism. It took time, perhaps starting with a 2005 cover story in *Time* magazine, and Vice President Al Gore's 2006 documentary, *An Inconvenient Truth*, both on global climate change, for the public to appreciate the economic consequences of carbon overshoot. That concern has not yet extended to biodiversity loss. But as contemporary threats to global biodiversity have been identified in professional journals since at least the 1970s and collated periodically for the general public by ecologists (e.g. Ehrlich and Ehrlich, 1981; Wilson, 1992, 2016; Levin, 1999) and writers (e.g. Kolbert, 2013, 2014). The pioneering work was Rachel Carson's 1962 book, *Silent Spring*, which drew attention to the way industrial chemicals and insecticides exterminate birds and insects (Carson, 1962). And that work faced not just scepticism in much of the media, but fierce resistance from chemical companies."

40 See annual Report Unilever, 2020.

41 Smith, Cr. & R. Soonieus, (2019), "What is stopping Boards from taking action on Sustainability". INSEAD Knowledge.
https://knowledge.insead.edu/responsibility/whats-stopping-boards-from-taking-action-on-sustainability-11436.

42 Former CEO, Paul Potman was adamant about Unilever's engagement to be more sustainable when he told The Guardian in 2012 – ahead of this time – that "What we firmly believe is that if we focus our company [Unilever] on improving the lives of the world's citizens and come up with genuine sustainable solutions, we are more in sync with consumers and society and ultimately this will result in good shareholder returns."

43 Pucker, K.P., (2021), "Overselling Sustainability Reporting. We're confusing output with impact", *Harvard Business Review*, May-June: 134–143. It is clear that many companies seem to confuse "output" with "impact". It is not because a company prepares an integrated ESG or sustainability report, that the company has genuine impact on reducing pollution or its carbon footprint. Independent of the many weaknesses of current ESG reporting that former Timberland COO, Kenneth Pucker, mentions in his critical paper (lack of mandates and 3rd party auditing; specious targets; opaque supply chains; complexity of the measurements in scope 1, 2 and 3); confusing information, and inattention to developing countries), what is worse is thinking that reporting (output) according to these ESG criteria seem to do the job (impact). On the contrary. The focus on (immature) ESG measurements and reporting has likely helped to delay much-needed structural transformation, Pucker convincingly argues. He approvingly quotes the young climate-change activist Greta Thunberg (2019): "The biggest danger is not inaction. The real danger is when politicians and CEOs are making it look like real action is happening when in fact almost nothing is being done, apart from clever accounting and creative PR." A reminder that we will need a real paradigm shift to get some real positive impact, reducing the moral hazards that organizations have created for so long due to lax or inexistent ESG rules and regulations.

44 "Greenwashing" is interpreted as making unsubstantiated environmental claims for the benefit of their companies. "Longwashing" is forging a long-term strategy primarily for the benefit of the firm's financial performance only rather than genuinely caring for the welfare of its current and future stake-holders.

45 See recent polemic essay on the "existential risks on the future of humanity" is: Ord, T., (2021), *The Precipice. Existential Risk and the Future of Humanity*, London; Oxford, Bloomsbury Publishing; and Zadek, S., and N. Robins (2018), *Making Waves: Aligning the Financial System with Sustainable Development*. We here refer again to the execellent summarizing Dasgupta review, (Febraury 2021) commissioned by the UK Treasury. It is important to note that a market price is the price at which a good, service or asset is exchanged for in a market. An accounting or shadow price is the price that reflects the true value to society of any good, service or asset. Obviously, most products only focus on the market pricing to determine the capital allocation and profit objectives, completely ignoring the often higher cost for manufacturing such products. Shadow pricing is mostly applied in Public Economics but should be part of any market decision to calculate the real cost-benefit of a product manufactured. In other words, we suggest to look at the negative externalities as well.

46 Larry Fink, (2018), "A sense of purpose", BlackRock, www.blackrock.com/hk/en/insights/larry-fink-ceo-letter.

47 Christopher Hohn – the CEO of his $38 billion The Children Investment Fund (CIF) who is defying the current industry trends, returning 14% in 2020 despite the coronavirus crisis, thanks to its profitable bets on Microsoft, Charter and Canadian Pacific – openly criticizes a number of asset managers for not doing enough against climate change. Hohn has a reputation for being a relentless activist investor. The New York Times called him one of the "most feared" investors in Europe. Hohn recently started picking a fight with his portfolio companies by forcing them to disclose their carbon footprint and slash their carbon emissions. Among whom, he criticised BlackRock for not pushing boards enough whose organizations have a high CO_2 footprint. Recently, his fund also donated $260,000 to Extinction Rebellion, an organization that strives to compel governments to act to stop global warming. Hohn highlighted the impact climate change was having on poverty, child destitution and destruction of the planet. This evidence has driven Chris to the creation of "Say on Climate" given that companies are responsible for 35% of global emissions. He describes the Say on Climate AGM resolution which requires annual disclosure of emissions, the plan to manage them, and how they will be judged going forward.

48 see Mazzucato, M., (2021), *Mission Economy. A Moonshot Guide to Changing Capitalism*, Dublin, Allen Lane – Penguin.

49 see Acemoglu, D. & J.A. Robinson, (2012), *Why Nations Fail. The origins of power, prosperity, and poverty*, New York, Crown Business-Random House; and Acemoglu, D. & J.A. Robinson, (2019), *The Narrow Corridor. States, Societies and the Fate of Liberty*, New York. We also like to mention the brilliant economist Chicago University Prof. Rajan: Rajan, R.G., (2010), *Fault Lines. How Hidden Fractures Still Threaten the World Economy*, New Jersey, Princeton Univ Press; Rajan, R.G., (2019), *The Third Pillar. How Markets and The State leave the Community Behind*, New York, Penguin; and Rajan, R.G. & L. Zingales, (2003), *Saving Capitalism from the Capitalists*, New Jersey, Princeton.

50 The academic research on carbon-tax or carbon-trading schemes is beyond the scope of this chapter, and book.

51 See Global Reporting Initiative (GRI) that issues its first set of guidelines in 2000, and by 2019, more than 80 percent of the world's 250 largest corporations used its standards to report on their sustainability performance. See https://www.globalreporting.org/.
52 See https://integratedreporting.org/. The International Integrated Reporting Council (IIRC) – previously the International Integrated Reporting Committee – was formed in August 2010 and aims to create a globally accepted framework for a process that results in communications by an organization about [shared] value creation over time. Sometimes this IIRC reports is also labelled as IAS Plus.
53 See https://www.sasb.org/. The Sustainability Accounting Standards Board (SASB) is created to develop separate standards for each industry so that companies report those topics and issues that are material and thus relevant for that particular industry. Instead of generic information, SASB intends to specify information that is material to the industry with "materiality maps" for each industry. At the moment, standards for more than 78 industries have been formulated. And research seems to indicate that these new material standards were positively correlated with longtime financial performance.
54 The information was shared during a SASB webinar on 10 June 2021, featuring the Senior Sustainability Director of BASF among others.
55 Verhezen, P., (2010), "Giving voice to a culture of silence: from a culture of compliance to a culture of integrity", *Journal of Business Ethics*, Vol. 96(2): 187–206.
56 The recent years, quite some progress has been made in ESG Reporting. There is a huge literature on ESG reporting which goes beyond the scope of this essay. We like to refer to some interesting practical overview by Epstein, M.J., (2008), *Making Sustainability Work. Best practices in Managing and Measuring Corporate Social, Environmental and Economic Impacts*, San Francisco, Barrett-Koehler Publishers, and we especially like to refer to the co-founders of SASB in the USA where material impact of any ESG measurement is emphasized making ESG quite practical for businesses: Eccles, R.G.; Miller-Perkins, K. & G. Serafeim, (2012), "How to become a sustainable company", MIT Sloan Management Review, Summer, Vol. 53(4): 42–50; Eccles, R.G. & G. Serafeim, (2013), "The performance frontier. Innovating for a Sustainable Strategy", *Harvard Business Review*, May: 50–60; and Eccles, R.G. & T. Youmans, (2014), "Materiality in corporate governance. The statement of significant audiences and materiality", *Harvard Business Review Working Paper* 16–023.
57 See www.cii.org/aug19_brt_response in 2019.
58 Kiel, F., (2015a), *Return on Character. The Real Reason Leaders and Their Companies Win*, Boston, Harvard Business Review Press, and Kiel, F., (2015b), "Measuring the Return On Character", Harvard Business Review, April: 20–21.
59 Bertini, M; Pineda, J.; Petzke, A. & J-M. Izaret, (2021), "Can we afford sustainable business?", *MIT Sloan Management Review*, Fall, Vol. 63(1): 25–33.
60 Savita Subramanian – A Director Investor Relations at the Bank of America – shared this insightful quantitative investors' information during a SASB webinar on 10 June 2021.
61 See Oberholzer-Gee, F., (2021b), *Better, Simpler Strategy. A value-based guide to exceptional performance*, Cambridge MA, Harvard Business Review Press. Taking care of your employees by offering better (than competitors') work environment creates more trust and loyalty, and decreases the willingness to supply knowledge or labour. It also increases productivity, and relatively speaking diminues the relative remuneration. However, very successful companies more often than not share this higher productivity with employees in the form of higher remuneration. In other words, focusing on the Willingness to Supply reflects every work-related activity. A comprehensive understanding of work lives is likely to reveal many opportunities to increase the satisfaction of the employees. In addition, digital technology can increase the flexibility of work, adding to increased satisfaction, and part of a virtuous cycle of trust. Working hours flexibility coupled with personal

passion of employees can be extremely powerful. The principle of value creation should become the moral compass of employers. Business practices are defensible as long as they create value for all parties involved, and thus make both employer and employees and independent contractors (like drivers of Deliveroo or Uber) better off.

62 See The Economist, May 22nd 2021: 8.

63 As reported in the Financial Times (10 June 2021), the district court in The Hague rules that Shell must cut its net carbon emissions 45 cent by 2030 compared with 2019 levels. Shell previously had made plans to cut the carbon intensity of the fossil fuels with 45 percent by 2035 compared with 2016 levels. However, carbon intensity is a measurement of carbon per megajoule of energy sold, rather than an absolute measure of carbon emitted. The Dutch court stipulated a total emission reduction rather than intensity targets. Shell's CEO, Ben Van Beurden, reacted with this statement: "Imagine Shell decided to stop selling petrol and diesel today, this would certainly cut Shell's carbon emissions. But it would not help the world one bit. Demand for fuel would not change." Although the majority on Shell's board supported its existing energy transition plan, the board may need to reconsider strategic options for more ambitious targets (after the court's ruling).

64 RSPO stands for the Responsible Sustainable Palm Oil.

65 Admittedly, Danone's sustainability strategy focusing on healthy food only, underperformed in comparison with its direct competitor Nestlé in the period 2015–2020, resulting in the board replacing the CEO.

66 If there is one thing that this covid-pandemic has taught us, is an overdosis of figures and stats, analog and digital, and not enough social contact and the freedom for us individuals to decide what we believe is our birthright.

67 The notion of bounded rationality and the dramatic negative external effects of pollution and social injustice for instance have taught us that we may mathematically be able to maximize one variable, profitability, but that does not justify our overzealous and often misguided rationality of selfish executives who maximize profitability at all costs that through a veil of a fair and responsible invisible hand hopefully result in an optimum socio-economic equilibrium. Unfortunately, there seem to be gap between such macro-economic aspirations and the micro-economic business reality on the ground. In a competitive market economy, performance is fundamentally relative, not absolute because the success and failure often depend on both the company's actions but also on those of its rivals. And even though a company could improve the quality of its product in many effective ways – be it better quality at a lower cost, faster throughout time, superior asset management and more – when rival companies improve at a faster rate, its performance may suffer. And admittedly, lasting success is largely a delusion or a statistical anomaly, corporate longevity associated with high performance is difficult to achieve because rivals are always looking to copy the leader's winning magic, or new companies enter the market and best practices are diffused while knowledgeable employees and executives move from one company to another.

Chapter 6
Is Your Boardroom Future-proof?
Preparing for shareholder & stakeholder engagement
in turbulent times

> We believe, as many business leaders do, that a company is more than a balance sheet. It is an expression of human bonds, a living entity that is sown and grown and whose harvest is lives and livelihoods. Stakeholder capitalism is a way to plant those seeds.
> Hunt, V.; Simpson, B. & Y. Yamada, (2020), "The case for stakeholder capitalism",
> *McKinsey & Company*

> It is very big deal to know what's on the mind of stakeholders. You need to understand what people are saying about you because that is best way to discover your vulnerabilities.
> Bruce Simpson, Senior Advisor to McKinsey & Company, 2022

Corporate leadership and Boards oversee three domains of corporate decision-making: *strategy*, *leadership* and *culture*, according to economist and international board member Dambisa Moyo.[1] Crucial for any board is to steer an organization through an uncertain future that is characterized by a VUCA environment. How to enhance its chances of success?

It may sound like a cliché, but true nonetheless: any organization's survival depends on the day-to-day leadership of senior executives, coached and supervised by an experienced board. It are the decisions made by the board that can lead to success or failure of the organization. A functional, decisive and wise board is essential for organizations' future. For those reasons, we argue that the following "issues" may need the attention of a well-functioning effective [supervisory] board:

(1) *addressing the longer-term risks* with much greater frequency. The board should get involved in preparing the future, and understand that future more intimately. Relying only on the executive team, a supervisory board will never be fully able to add value – because of the asymmetry of information between management and board members – unless they can make more informed decisions by having access to information from third parties (consultants, experts in particular fields). Once it is understood what is at stake, supervisory boards need to be more involved in investing in continuous or disruptive innovation which also implies that the board acknowledges the changing context with new technology like artificial intelligence (automation, data-driven algorithms and machine learning), and new social trends.

(2) preparing *the development of the next leaders* amid an increasing "fight" for (international) talent – especially in STEM (science, technology, engineering and math) related competencies, but also with leaders educated in liberal art who know how to "connect" in a global world. At the same time, in the recruitment process of new leadership, one should incorporate particular metrics to gauge

the potential CEO's ethical values. Does his or her moral compass (or lack thereof) match the expectations of the board. And what about the recruitment process of the board members themselves? Is it politically inspired, or based on seniority only, or can merit and real expertise thwart any political mingling. This second part focuses on training and leadership development that aspires to make a board more effective in a fast changing world. We may need a different kind of leader today, compared with the traditionally trained MBA-type leader who often is elevated to the boardroom. We now need team-players who understand a broader socio-ecological context.

(3) How about *the "cultural" sensitivities that boards need to address these days?* We are referring to the increased demand for scrutiny on *environmental and social issues* that now have entered the radar of the board's attention. Is there expertise available on the board. Should the board establish a separated Ethics Committee to effectively address those challenges? What about the proper use of AI systems and not falling into the trap of biased data or unfair outcomes by this automated data-driven systems? How to address the enormous reputational danger of cyberattacks: is the board and management prepared for such an event? Let us address those three issues, crucial for any board to sustain the competitiveness and relevance of the firm in an ambiguous and complex future.

1 Preparing for the Future and its Risks

How do boards effectively deal with the criticism of complacency or short-termism? How to create value for all stakeholders and not just to top executives and shareholders? Today, we live in an extraordinary messy world. The traditional approach to strategy, based on data research and analysis, may possibly be a little "outdated" or not too useful for what is coming. Can strategy be reframed so that companies can thrive in the face of current and future challenges?

1.1 Openness for Technological [digital] Innovation and Implementation

Although we are big proponents of firms embracing innovative technology like machine learning and icloud technology, no artificial intelligence algorithm could have predicted the pandemic, or even have known at beforehand how the covid pandemic has affected a world in a connected manner by the use of digital technologies. War- and scenario planning, and risk outliers analysis, could have warned firms to be ready for the potential destructive force of a potential pandemic. Not *hineinseit* or *postmortem*, but at beforehand, ready and prepared. Similarly boards need to give attention to human creativity that engenders innovation, and have the pulse on the heart to know why people join, stay or leave the company.

Many businesses still see the organization as an information processing mechanism that can be fully controlled, as long as one understands the information processing like in a computer. However, we believe that an organization has evolved from a mere information processing machine to a living organism that continuously create new knowledge and makes progress. Digital technologies are nothing but very useful tools. The essence remain people and the leadership in organizations, which is more than the sum of innovative controllable [technical predictive] tools. And yes, digital technology has allowed us to remain connected during this pandemic, to explore new business opportunities and online solutions. But it is no coincidence that at the same time, many people are leaving organizations today because they are dissatisfied with organizations for what they stand for. Many organizations miss a clear strategy to move forwards and miss a purpose to "enlighten" the people working in the organization.

Current organizational structures remain too mechanic, based on the old traditional management perspective of Taylorism that assumes that people's behaviour can be controlled by extrinsic motivators, like salaries. Often, such a perspective seems to forget the importance of having a feeling to really contribute, to be intrinsically motivated by the job.[2] Again, it is the board that needs to monitor such sentiments and adapt the organization – indeed, a living organism – to a sensible organism that continuously adapts and connects through a feedback system with its smaller parts that constitute the whole. Many interesting developments are taking place in the field of innovation and for bigger companies to remain agile, or showing ambidexterity, both in the B2B, P2P and B2B arena.

In the autocar manufacturing for instance, meeting the new demands for electrification and connectivity can be quite daunting, especially when faced with more nimble competitors. All those trends are speeding up the innovation in every facet of the automotive industry. R&D at Mercedes in Stuttgart realized that efforts to collaborate with start-ups were being hampered by the company's existing innovation processes, potentially missing out on new creative ideas that drive competition. In response Mercedes digital business managers and R&D developed the Startup Autobahn, an "open corporate accelerator", that could attract a broad array of mature startups.[3] It allowed Mercedes to expand and accelerate innovation. Incumbent companies in retail, financial services, health care, and many other industries are aware of the competitive risks posed by limitations of their innovation chains and startups' ability to rapidly exploit digital technologies. Mercedes' experience shows how an open inventive collaborative model can enable effective integration of new ideas into corporate R&D processes and accelerate innovation efforts.

Fuelled by the rise of digitalization and technology-mediated platform markets, our consumption of goods and services is evolving into *servitization* of products.[4] Indeed, we are replacing private ownership of goods with temporary access rights, and we are also exchanging material goods for their experiential substitutes.[5] Long-term ownership of a car has been replaced with car- and ride-sharing platforms like Zipcar, Lyft and Uber in the USA or Grab versus Gojek in Southeast Asia. We are increasingly favoring subscription platforms where we stream digital instead of owning movies for instance. Indeed, over the last couple of years, there has been an increasing emphasis on "experience". Access-based as-a-service consumption models offer many benefits, especially for those with less disposable income. But brands react and attempt to re-cultivate a new sense of ownership. Automakers like Volvo with their Polestar are directly offering their cars on a monthly subscription basis to fend off commoditization in the B2C business. In B2B that 'servitization' is less blatant and translated in different forms such connectivity that is based on long-term relationships. In the same vein, B2B follows in the footsteps of B2C businesses where customized personalization is becoming the new normal. Providing omichannel experience is now part of the B2B strategy roll out.[6] Customers want a right balance between online and offline possibilities, not just in the B2C arena that became a must during the pandemic, but also in the B2B context.[7] As more companies enable face-to-face, remote, and e-commerce interactions, satisfaction with the sales model has grown exponentially. More than 90 percent of B2B companies in the West say their go-to-market model is just as or more effective than before the pandemic began. Not all countries react the same way, new emerging power houses in South Korea and Brazil are more favorable to this personalized omni-channel experience offered in B2B, whereas Japanese and French prefer a more traditional approach. Indonesian boards better be warned that their emerging neighbouring markets are in the process of embracing these digital potential business opportunities.

Moreover, good governance often supports an ecosystem's ability to create value, manage risk and optimize value distribution among its partners. Today, researchers are saying that by aligning the firm's ecosystem's governance model with the firm's strategic priorities, the company can position itself to stand apart from competitors. Apple has applied that successfully vis-à-vis Google, Samsung and Facebook: it established a rather closed governance and ecosystem model by including stricter access rules, extensive quality control for new applications, and more restrictive data-sharing policies.[8] The company is trying to differentiate itself with a more coherent user experience, even though this could limit its growth rate. Apple's narrative of being different is apparently appealing to many customers. A board can even use governance to ensure social acceptance. Indeed, good governance is rapidly becoming a prerequisite for building social capital and securing the social legitimacy required by business ecosystems. A good governance model must be designed to engender and maintain social and investors acceptance, as well as legal compliance, over the long term and meeting changing demands. Superior governance must be consistent and fair. Only then a purposeful narrative will be credible and effective.

1.2 Establishing a Clear Purposeful Narrative

We even go a step further and claim that it is beneficial for any organization to be inspired by a clearly communicated purpose or narrative, more particularly, a purpose that is engrained in a moral beacon that can guide us.[9] The essence of a situation or a company's vision is often hard to express, that is why smart and wise leaders use metaphors, stories and other figurative language to communicate extensively and effectively with people. Such narratives enable individuals and groups that may have experienced different contexts to grasp things quickly and intuitively. In fact, the corporate governance principles – transparency, fairness, accountability and responsibility – provide the basis to function as such a guiding beacon. As mentioned, any board needs to cultivate a certain organizational culture that allows potential reinterpretation of these principles. The translation of these guiding principles can then steer the behaviour in an appropriate manner. It is up to the board to fill in or to contextualize those principles. Some may find it useful to formalize them in a code of ethics, whereas others may prefer to stick to generic emotionally powerful narratives – like the famous Johnson & Johnson *credo* (the Latin for "I believe") that has withstood time and crises. Whether this purpose is grounded in a moral goal [whatever its philosophical nature] or in human reciprocal agreements, it is clear that anybody will acknowledge that people are compelled to form teams as in a social connection. Even our brain is constituted along that line, exhibiting a predisposition to seek the common good via egalitarian and altruistic behaviour.[10]

The capacity to empathise, to emotionally connect, allows a leader to understand reactions and expressions at a deeper, emotional level. Subsequently, a leader should be able to clearly communicate the "essential soul" of the organization with others since that would reconfirm that groups are dynamically connected to others. For instance, Steve Jobs, Apple's iconic late founder, delivered a memorable narrative during the Stanford's commencement speech in 2005: he told a rapt audience three stories from his life, capturing the essence of what constituted him – and by extension Apple. But it also contained numerous contingencies, idiosyncracy and choices made. The power of this story lies in Steve Jobs sharing the essence of what life is about. Powerful, eloquent, simple but engaging, logic and emotional, and above all memorable because of its essence well communicated. To use narrative and stories effectively, leaders learn to see the relationship between one thing with another, between themselves and someone else, or between the present and the past or the future.

An example of a strategy guided by clear purpose is the Japanese company Kyocera, founded in 1959, which interprets itself as a collection of human beings, striving to operate in a way that is good and right, practising self-reflection and self-discipline, refining their minds and elevate their character in everyday life.[11] Interestingly, the management researchers Nonaka and Takeuchi labels this guiding beacon the "soul" of the company – which they define as "the simple truths and principles that guide us to do what is right as human beings, representing a living philosophy born from experience and practice. A 'soul' helps us find our way every day through uncertainty and hardship – it is a way of life."[12] We have put the argument forward in previous chapters that this kind of "philosophical purpose or company narrative" should be exemplified or incarnated by the exemplary behaviour of board members of the firm. They steer, guide, control and coach. The (non-executive and executive) directors set the tone at the top. The board is closely watched as they represent the organizational exemplary for stakeholders.

Now, why this explanation about an organizational soul or purpose in relationship to strategy? Simple, strategies are informed bets or choices. In a swiftly changing environment, one needs to adapt to an emerging reality where intended strategies may need to be reinterpreted into a new realized strategy. However, behind the adaptation – almost continuously – people seek some steadfast beacon to relate to, to understand what the company's essence stands for. That can be found in the soul or purpose of the organization. And a board needs to take care of that 'soul', they are the legal representatives of the organization and guard over the legacy of the organization, often found in that purposeful soul, expressed in the narrative of the firm that reflects its essence, as any "*credo*" does.

In other words, how to make strategy to come alive? How to infuse strategy with soulful purpose so that employees can be emotionally tune in to the organization? How can one retain talented employees? By tapping into some fundamental emotion of *thumos*,[13] respect and pride of people, which goes beyond mere competitive remuneration packages. This notion of recognition and respect – a deep emotional desire of human connectivity – can only be satisfied when an organization acknowledges this need and embraces it through self-development and providing career opportunities.

1.3 Consensus on Trust and *Thumos* that Underpin an Appealing Narrative

That consensus on organizational principles – to be closely aligned with the generic corporate governance principles – can be summarized as:[14] (1) coping with complexity by tapping into both analytical and intuitive thinking, (2) adapting to change to new socio-economic circumstances as well as anticipating accelerated technological progress that needs to be embraced, (3) embracing the dynamic duality of a learning organization as in acknowledging distinguishing explicit and tacit knowledge creation, (4) empathizing with on a deeper level with others' perspectives in the organization and beyond, as well as cultivating that attitude of compassion, (5) telling narratives and stories that reflect the essence of the organization's beliefs and ideals, helping to internalize strategies, and finally (6) living in harmony with our environment which confirms the importance of ESG issues for any organization today.

Surviving an ambiguous future is based on strategies that is driven by human beings' needs, often crystalized in that notion of *thumos*, the desire to be acknowledged and respected, including the deep connection of humans with nature. Such a connection requires practical wisdom, *phronèsis*, allowing boards to connect with that fast changing business context.[15] Indeed, strategy is driven by practical wisdom, that is based on experience and proper guidance. Strategy is about future-making, about creating a future that is hazy, messy and very unpredictable. Hence why leadership needs narratives to navigate through the muddy waters of business, to steer the organization away from morass to more open waters. Those narratives illustrate the beliefs of the organization, of what the company really stands for, of the essence of the organization. Without that soul, it will be hard to guide and motivate people in the organization. And yes, strategy, once more, is about making the right choice, choosing a future that should go beyond narrow self-interest of maximizing profitability only.

By making an organization a real organism in which all the elements are connected and genuinely interdependent, the board can help an organization to thrive on those fundamental "feelings" of excitement to be really driven by a moral compass, by creating something greater than ourselves, something we can believe in. Creating an organizational culture of candid honesty and openness gives credit to both the individual, the team and the organization as a whole. Real topics of importance are sincerely discussed in an open manner, and not under the veil of a hierarchical system where political and organizational correctness prevails over genuine debate and the possibility for change. Do we not all know of cases where the messenger is shot for bringing bad information – because the boss "doesn't want to hear anything bad"? The result is that such leadership gets filtered information – not the real raw data – tripling from underneath to the CEO and the board. And to make things worse, in such hierarchical non-open environments, one often sees tit-for-tat tactics that helps employees and managers, and even board members, to survive. It's a natural phenomenon to apply such strict reciprocity that helped us to survive in evolutionary terms. When push comes to shove, loyal people stands together, but such an (natural) attitude can undermine real discussion that is supposed to prepare the organization for the future. Moreover, such reciprocal behaviour may even contradict the implementation of an ethical organizational culture with fair processes and procedures. Nepotism and cronyism does establish the opposite. Studies have proven that fairness is well regarded. Avoiding such opaque processes is part of good corporate governance. For people to believe results to be fair, they have to be confident that the process by which these outcomes are achieved according to predetermined procedural governance processes. If an opaque process produces a good outcome or more specifically a well-regarded appointment, people may still cry foul, even possibly undermining proper collaboration.

Adapting to changes requires wise leadership who understand how to become more agile to adapt the strategy where necessary to a new situation, to continuously innovate to remain competitive. Only smart and wise leadership will be able to achieve to integrate short term demands with long term visionary objective. This kind of leadership understands how companies can operate more sustainably.

Leadership and their organizations won't survive unless (1) they create a future that rivals cannot, (2) they offer more value to customers who are willing to pay for that, in a way that competitors cannot, (3) live in harmony with society, which make them distinctive from competitors, (4) have a clear moral compass and purpose mind when pursuing strategic objectives, that incites energy among the people in the company, and finally (5) to pursue a common good as a way of life that characterizes the organizational culture, allowing anyone within the organization to succeed and strive for something that may excite them as touching an inner energy that is palpable in the organization.

At the end of the day it is about a board that makes enlightened decisions that create excitement and belief in a great future. Such a leadership cultivates wisdom in each of us, making practice converted into knowledge and knowledge into wisdom by making it a habit, as in intuitive tacit knowledge. Somehow, we shade the old management adage that says that only what gets measured will get managed. The chemistry among leadership at boards can only be partially "measured"; but the functioning of a board depends on that perceived collaborative unity at a board. The outcome of those synergies may be visible and measurable, but the input and the underlying feelings that constitute certain behaviour remains a subtle reality which may partially escape the deciphering power of analytics.

1.4 External [Technological] Forces Putting Pressure on Governance Principles

So far the internal parts of what affects strategic planning. What about the external forces affecting or even shaping strategy? Macro-economic changes and geopolitical issues, the threat of changing customer preferences have all become part of long-term risks that leadership at boards cannot ignore any longer. In addition, board members should scan the horizon for slower-moving issues that may reshape the landscape of the business over a longer period. Hence why leadership need to anticipate some of those critical issues while also developing plans for potentially navigating them accordingly. How to make the firm more future-proof? Organizational culture that embrace profit through purpose and corporate governance itself may help organizations to be better equipped to go through such transitions that will take place, whether we like it or not.

Besides the macro-economic context, organizations and their boards assess micro-factors, based on internal data that should give a sense of the company's financial and operations' performance. Boards determine whether or not the organization is overly "revenue reliant" in its pursuit of profitability. In other words, does leadership understands whether or not the firm shows an overdependency on the revenues stream of one particular unit or line of business. At the end, it is the board's obligation to allocate capital to those projects that are priority and such allocation decision usually remains an art of balancing priorities. In economic terminology, it is answering the question what firms do with each marginal rupiah or dollar earned. Corporate leadership decides how to optimize the firm's assets and capital, or makes a judgment about the best use of the firm's marginal rupiah, euro, yen or dollar. Does the board decide to reinvest the profit earned (as retained earnings), or does it pay back the shareholders as dividend pay-out or share buybacks, or reducing debt, or does it buy or sell assets as in entering M&A activities?

Today, no company survives without taking data and data protection seriously. Nonetheless, cybersecurity remains an area that indicates that many boards are not fully prepared for those kind of risks. Data is swiftly becoming the new oil of the digitalized economy. Boards cannot be left behind to embrace this fast growing field of digitalization of our economies. And they urgently need to get the expertise and experience to be able to make informed reasonable decisions about the future of the company. The future is for the youth of this world, who have been brought up with a digital world. Soon a virtual reality may be perceived as equally important as our real physical world – if one may believe technology companies like Meta, Microsoft, Tiktok, Google and a number of others.[16] Should boards not understand what is going on if they cater for a younger population? Even fashion houses like H&M, Zara, GAP and Mango have hired data analysts to predict the next fashion attributes or colours. No company can afford to ignore artificial intelligence, machine learning or any form of optimal usage of available data and data analytics.

Along with the digitalization of our daily life, *cybersecurity*[17] has risen in importance – as expressed in Figure 33. Every day, we hear cases of companies attached by malware, by hackers of whatever sort and nationality, asking ransom to set them free again.

Figure 33: Who practices modern governance?.

Figure 33 summarizes this technology trend to be embraced by 'modern governance'. Effective boards will have experts available to inform them on how to protect the crown asset jewels of the company against digital intruders, and how to protect data privacy. Today, companies like Facebook (Meta) and Google (Alphabet) are criticised for taking the individual data privacy too lightly. This privacy is exactly what constitutes the core strategy of Apple which has made it its reputation to protect its eco-system and the billion customers using it.

1.5 Do Firms Lack a Vision to Invest in Promising Projects?

Another troublesome feature is that stock buybacks in the USA is another tool to keep share prices up. More, stock buybacks has become the norm and it is sucking up an incredible amount of capital. From 2009 to 2018, the major S&P 500 companies spent about USD 4 trillion in buying back stock while paying out USD 3.1 trillion in dividend. In other words, firms used capital and about 92 percent of profit to buy back their own stock on the exchange. In comparison, in early 1980s, firms only bought back about 5 percent of the profit.[18] Is short profit preferred to long term productive investments? Does this mean that boards and executives are focusing on optimizing the short-term stock price at the expense of investing in potentially promising longer term projects? Or worse, boards and their management are *not able to find those promising productive investments that will create cash flow in the future?* This is in sharp contrast to many younger technology companies that hardly pay out any dividend, and are busy to re-innovate their business models.

Worse, about 30 percent of the stock buyouts in the USA were funded by corporate bonds. In other words, firms take on debt to finance buying back their own stock, instead of revenue-creating investments that pay off the debt.[19] According to that same research, hardly 55 percent is investing for the future. Call it whatever you want, bad management, lack of vision. But definitely a bad habit that Asian firms should not follow. The aircraft manufacturer Boeing spend USD 43 billion on purchasing their own stock on the NYSE versus USD 20 billion on R&D in the same period 2013–2018.[20] Not exactly reassuring, especially if you take into account that Boeing ended up taking major shortcuts on design and safety that resulted in the Lion Air and Ethiopian Air crash disasters of a 737 Max. One should not chase stock price above the company's future.

In an academic survey, 80 percent of CFOs admitted that they would decrease spending on R&D, advertising, maintenance, or hiring to ensure meeting the expected quarterly investment targets.[21] Fortunately, Asian and Indonesian firms are not under the same quarterly short term pressure. But with international investors in their investment portfolio, there is likely an increasing pressure to meet targets in terms of revenues and return on invested capital. That is not necessarily a bad thing, as long as the basic longer term philosophy of family businesses and potentially also of State-owned Enterprises can be kept intact. It has been empirically proven in some studies that companies that plug back their earnings into the organization outperform their peers in return on invested capital by an average of 9 percent per year. We can conclude that more often than not, short term investors, speculators and instant traders benefit the most of these stock buybacks. From a strategic and business perspective, it is not really rational to focus on this kind of activities, that hardly create any real organizational value, unless to boost the stock value.

Boards should refrain their CFOs to get too much involved in these kind of practices. Boards should expand the reporting timelines to three to seven years, instead of focusing on quarterly or annual financial performance. Unfortunately, most time horizons of investors have dramatically shortened over the years. The average holding period of stocks has plummeted from up to eight years in the 1960s to about five months in 2020. It creates "hot money", something Indonesian stock market – but also exchanges in other emerging economies – has suffered from during the pre- and after Asian crisis. And even today, this "speculative" investors are not necessarily the investors an Asian firm is looking for. In fact, such extremely short perspective is contradictory to the longer term perspectives that most family enterprises or state owned enterprises take.

To prepare the future one needs a clear long term vision and a well thought through strategy and risk assessment. Hence why stories are powerful because they explain both the "why" by describing the causality between the past and the present, and the "how" as in how did this happen. Stories and imagination are especially effective during times of crisis; it enables leaders to develop wide and deep insights on what's behind the phenomena in a given time and place, and to make judgments that transcend superficial challenges to create the future.[22] Grasping and communicating the essence of what the organization stands for is one thing. However, effective leaders must also know how to bring people together, and get them to act, combining and synthesizing everyone's knowledge and efforts in a single-minded pursuit of the board's goals. Boards enable people in the organization. And a story or a narrative is nothing but "data with a soul".

2 Development of the Next Leadership with the Aim to "Innovate or Die"

Investing in technological and business innovation is crucial to survive the fierce competitive battle. At the organizational level, the board's task, directors prepare themselves to act efficiently and effectively in pursuing those strategies. That will require talented and experienced board members. Are organizations ready to secure some continuity in leadership? Research has shown that boards composed predominantly of individuals with the same kind of background risk engaging in groupthink, that over a longer period is often detrimental to the organization.[23] Ultimately, only someone with relevant expertise and experience, and proven to be an independent thinker can warrant a seat on a board.

2.1 The Global War for Talent

The current pandemic crisis may have aggravated the ongoing challenges. Therefore, the role of an effective boardroom cannot be underestimated, and the choice for the right diversified and effective team on that board who chooses the top executive in charge remains a difficult task. We even dare to state that in times of turmoil and crises, boards function as custodians of the organization and its corporate assets, and by extension has a responsibility to its shareholders but also to the society as whole in which it operates. One cannot do it alone; both governmental institutions, civic society and businesses need each other, they need to collaborate in a way that benefits society. Being a board-member can be tough and very stressful. But it is as true that effective leadership at boards can transcend conflict and challenges as long as they feel united about the basics, about the challenges the organization faces, especially if it becomes an existential fight to survive. That is where courageous boards make a difference, where talented teams have a real impact.

A. Retaining Talent
Then, how to retain top talent without overpaying its top executives? Instead of trying to redistribute the pie in favour of highly paid top managers – even in times of crisis as this covid pandemic – we opt to defend a position to pay executives well and fairly according to industry standards. That include bonuses that are linked to long term value creation. The core challenge to retain top executives in the USA and the UK has been the meteoritic rise of stock options as compensation. These options were meant as a neat answer to the traditional agency problem to align executives incentives with those of shareholders, as in optimizing the stock price of the firm. It certainly worked, but it created the vicious side-effect of managers focusing on short-term shareholders' value creation (as in short term profit) and unintentionally allowed managers to rig or abuse the incentive system. It aggravated the problem of short-termism in the USA and other Anglo-Saxon countries which adapted this remuneration system. It looks like this short-termism is slowly encroaching into Asian boards now, likely under pressure by foreign institutional [activist] investors. But we should not exaggerate this tendency either – especially with the counterforce of increased stakeholders' demand for more sustainable business practices that imply a longer term perspective. It is a dilemma or paradox between two opposing trends that boards will need to resolve.[24]

Staffing a board requires to attract members who have the necessary expertise and experience to contribute to make informed decisions. Individuals who have been CEOs themselves bring a wealth of transferable experience and knowledge to a board. And of course, specific technical expertise is required to lead an audit committee or a nomination and remuneration committee. Also operational knowledge to advise on how products work or individuals intimately understanding risk management should be mandatory. When companies derive substantial revenues from export or international business, some international expertise should be obtained to staff the board's governance or risk committee. Also here, achieving a certain balance of expertise and experience in the boardroom is crucial. For instance, Boeing's board was recently criticised for two fatal 737 MAX crashes because most board members had financial backgrounds and allegedly too few who had engineering or technological expertise. Increasingly, the need for technology skills as well as the need for geopolitical expertise – for instance understanding intellectual property rights amidst mounting economic protectionism – and the need for diversity may be on the wish list of a board.

To prepare potential leaders to follow in the footsteps of current leadership at the board, different methods can be applied. One with a proven record is mentorship and modern-day apprenticeship. Those methods of mentoring (top management level) and apprenticeship (middle level management) allow a board and its leadership to disseminate some of the tacit practical knowledge and explicit knowledge within the organization.

Internationally, we see that the share of newly appointed directors who come from a traditional CEO/CFO/COO background is declining – dropping from 59.4 percent to 56.0 percent since 2019. Over the same time period, the share of newly appointed directors who come from non-traditional backgrounds has increased from 13.0 percent to 18.9 percent in 2021.[25] The group of newly appointed directors with nontraditional backgrounds is split almost evenly along gender lines. Newly appointed directors from traditional C-suite backgrounds are twice as likely to be men, while women represent the majority of new appointments in technology and marketing, and the vast majority of new appointments in human resources and ESG.[26] We foresee a similar trend in some Asian boards, though it may take a little more time.

Globally, but especially in both the US and Australia, scrutiny has increased for companies whose boards lack diversity. Companies are responding to this external and internal pressure in different ways, but the net impact is that boards are becoming more diverse.[27] Japan, however, scores quite badly on this diversity criterion in corporate governance standards: women form a real small minority on boards (<3 percent); the opposite are Scandinavian boards where roughly about 40 percent are women. Again, diversity generally contributes to better decision-making and for that reason, boards could improve their corporate governance rating by adhering to those best practices.

B. Appointment of CEO and Succession Planning

The problem with identifying top candidates often lies in how a short list is generated by the board or its shareholders. Traditionally, the focus is on *who* the leader is without significant weight put on what skills he or she needs to deliver on the company's strategy preparing the future of the company. If succession discussions are to be transformed into more of an upstream process for the board – and members are to have a clear understanding of what the company needs before discussing the best candidates – then the process must account for three distinct and entirely predictable challenges. They are predictable to a certain extent because these challenges can be anticipated and overcome.[28] First, a board should start with the *what* and not the *who*. Doing so will lay out a more realistic and substantive framework. Second, from this vantage point, boards may try to explicitly minimize the noise[29] in the boardroom. Ensure that the directors are using shared, contextual definitions of core jargon, such as *strategy, agility, transformation*, and *execution*. Third, board may root the follow-on analyses of the candidates in that shared understanding, and base any assessments on a factual evaluation of their track records and demonstrated potential in order to minimize the bias of the decision-makers themselves.

The CEO succession – hiring and firing when warranted – is one of the major tasks of a board. The selection of leadership is one of those functions over which the top executives have no say or debate. Some argue that this function is among the most important of a [supervisory] board. Each new CEO (or President Director) who is responsible for the day-to-day management of the firm has his/her own style which obviously can affect the organizational culture. A great deal of turnover in the CEO position is often disruptive. Indeed, frequent changes in the position of CEO, can be quite destabilizing and confusing to employees and other stakeholders. The example of Pertamina a couple of years ago reminds us of such a destabilizing force.

Despite this important duty, many boards do not have a proper detailed succession plan in place – even though the CEO tenures on Western MNOs have dropped from eight years in 2000 to just five years today.[30] To remain factual, despite the decreasing average CEO tenure, the top 100 best performing CEOs remain in power for an average of 20 years, a multi-fold for their less performing peers.[31] It should not surprise us that there exists a correlation between long term and performance. Continuity aligned with innovation, consistency and unexpected novelty, stability aligned to agility all help organizations to better perform over a longer time frame.

An additional complicating factor is that one can distinguish two kind of top executive profiles. A "peacetime CEO" focuses on expanding market share and on setting big ambitious goals that may even reflect a high risk appetite supported by the board. Another type, a "wartime CEO" must avoid taking on significant new risks, and is focusing on defending the position of the firm while executing a survival plan, which may include some cost-cutting.[32] The board should be clear about what type of CEO is needed. Recruiting the right CEO requires finding someone with a range of skills, a deep understanding of organizational management, industry experience, and character of high integrity and temperament of confident humility that is also resilient in adversity.

Keeping or getting talented managerial talent has become a very hard game today. It may be less of an issue within a family business, but it definitely is a big one at state-owned enterprises in Indonesia where the tenure is on average four to five years – if that long. How to resolve this potential lack of leadership succession? Obviously, developing the next talent, preferably in-house. That may require more women and younger talent to take on leadership positions within the firm before giving the opportunity to grow into a board membership role. And that also implies being ready for addressing some of those new demands by the community, including to handle ESG issues.

When you talk about good corporate governance, you clearly must include the goal of minimizing corruption[33] and nepotism within firms, especially within state-owned enterprises with a reputation of red tape and long ranging nepotistic habits or even outright unethical behaviour. Some estimates infer that corruption can add ten percent to the cost of doing business globally, and up to twenty five percent to the cost of procurement in some developing countries. And although "the envelope of money under the table" is still a serious challenge in many emerging markets, quite a number of the corruption cases involve companies whose ownership is hard to identify. Often these "envelopes" go through shell companies that function as "getaway vehicles" for corruption and money laundering.[34]

And let us be clear: corruption is not just an emerging country issue; half of the international foreign bribery cases since 1999 have involved public officials from developed countries.[35] One of the solutions for companies – both in developed as well as in emerging countries – is to develop strong codes of conduct that are fiercely implemented. Unilever is such an example. One of the authors, Peter remembers talking to a former chair and a former board member of Unilever Indonesia who explained him that there is zero-tolerance for corruption. When five middle managers – a top sales team – were caught to bribe a distributor in Surabaya (Indonesia) – the team was unceremoniously fired from Unilever without warning letter (since this top sales team breached the signed code of conduct that functions as a legal agreement). And in Unilever, everyone knows that success without integrity is a failure. Nobody makes a career within Unilever and other great companies by focusing on outcomes only. The process is as important as the profitable output itself.

2.2 Boards Overseeing Top Executives to make Organizations Competitive

Boards are tasked with overseeing strategy and leadership supervision and securing a proper organizational culture that ensure that companies remain competitive over a longer period. Only a relentless pursuit of excellence, both strategic and operational, allows a firm and its board to realize their aspirations. This pursuit of excellence has always been the trademark of Toyota, the Japanese automobile manufacturer in Japan, today still one of the most innovative and leading car companies in the world – rooted in its notion of *kaizen*, the habit of doing a little better every day by eliminating waste and continuously becoming more efficient. It is an attitude of never being satisfied with the status quo.[36] It was *kaizen* that enabled Toyota to turn the Toyota Crown into a Lexus by 1989, today competing with the best of class. Behaviours that are practiced every day become a way of life, they become the organizational culture. It is culture that "carries" a strategy that is planned by the board and executed by its executives. Some organizational cultures are proving the food to become flourishing gardens, allowing people to mature and thrive. Such a place does not come automatically, it requires practice and resilience as with everything worth striving for in life. Toyota for instance has built such daily routines based on guiding principles, called '*kata*', that eliminates waste to streamline operations and seeks to continuously make improvements of the process of production.[37] Indeed, such a philosophy of continuous improvements have been built into the Toyota Production System.[38] This *kata* can be described as a way to keep individual thoughts and actions in sync with dynamic unpredictable conditions. These routines are embedded in a close human network of respect or *thumos*, but also a certain level of openness. The team attempting to achieve excellence through open dialogue and candid debate is also practiced at Toyota which uses the phrase "let's *yokoten*" – an abbreviation for *yokoni tenkaisuru* which literally means to unfold, or open out sideways.[39] At Toyota, communications are viral, and knowledge is diffused in all directions. We only guess that PT Astra, representing and manufacturing Toyota cars among others, has been a consistent top performer in the Indonesian economy - whereby its managers were mentored by Japanese executives. This Indonesian company may have learned to apply some of those [Japanese] practices in its benefit.

These process-related practices ensured that the company followed the desired behaviour, that things were done the right way. Strategy formulation – whatever the stormy complex uncertain circumstances – then becomes much easier; strategy becomes a clear expression of those practices, guided by that organizational soul that almost always gives *thumos* a real place for everyone in the organization. In a way, we believe that this notion of respect requires a certain level of consensus on the principles with explicitly giving due attention to the individual aspirations and expressions.

Asian companies – emulating what Toyota and other Japanese companies achieved in the 80s and 90s of last century – often face fierce competition at home and globally when trying to expand beyond their home borders. Many Indonesian and Asian firms have been well engrained in the global supply chain, but not yet at the end of the chain where most of the innovation is captured by firms. Unfortunately indeed, only a few Indonesian companies have followed in the global steps of Japanese firms – likely due to an institutional context of less developed status in terms of education and related innovation.

Yet, any company specializing in a certain skillset and unique value proposition can succeed. Having both travelled quite a bit, and having lived abroad in a number of countries, both authors believe that in the hospitality business for instance, the Indonesian and Thai hotel service and resort hotels are likely among the champions in the industry, partially because of its service-orientation and partially benefiting from applying international best hospitality practices. Corporate performance is dependent on an organizational culture aligned with proper management meticulously executing the firm's strategy, not on a more vague perception of a national culture.

However, the covid pandemic and the new cold war between US and China, and Russia versus the West, is changing the global business climate. How will Asian and particularly Indonesian companies fare in a business word where decoupling is on everyone's lips? Should it surprise us that Didi's delisting revives US-China decoupling risks? Or is Wall Street – despite still being one of the most liquid capital markets – something that does not excite Asian companies anymore. The decision of by the Chinese ride-hailing group Didi Chuxing to delist from the New York Stock Exchange, just after its $4,4 billion initial public offering in June 2021 – one of the biggest listings by a Chinese company in New York since Alibaba in 2014 – was likely driven by CCP's desire to exert greater control over those important tech companies. One way to do so is by "forcing" them to list closer at home, on the Hong Kong Stock Exchange. It obviously will hurt Western investors in Didi's delisting, and may accelerate a self-fulling prophecy of such US-China decoupling.

A dangerous [geopolitical] trend, to say the least. Till now, global capital has been deliberately blind about political institutional differences. China but also other Asian countries continue to attract amounts of foreign direct investment. However, there is high probability of political pressure in the USA to curb on investments in China because of alleged unfair trade practices, facilitating human rights abuses, military and high tech modernisation that may harm US national interests. Many Western observers start to consider China's "opening" as a careful managed process that is designed to keep government control over important industries and capital markets towards fulfilling national objectives.[40] Maybe, ASEAN countries could benefit from some of this re-location of US and European companies. At the same time, the Securities and Exchange Commission (SEC) in New York is prodding all companies who do not fulfil the stringent information about audits and full disclosure of government control over their operations to delist.

Modern governance involves the practice of empowering leaders with the tools, processes and insights required to fuel good governance. And companies' practices and technology evolve with the business landscape. In this era of artificial intelligence, organizations must be all at once more informed about the latest technology, more secure against potential hacking, more transparent to fulfil the increasing institutional and individual investors' pressure, and more purpose-driven to inspire customers and employees alike while placating investors and especially the community at large.

We see today a few common governance deficits: (a) a lack of visibility in terms of who are your shareholders, really, (b) lack of security with respect to confidential material, conversations and data, and (c) the lack of speed in the event of a corporate crisis. Translating these deficiencies into a workable modern governance framework, it implies boards to focus on installing a proper subcommittee authorized and accountable to provide a proper security ICT framework, as well as securing proper executive communication with its stakeholders, having proper risk and compliance policies in place, being clear about strategic growth and expansion. And last but not least, modern governance highlights the importance of implementing ESG policies impacting the community at large, while also gathering intelligence and benchmarking about financial and non-financial performance – that is expected from the firm.

Answering whether an organization is "future-proof", a board has to adequately think through long-term risks. While it is the management's obligation to oversee an organization's day-to-day operations, it is the board's duty to heed potential new transformations that may be underway, or trends that will drastically alter how business is conducted. Culture and governance go hand in hand, and when aligned, the organization will benefit and be better equipped to face new challenges and new trends of whatever sort. With almost certainty, we can claim a deep form of uncertainty will be inevitable. However, good corporate governance and better prepared boards are better equipped to address those inevitable changes.

3 Addressing Sensitive Socio-Cultural and Eco-systemic Risks

Without a strong organizational culture that reflects the purpose and mission-vision of the company, strategy may be idle and nonsequential. Culture goes further than the governance principles, it keeps an openness to the world, not just keeping track of new technological innovations, but sense the broader and often sensitive trends in society, be it #metoo, or climate change, or investor activism versus communal activism, or any other issue that could have an impact on the reputation of the firm. Boards need to keep a *growth mindset*,[41] founded on the principles of continuous learning and innovation.

3.1 Practical Wisdom should Prevail Over Short-Termism

The neoliberal goals of profit maximization has become the main doctrine of business in the Western hemisphere. But times have changed and in 2019 the Business Roundtable, a body of CEOs of major US companies, publicly stated that a corporation should not just adhere to the old philosophy of shareholder primacy, but should operate with the benefit of all stakeholders in mind – customers, employees, suppliers and communities – and generate a fair long term value for its providers of capital, its shareholders.⁴² The days before ethical values like integrity and honesty and fair dealing with customers were assumed, today, a much broader idea of social responsibility is making it much more tricky for any board to function and to make appropriate decisions. From a boardroom perspective, companies both in the West as well as in Asia feel the pressure to collectively take a broader societal view and make ecological and social mindfulness part of their operating principles – which we have explained in the previous chapter.

Today's global organizations are being called to take more responsibility about emerging societal issues, such as racial equality, gay rights, pay parity, parental leave and health leave, workers' rights, sexual harassment, human rights etc. Nike and Louis Vuitton have experienced what it means to be pressed by their customers at home to comment on alleged human rights violation in China and the reaction by the Chinese to boycott these Western products. How to address the risk of a more siloed and protectionist world? No real straightforward black- & white answers here. Again, balancing the often opposing opinions and finding commonality to reach some form of minimal consensus, allowing organizations to continue to do business while not jeopardizing their own values. And we repeat, boards are charged with ensuring that management finds that right balance between short-term financial performance – which may be to give in to the Chinese government's pressure – and long term value creation which is grounded in its purpose. And if that purpose and the accompanying values include deep respect to individual human rights for instance, than the board will need to make some difficult decisions.

Making the right decision under extreme difficult circumstance remains a huge challenge, even for the bravest. Using a metaphor or narrative to make a decision may sometimes help. Indeed, good moral judgment can be expressed in a story that enables audiences to appreciate the particulars that no theory can fully capture. Yes, a good decision is often a matter not of theoretical or logical reasoning – what Aristotle defined as *epistémè* – but of practical wise reasoning (or *phronèsis*) which comes from sensitive reflection on and integration of a great deal of experience (or tacit intuitive knowledge), expertise (or explicit knowledge), and close attention to the unforeseeable and unrepeatable particularities of many individual cases.

Nonetheless, many boards are unprepared for those rising expectations of the outside world. Not many boards have extensive knowledge on ESG issues: while 29 percent worldwide had some relevant ecological, social -ethical or governance experience or background, they mainly focused on social topics. Only a very small minority of directors across the survey's 100 global companies has considerable climate knowledge.⁴³ And boards without the relevant expertise will likely not know the questions to ask, or to understand what potential risks might exist. And although may firms may have created subcommittees that attempt to assess the ecological and social risks, most of their members are not qualified to understand or analyse those new questions that the public expects firms to address. Given the role of boards as safeguards of business, board members often remain very short-term focused, partially because of the external pressure by investors – though that is slightly less the case in family businesses and state-owned enterprises who inherently aim for a longer term focus. Nonetheless, a considerable number of CEOs – be it in Western MNOs or Asian family business or state-owned enterprises – may not feel the need yet to give attention on sustainability issues. The wind is changing swiftly though.

For instance, a surprising court ruling in the Netherlands has imposed strict CO_2 reduction to Shell over the next decade. A soft law just became a hard law in 2021 that may influence [Western] court actions in the future. Meanwhile, Shell's board, under pressure by financial analysts, has moved its headquarters from Amsterdam to London, to soften the immediate blow and reduce some of this external pressure. That won't change the fact that the socio-economic context is changing, demanding more ecological responsibility, and now also some more accountability vis-à-vis ESG criteria from boards and their companies. Especially in industries like energy which are scrutinized even more extremely today considering the sensitivity of the matter to a broader public. Investors may temporary succeed to escape some of that stakeholder pressure, but our guess is that the more innovative and sensitive energy companies will likely outflank these traditional corporations in the next decade or two.

3.2 Boards Being Sensitive and Inventive

Innovative companies usually survive. When CEO, Hubert Joly, former CEO and Chairman of US based Best Buy, was brought in at Best Buy in 2012, the situation was bleak: the company was close to failure and Joly was advised by many to cut stores and headcount. His response was doing the opposite of cutting costs by firing people. He wanted to fix what was broken, instead of "getting the people out". Indeed, his first step was listening to the people that made up the organisation. The next phase was to figure out how to accelerate growth: *"The essence of the turnaround was building the right team at the top and listening to the people. People are not the problem; they are the solution,"* according to Hubert Joly, former Chairman and CEO of Best Buy. One of the clever strategic and emotional moves of Best Buy to save itself from ruin was to become a strategic partner of Amazon for physical display of Amazon products and as a preferred "pick up" place for online bought products. In the process, the board enabled the company to become one of the best places to work for in the USA. Talking about a turnaround.

What about transforming Asian organizations to become more competitive? Especially state-owned enterprises. When innovation is called for, leaders need to create environments in which their people can find answers on their own. Let others make decisions.[44] Create a space and psychological safety in which creative and innovative minds can thrive. Hierarchical order style won't succeed in fast pacing contexts, where risks loom behind every corner. Agility here means to trust and delegate the authority to those who are in touch with that changing reality on the ground.

Companies experience every day how culture can make or break the company. The value of a firm depends on tangible and intangible assets. We go even so far by advocating that the worth of an organization is increasingly determined by intangible assets like culture and values – a worth that often exceeds the tangibles. The accountancy firm EY recently has calculated that "intangible assets" such as culture constitute on average 52 percent of an organization's market value, and in some industries as much as even 90 percent.[45] A board taking interest in assessing and implementing the "right culture" not only supports a company's strategy, but will be essential to a more sustainable and long-term value creating company.

Consider the following Take Away Ideas of Chapter 6:

---

1. Boards need to (1) address the longer-term prospective of the firm, (2) guarantee continuity in leadership by having a clear succession plan, and finally (3) making sure that the cultural sensitivities are taken seriously and addressed in the firm's policies and or strategies.

---

2. Avoid short-termism & create entrepreneurialism in the organization. However, a board paradoxically synthesizes and integrates opposing ideas: short term and long term thinking, present exploitation of assets and continuously exploring new opportunities to invest in. The best performing companies likely have achieved this kind of integration of opposing ideas. They think in terms of both/and, and not in terms of either/or.

    One clever way to achieve this difficult dialectic process is embedding those opposing ideas in a narrative that appeals both to the mind and the heart, expressing the idea in a more powerful manner than in pure logic.

---

3. Innovation is necessary => embracing digitalization and socio-ecological challenges. Boards need to think in a more systemic way where interdependencies and connectivity play a crucial role.
   Only by embracing new trends and technology will boards and their organizations being prepared and become more "future-proof".

Notes

1 Moyo, D., (2021), *How Boards work. And how they can work better in a chaotic world,* London, The Bridge Street Press.
2 Deci, E. L., & A.C. Moller,(2005), "The Concept of Competence: A Starting Place for Understanding Intrinsic Motivation and Self-Determined Extrinsic Motivation", in Elliot< A.J. & C. S. Dweck (Eds.), *Handbook of competence and motivation* (pp. 579–597). Guilford Publications.
3 Bettenmann, D.; Giones, F.; Brem, A. & P. Gneiting, (2022), "Break out to Open Innovation", *MIT Sloan Management Review,* Winter, Vol. 63(2): 39–43.
4 See Coreynen, Matthyssens & Van Bockhaven, 2017.
5 Morewedge, C.K., (2022), "When we don't own the things we use, will be still love them?", *MIT Sloan Management Review,* Winter, Vol. 63(2): 16–18.

6 Arora, A.; Harrison, A.; Plotkin,C.L.; Magni, M. J. Stanley, (2022), "The new B2B growth equation", *McKinsey & Company*, February.

7 *Ibidem*. B2B companies that assume they've cleared the omnichannel bar in sales and marketing will need to think again. Among the headlines: (1) Omnichannel is a path to share growth. The more channels a sales organization deploys, the bigger the market share gains. (2) There are no exceptions. *All* B2B customers prefer omnichannel, no matter their industry, country, size, or customer relationship stage. (3) B2B loyalty is up for grabs. Customers are more willing than ever to switch suppliers to gain exceptional omnichannel experiences. (4) Make your numbers. The new bar for omnichannel excellence is ten or more channels over three engagement modes (in-person, remote, and self-service), delivered 24/7. (5) Master the five "must dos." Customers are resoundingly clear on the five capabilities they *most* want from omnichannel – and they want all of them, from performance guarantees to real-time customer service. But good news is buried in the more than 300,000 data points we've gathered in our latest B2B Pulse. If keeping up with customers' omnichannel expectations has felt like a game of two steps forward, one step backward, B2B companies now have a once-in-a-generation opportunity to shift share meaningfully – through greater orchestration, integration, and personalization.

8 Pidun, U.; Reeves, M. & N. Knust, (2022), "Setting the Rules of the Road", *MIT Sloan Management Review*, Winter, Vol. 63(2): 44–50.

9 It is clear that our natural instinct to collaborate with teams (within the organization, but even outside) has allowed us to survive and to thrive, but it also creates a potential for conflicts of interest. Such potential breaches jeopardize the fiduciary duty of care, loyalty and prudence. Especially the enormous challenges to be able to openly discuss future strategies is making ethical responsibility engrained in the organizational culture so important.

10 See Churchland, P.S., (2019), *Conscience. The Origins of Moral Intuition*, New York; London, Norton & Company.

11 Nonaka, I. & H. Takeuchi, (2019), *The Wise Company. How companies create continuous innovation*, Oxford, Oxford University Press.

12 Nonaka, I. & H. Takeuchi, (2021), "Strategy as a way of life", MIT *Sloan Management Review*, Fall, Vol. 63(1):58.

13 *Thumos* (also commonly spelled 'thymos'; θυμός) is a Greek word expressing the concept of "spiritedness" (as in "spirited stallion" or "spirited debate"). The word indicates a physical association with breath or blood and is also used to express the human desire for recognition. The notion thymos partially constituted the driving force behind the philosophical force of History as explained by Hegel, and taken over in the often cited work of Francis Fukuyama: The end of History.

14 Nonaka, I. & H. Takeuchi, (2021), "Strategy as a way of life", *o.c.*, Vol. 63(1):56–63.

15 See Verhezen, P., *Wising up. Responsible Leadership in an era of Artificial Intelligence*, forthcoming in 2022–2023.

16 For a more philosophical insight whether a virtual reality will become as important and "real" as our physical known reality, we like to refer to Chalmers. D., (2022), *Reality+. Virtual Worlds and the Problem of Philosophy*, Dublin, Allen Lane – Penguin.

17 Pearlson, K. & K. Huang, (2022), "Design for Cybersecurity from the start", *MIT Sloan Management Review*, Winter, Vol. 63(2): 73–77.

18 Polman, P. & A. Winston, (2021: 202), *Net Positive. How courageous companies thrive by giving more than they take*, Cambridge MA, Harvard Business School Press.

19 Lazonick, W.; Sakinç, M.E. & M. Hopkins, (2020), "Why stock buybacks are dangerous for the economy", *Harvard Business Review*. January.

20 Ford, J., (2019), "Boeing and the Siren call for Share Buybacks", *Financial Times*: August 4.

21 Graham, J.R., Harvey C.R. & S. Rajgopal, (2005), "The economic implications of corporate financial reporting". *Journal of Accounting and Economics*, Vol. 40: 3–73.

22 Nonaka, I. & H. Takeuchi, (2019: 189), *The Wise Company. How companies create continuous innovation*, Oxford, Oxford University Press.
23 See Sibony, O., (2019), *You're about to make a Terrible Mistake! How Biases distort decision-making – and what we can do to fight them*, New York; Boston; London, Little-Brown Spark; Lovallo, D. & O. Sibony, (2006), "Distortions and Deceptions in Strategic Decisions", *McKinsey Quarterly*, April, Vol. 1: 18–29; Lovallo, D. & O. Sibony, (2010), "The case of Behavioral Strategy", *McKinsey Quarterly*, March: 30–343; Kahneman, D. & D. Lovallo, (1993), "Timid Choices and Bold Forecasts: A Cognitive Perspective on Risk Taking", *Management Science*, Vol. 39(1): 17–31; and Kahneman, D.; Lovallo, D. & O. Sibony, (2011), *"Before You Make That Big Decision"*, Harvard Business Review, June: 50–60.
24 We have developed a theoretical and practical framework to overcome this kind of paradoxes in business. See Verhezen, P., Wising up, a forthcoming publication in 2022.
25 See Diligent Institute July 2021: https://www.diligentinstitute.com/wp-content/uploads/2021/07/Beyond-the-C-Suite-Trends-in-Director-Skill-Sets-2.pdf. When looking at the breakdown of new appointments by discipline, we can see that the share of those with technology, HR, and ESG experience is on the rise. Since 2019, the share of new appointments with technology backgrounds has increased from 12.1 percent to 15.5 percent, the share of new appointments with HR backgrounds has increased from 5.5 percent in 2019 to 7.7 percent in 2021, and the share of new appointments with ESG backgrounds has increased from 2.7 percent to 4.4 percent in 2019 and 2021 respectively.
26 *Ibidem*. The most illuminating breakdowns are in HR and ESG, where women represent the vast majority of new director appointments with those skillsets. For new director appointments with HR backgrounds, women accounted for 83 percent in 2019 and 72 percent in 2021. The proportion of new appointments with ESG backgrounds who are women has been steadily rising over the last two and a half years, skyrocketing from 64 percent to 84 percent female in 2021.
27 *Ibidem*. In the US, companies are feeling pressure from governments, institutional investors, proxy advisors and asset holders alike – and they are seeing a sharp rise in issue awareness and social activism among their employees and local communities. In response, companies are interested to seek directors with diverse perspectives – both as a bulwark against risk, but also to take advantage of potential new business opportunities. In Australia, although the banking Royal Commission produced its final report in 2019, the new requirements are still creating ripples. Companies are more keenly focused on corporate culture, ethics and accountability across the board. In line with this trend, the Australia Institute of Corporate Directors (AICD) has issued guidance to corporate boards to strive for a minimum of 30 percent female directors and ensure the inclusion of indigenous and other ethnic minorities on their boards. These efforts are picking up momentum and Australia listed companies feel intense pressure to uphold these standards. The UK is a bit behind the other two countries in terms of skill set diversity, but changes are likely on the horizon. We are likely to see an increase over the next three years for UK boards in terms of skill set, gender and ethnic diversity with the implementation of the targets set by The Parker Review last year, especially for FTSE 100 and FTSE 250 companies which will be required to disclose their board's ethnicity and gender data, proving they have 30 percent female directors and to have at least one ethnic minority on the board.
28 Reimer, D. & A. Bryant, (2022), "The new rules of succession planning", McKinsey & Company, February.
29 Kahneman, D.; Sibony, O. & C.R. Sunstein, (2021), *Noise. A Flaw in Human Judgment*, London, William Collins.
30 Cheng, J. Y-J; Groysberg, B. & P. Healy, (2020), "Your CEO Succession Plan can't wait", Harvard Business Review, May.
31 McGinn, D., (2016), "The best performing CEOs in the World", *Harvard Business Review*, November: 41–51.

32 Moyo, D., (2021: 69), *How Boards work. And how they can work better in a chaotic world*, London, The Bridge Street Press.

33 Verhezen, P. & N. Soebadjo, (2013), "Is there hope for corporate governance in Indonesia?", *Strategic Review*, Vol. 3(3): 67–73.

34 "Partnering against corruption initiative", *World Economic Forum*, accessed in March 2021: https://www.weforum.org/communities/partnering-against-corruption-initiative/.

35 Polman, P. & A. Winston, (2021: 198), *Net Positive. How courageous companies thrive by giving more than they take*, Cambridge MA, Harvard Business School Press.

36 Nonaka, I. & H. Takeuchi, (2019), *The Wise Company. How companies create continuous innovation*, Oxford, Oxford University Press.

37 Rother, M., (2010), *Toyota Kata: Managing People for Improvement, Adaptiveness, and Superior Results*. New York, McGraw Hill. Rother spent six years observing Toyota's continuous improvement process in action. The idea behind Toyota Kata Framework is that by practicing improvement routines consistently, the process becomes second nature. Over time, one will develop a scientific approach to thinking critically, solving problems, and making quick decisions about what comes next. In the Knowledge Literature, one could compare *Kata* with a form of *Tacit Knowledge*.

38 Crucial in the *kata* process are four steps that may allow to continuously improve and innovate: (1) understanding the direction or challenge; (2) grasping the current condition (what we do know and what we don't yet know); (3) establishing the next target condition, whereby the target condition brings us one step closer to the actual challenge; and (4) experimenting against obstacles which allow us to define and run experiments against them in order to learn what works, and what does not.

39 Nonaka, I. & H. Takeuchi, (2019: 209), *The Wise Company. o.c.*

40 Blender, J, (2021, December 4–5: 20), "The Long View", *The Financial Times*, London.

41 Dweck, C.S., (2006), *Mindset: the new psychology of success*, New York, Random House.

42 Neves, P. & J. Story, (2015), "Ethical leadership and reputation: combined indirect effects on organizational deviance", *Journal of Business Ethics*, Vol. 127: 165–176.

43 Whelan, T., (2021), "US corporate boards suffer from inadequate expertise in financially material ESG matters", *NYU Stern Center for Sustainable Business*, January. https://ssrn.com/abstract=3758584.

44 Hill, L.A.; Tedards, E. & T. Swan, (2022), "Drive innovation with better decision-making", *Harvard Business Review Special Issue*, Spring: 86–93.

45 Moyo, *o.c.*, p135.

Concluding Remarks
Mindful Leadership & An Effective Boardroom Impacting Performance

The pressure on boards and their organization to perform can be overwhelming. Especially if internally, investors want continuity or even improvement of financial profitability, while the community seeks more accountability and responsibility for respecting ecological and socio-ethical demands. Board members are increasingly expected to be seasoned professionals who take risks to exploit the current competitive position and explore new opportunities. Today, leaders are also assumed to be mindful to the broader community with its continuously evolving ecological and social-ethical concerns. Add to that equation the expansive international trade – though the US-China cold war may slow down this globalization process a little -, operationally complex and culturally always evolving features, and any board is confronted with a really difficult task ahead. How to address the impact of a changing reality?

Corporate governance is the oversight system that removes people and processes when they do not function well within the organization. Governance is a system of check and balances on power, designed to safeguard the interests of the organization which should always prevail over individual interests. Basically, corporate governance provides the foundational framework in which an organization and teams function. The decision-making body is the board that governs the organization. The board is fundamentally a structure of governance that steers and supervises, while the CEO is the day-to-day-leader who with management executes financial goals and non-financial objectives. The non-executive directors (commissioners) of the [supervisory] board are not employees of the organization. They are engaged on a contractual basis for a predetermined period and paid a flat fee – in the US the remuneration package of these 'directors' sometimes includes stock options – for serving on the board of the organization. For the most part, boards share commonly accepted standards of operating – which are 'codified' in articles of association or the constitution of the firm. That governing document ensures that the duties, constraints and limitations are well defined at beforehand.

Board members are custodians whose main job is to strengthen the firm's foundation – rooted on the "steel-cement-foundations" of the four corporate governance principles – upon which "the boardroom" can continue to grow and steer the organization's future direction. A good board is incredibly important and adds enormous value to the organization. Admittedly, rubber-stamping boards hardly add value, and even may destruct organizational value by allowing misbehaviour and misjudgements. Boards need to take smart and wise decision, based on sound judgments that requires a minimal level of expertise, experience and a broad perspective. Board members are paid to watch from a helicopter view, where top executive leadership is viewing at a much lower altitude closer to the operations. Operational management is running the show in the ongoing activities of the organization. All three levels are needed to keep an organization competitive, to steer and manage the organization in an appropriate and effective manner.

For a very long time, corporate governance has been a mere legal matter for most organizations to interpret limited liability and to resolve the traditional agency problem. That agency challenge resulted from the separation between ownership and management, which historically took first precedent in the USA in the 1920s. Indeed, at that moment, professionals with access to information that even owners did not have, became quite powerful. We entered a period of managerial capitalism where those hired guns had the advantage over owners and investors to asymmetric information that they could use for their own benefit. The agent could easily misuse this asymmetric information in his advantage at the expense of owners. That's when corporate governance became a financial incentive issue, not just a legal matter. From the late 80s, institutions became more predominant in owning shares at the New York and London stock exchanges, resulting in an institutional capitalist neoliberal system. A number of international and local crises have turned corporate governance into mainstream economics and business, and making good governance practices now also a management and oversight board issue, not just a financial and legal matter, but also a socio-economic and increasingly an ecological systemic issue. It is clear that boards do have a fiduciary duty to look after the interests of the company that cannot be delegated to other people in or outside the company. Governing an organization implies adhering to the four main governance principles – transparency, fairness and equal shareholders' rights, accountability and responsibility – that allows a board to steer the organization with the aim to reduce risks and to optimize business opportunities that are translated in profitability. In short, governance now is seen as a practice that embraces legal duties, ensures financial performance, but now also implies clearly defined management responsibilities that are supposed to preserve the reputation of the organization, in terms of ecological and socio-ethical objectives and constraints.

However, corporate governance in Asia does not necessarily focus on the traditional agency challenge where the objectives of investors and managers or financial analysts need to be aligned with the owners and investors of the organization. What is the focus of corporate governance in Asia? Most of the time, Asian organizations are either family-owned or state-owned, both with a high level of concentration in ownership. This is the opposite situation in most Anglo-Saxon jurisdictions where the capital markets are characterized by dispersed ownership. When foreign investors take a financial "stake" (or participate in stock) in an organization, their concern boils down to the fact that majority powerful owners may not treat new investors equally as the law prescribes. Those foreign (or even local) minority investors may face specific risks in those Asian firms, because the "rules of the game" may not be equally implemented or followed in those family empires or state-owned enterprises. In other words, the major governance challenge in Asia is related to the majority versus minority ownership treatment, and the weak implementation of best governance practices, due to a less sophisticated capital market, and may we add, institutional voids. Indeed, prevailing nepotism, cronyism and even corruptive behaviour may aggravate the situation in Southeast Asia, and equally in China where the "rule by law" is often not the same as "the rule of law" (that supposedly guarantees equal and objective treatment). At the other hand, what works for the US or Europe may need some "contextualization" in an Asian environment.

A Western epistemology tends to accord the highest value to abstract theories and hypothesis that contributed to the development of sciences. An Asian epistemology, on the other hand, emphasizes pragmatism that tends to value the embodiment of direct personal experience, *hic et nunc*. For instance, the Japanese notion of *genchi genbutsu*, which literally translates to "real places, real thing", but figuratively translates to "have you seen it". Reality for Asian managers lies in a delicate, transitional state of permanent flux, and in visible and concrete matters, rather than the prevailing Western view of reality as an eternal, unchanging, invisible, and abstract entity.

Instead of convergence of corporate governance principles in a "global flat" world, we see a reality on the ground that acknowledges the uniqueness and idiosyncracies of social cultures or markets that absorb and thus "adopt" those general "universal" principles. Only a combination or integration of our desire to embrace some principles allowing us to enter a global world and its "rules of the game" while fully acknowledging and integrating them into our own deeply rooted "emotional" socio-historical values will make us feeling "home". Companies are not different. Its leadership likely endorses aspects of a national culture, but as in any global competition, some universal rules need to be accepted and respected as well. Such potential dichotomy occasionally causes some confusion.

Governance rating agencies consider independence in organizations with dispersed ownership as crucial and positive for the good functioning of the boardroom. That makes organizations with block-holding owners – often families – less favourable in the eyes of some American governance experts because perceived as less independent. However, others like S&P Global may consider such block-holding participation as a certainty for continuity and consistency. In other words, even about one criterium as independency, Western governance experts do have different opinions. There is ample empirical research that proves each point (often because of subtle different assumptions). Because Asia is characterized by family or state-owned enterprises, we have focused on providing arguments to make a board more effective within the existing institutional constellation. Of course, we believe in the independency of decisions made at boards. Interpreting this independence as less a formalistic and rather an individual mindset to speak out, to avoid groupthink and to be candid in the interest of the organization.

Although the Western and Eastern context may differ enormously, the underpinning principles of good corporate governance remain "universally" applicable. These principles function as the governance beacons across borders and even time. It is equally true that those generic principles need to be contextualized or translated into a concrete legal framework of corporate law and organizational rules. What may function very well in a Western context may not be fully relevant in an Asian context. For instance empirical academic research by one of the authors indicated that (1) not accepting party related transactions, or (2) making sure that reputable auditors are hired to verify the financial auditing reports that will subsequently be transparently disclosed to the public in case of a public listed company, and (3) properly disclosed ownership details and financial data to the financial tax authorities were all features that had a positive impact on the return on assets in Indonesian listed companies.

And yes, the "surrounding" institutions will partially determine the quality of corporate governance on a national level. Similarly, the lack of good functioning institutions will not necessarily preclude some outstanding organizations to shine and to outperform other competitors. Often those performing organizations (like Telkom or Astra in Indonesia e.g.) have adhered to and implemented proven foundations of good corporate governance. And this despite or in spite of weaker surrounding institutions or regulators.

When talking about boards, we refer to the *fiduciary duties of care*, *loyalty* and *prudence* for which each of the board members will be accounted for. Those duties cannot be delegated and board members – once they accept to serve on a board – will need to discharge those duties. They are liable to fulfil to be guardian of the organization which they steer and govern. This book has equally emphasized the importance of prudent decision-making which implies that the board understands proper risk practices, and take their time to determine the risk appetite and assess the major preventable risks, next to the not-preventable external risks. Important for any board is to debate the strategy, and its flip side, the risks attributable to those strategic choices. Without taking risks, no innovation would take place, and without innovative moves, no profit can be made. Hence why we believe that intrapreneurial and entrepreneurial activities are crucial for any organization to succeed. It is clear across borders that a too bureaucratic management style – driven by hierarchical oriented boards, especially in state-owned enterprises – will kill emerging ideas and entrepreneurial leadership. Without such built-in agility, an organization likely become morose and will die over time. In case of state-owned enterprises, governments may keep those organizations alive, but they may remain organizational zombies, not able to withstand real headwind. They still stands, barely, because of monopolistic protection by the government. Some of those organizations are not competitive or dynamic, and from a pure evolutionary perspective, one could argue whether such organizations should be kept alive, draining money and assets away from younger and more adaptable emerging firms.

Understandably, hierarchical bureaucracies do not adapt quickly to changing circumstances in the market. To overcome such changes, business needs to bypass those organizational constraints by tackling selected (pilot) projects that demand speed, flexibility and experimentation. Typical characteristics of an entrepreneurial spirit, such as the big corporations Novartis and PepsiCo for instance managed to apply. But that flexibility is not exactly the *forte* of any bureaucratic organization, as typical state-owned enterprises.

Figure 34 visualizes how the board creates and safeguards an organizational environment in which executives and employees immediately feel that they can have an impact. The efficiency and effectiveness of a board is dependent on (1) a proper definition and understanding of roles, tasks or duties of each of the board members, (2) implementing good practices within the legal board structure, (3) choosing the right people with the needed skillset and the right team (composition), and (4) guaranteeing good decision-making based on the right information following the right processes that could be codified into formal procedures.

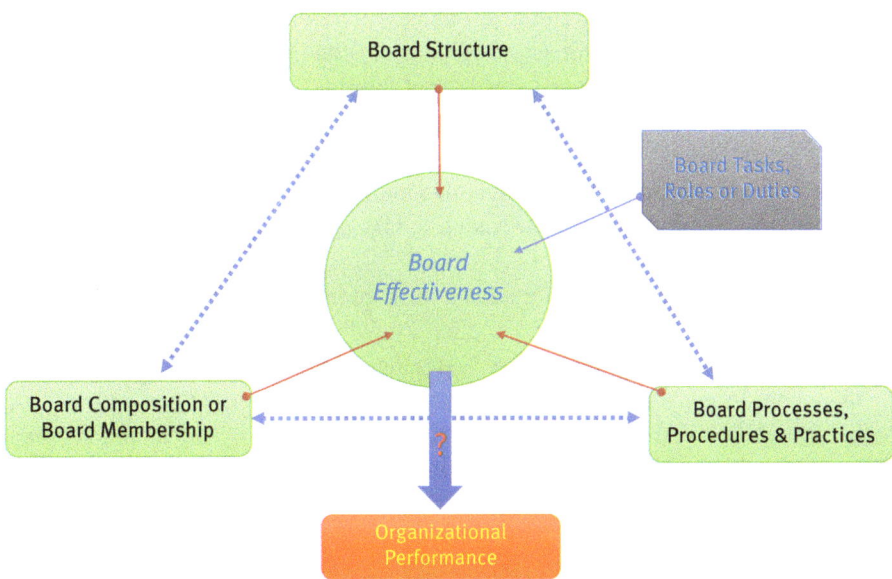

Figure 34: Variables of board effectiveness.

Organizations do not operate in a vacuum, but optimally function in an institutional context where the rule of law is assumed. Though not the focus of this book, any investor you speak will confirm that one prefers stability in terms of legal and judicial constraints. When governments change policies or rules too often without clear economic justification, investors stay away. When institutions cannot be relied on, it creates fundamental voids that add to the overall risk of an economy.

Nobody really benefits from such institutional voids over a longer period. Short term, some business may be able to take advantages of such particular voids, but such windfalls remain *ad hoc* and often depend on serious risk-taking with an expected relatively high profit in return to make it worth it.

In order for a board to be effective at the organizational level, leadership needs to make sure that the tasks and duties are well defined and understood. Moreover, a board structure and its effective implementation needs to be well understood by all the board members. The composition is advised to be as diverse as possible with the needed expertise and experience, to properly supervise and coach top executives. Finally, one assumes processes and practices to be properly determined and defined, and where appropriate to be formalized in specific procedures.

One important feature fundamentally affects the (non-) functioning of a boardroom: the *chemistry* and the mix of *behavioural* characteristics – that includes the *integrity* – of each of the non-executive and executive directors. That coherent and unified decision-making as a team obviously impacts the effectiveness of the governance of the organization.

Because of the enormous confusion about board structures we have seen during our tenures, we have emphasized to consider the pros and cons of a dual-tier board as it exists in Indonesia and some other civic law jurisdictions, in comparison with a single-tier board structure that prevails in the Anglo-Saxon jurisdictions, following a common law system. In case of a *de iure* double-tier board structure, it is adamant that the supervisory and executive board members team up as a *de facto* unified board – precluding an organization to take excessive, unreasonable or inappropriate risks.

Combining all these characteristics and features (as visualized in Figure 35), boards will establish the tacit and explicit knowledge to organize themselves in such a way that the chance for success is significantly enhanced.

Any board member, especially the chair of the board – needs to address and probably align to a certain extent to the institutional pressure by capital market players, that often boils down to expected profitability in line with peers or preferably above the industry average profitability. A corporate leader will address some of the basic concerns of investors to optimize return on investment, while also giving attention to the ecological and social-ethical demands of stakeholders and community.

When focusing on the internal abilities of the organization, a board needs to get well organized. An often proven concept is to divide the work at a board with installing subcommittees authorized with specific tasks and duties. Secondly, although the specific structure of board is almost always determined by the law and thus automatically imposed by the legal jurisdiction of the place in which the organization is incorporated, a board should optimize the advantages of such a board structure and amend the weakness into opportunities to improve the board functioning. Subsequently, in order to be able to steer the organization into the right direction, having the right individuals and the right team in place is crucial to

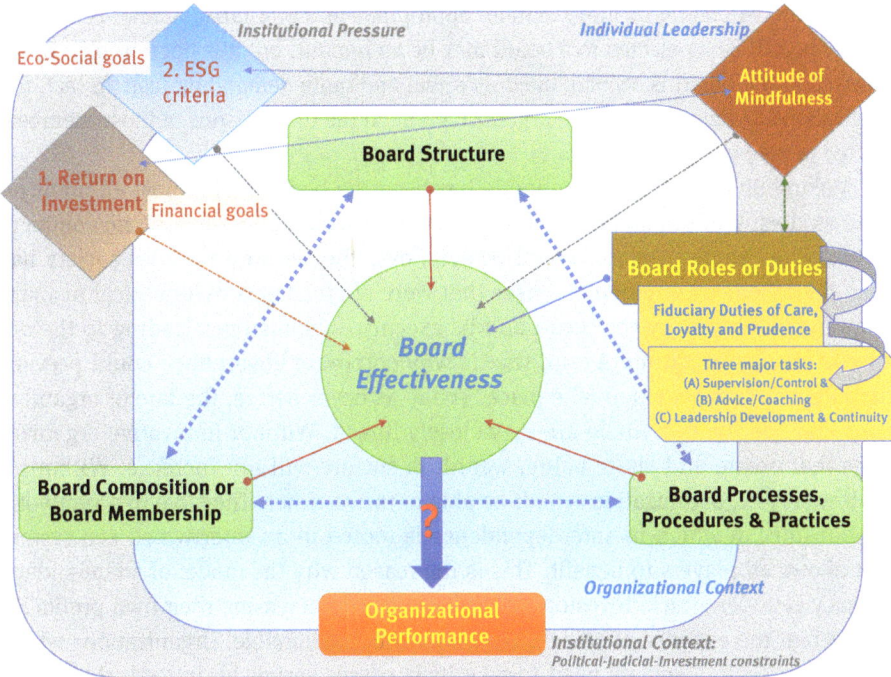

Figure 35: An integrated perspective in determining effective leadership within functioning boards.

succeed. Hence why the choice and the composition of the board members is a very important task, led by the lead director or chair/CEO (in case of a single-tier board structure) or chair (in case of duel-tier structure) of the board. The boardroom requires a certain formalistic approach with codified procedures to protect the actors involved while still able to function as a well-oiled team in which each trusts the professionalism of the others. Because of these formalities, certain processes will need to be strictly respected and followed like the way an annual shareholders' meeting is called and organized, or how to organize the voting about particular decisions to be taken. It also includes the formal appointment of a corporate secretary who looks after the implementation of the processes and procedures and who assists the chair of the board. Only by respecting formal rules and procedures, while also be able to informally discuss and trust each other, a board will be able to function as guardians of the organization and its assets. Each board member will benefit by being very mindful of different aspects and perspectives about the organization, by being attentive to the processes, to the ideas and challenges that the organization face, and especially to the way decisions are taken. Only attentive and honest candid discussions within a board will allow a board to be really successful to fulfil its fiduciary obligations and to steer the organization to the right direction where opportunities will emerge and unfold. Safeguarding the interest of the organization's survival and extending its lifespan in an appropriate and profitable manner is sensible for any board. Being elected to a board may be an honour, but it is not a trophy. Being asked to join a board is accompanied by a real and quite demanding task. In fact, the survival and sustainability of the organization lie in the in the hands of those members elected to the board.

Making an organization profitable has been the bedrock of almost all management studies. Without creating value that generates enough cash flow, no company will survive. No discussion there. However, over the last four decades society has been burdened with numerous crises that were often caused by unethical or inappropriate behaviour by the board and its executives, sometimes leading to the demise of the organization. Again, that is why corporate governance could prevent such unfortunate events to take place. Today as never before, the fate of organizations and society as a whole are very closely linked. Without innovative organizations that create and share value, wealth in society will not increase. Without a healthy society, organizations won't be able to thrive either. They live in a symbiotic relationship, in which its interdependence is rooted in an intertwined eco-system that allows all players to benefit. This is the reason why the model of shareholders' primacy is under attack. Investors solely focusing on increasing their own profitability, even at the expense of other players, won't be sustainable. Organizations which are embedded in a society need to take its concerns seriously. Indeed, those concerns, expressed in ESG criteria cannot be ignored anymore. Practitioners at boards know how to strategize and to build in ecological and social-ethical characteristics that could increase demand and or reduce cost, and please both impact investors and regulators. Such strategies will be translated into becoming more circular, and thus more ecologically and socio-ethically sustainable.

The authors have spent quite some time to argue for expanding the board obligations. When boards do not take the stakes seriously of all those involved, again, a firm won't survive. Like any organism that is based on different elements, all those separated entities need to be in harmony to survive or to thrive. It should not surprise anyone that business is using scientific insights to churn out new innovative products and or services. But above all, boards that govern a business are action-oriented. A scientific analytical mind analyses and deciphers a problem. However, only when knowledge turns in actual business activities can an organization thrive. In other words, science is organized knowledge, but wisdom is organized life. What we really try to say is that practical experience (tacit knowledge), intellectual expertise (explicit knowledge) aligned with the notion of purpose and wise judgments will result in reasonable but also responsible decisions. Such decisions must make sense, and serve a clearly communicated purpose that creates intrinsic motivation. Founding fathers of an organization – often evolved to conglomerates in Asia – carry that wisdom, expressed in the company's values, vision-mission and philosophy. At that moment, an organization – rooted in an effective board – may have a chance to thrive over a longer period, creating and capturing value. Nothing wrong with making a decent profit while being driven by an "emotional" purpose that intrinsically provides the needed energy to continue to resolve challenges, day in, day out. That is what we have described as the organizational culture without which one won't sustain over a longer period. It is likely also the hardest to achieve, because its intangibility requires a different mode of governing, managing and execution. It requires practical wisdom that immediately grasps the essence of a challenge, able to communicate it and jointly search for solutions. It should not be forgotten that true wisdom of knowledge manifests itself in concrete action, materializing a visionary dream communicated in an appealing narrative.

Allow us to refer to an the example of Japanese Airlines' debacle and its turnaround. Why JAL? Because the Japanese culture is based on certain "Asian" features of discreteness, harmony conscious, and consensus-oriented, still quite hierarchical, and where necessary candid and always pragmatically purposeful. All ingredients that could be useful for a slightly different context like Indonesia with nonetheless similar commonalities to share. Japanese Airlines' turnaround in 2010 illustrates the interactions that took place at the board, the organizational, inter-organizational, team and individual levels. It is obvious that the leadership of chairman Kazuo Inamori (who had founded the successful Kyocera corporations in 1959)– as chairman, taking the lead in this crisis – played a pivotal role in the turnaround. He took a very hands-on approach and started monthly meetings with the top 30 managers of JAL, and "educated" those top executives in accepting a business philosophy that was less aloof than the usual state-owned enterprise attitude that characterized JAL before. The main underlying idea that was newly installed in JAL was to take full accountability and responsibility for the organization. Till 2010, no one had taken responsibility for making profits which had resulted in JAL mounting huge losses that led to its bankruptcy. The whole turnaround exercise that took two years was steered to introduce self-supporting management systems and rehabilitate the trust between top executives and unionised labour. JAL's philosophy successfully took over, adapted and internalized Inamori's adage which he originally developed at Kyocera: "the Result of Life and Work = Attitude x Effort x Ability". *Attitude* refers to the state of mind and belief system and philosophy of each individual; the *effort* was the passionate involvement in what people do and the dedication of one's work; whereas the *ability* implies the talent and intelligence of the individual. Relentless pushing forward with embracing the work ethics demanded, aligned with each one's ability and an attitude of resilience and strong ethical values as a team enabled the turnaround of this venerable airline. Maybe the Indonesian national airline Garuda could learn a thing or two from this example.

This book has outlined the importance of practising good corporate governance for any corporation or organization. Be it because of reduction of risks, or because creating a certain feeling of procedural justice among all shareholders and stakeholders for properly following and applying processes for important investment decisions, or making sure that the board has the necessary expertise and experience in house to make informed decisions, or take advantage of the legal board structures. All that contributes to realizing the purpose of business, as in creating value for customers, partners and their employees alike. Such creation and sharing of value is quite sensible from a business view, and contributes to daily life of all those [stakeholders]. An organization will survive and thrive because its strategy is embedded in a greater cause beyond mere profit maximization that only benefits the capital providers. Having said that, those investors should be decently rewarded for the risks they took to invest in the organization, together with the founding owners who may still have a "stake" (in this case, literally, assets or stock) in the organization. Business – like any living organism – is about finding a balance between self-interest and fitting into a bigger eco-system. Only in this balancing dialectic act of synthesis one can hope that a feeling of harmony within boards and their organization – embedded in a cultural and broader context – may arise.

And yes, success is only possible through the trial-and-error method. As any entrepreneur will admit, the success of a product is usually the result of many misses and mistakes. The famous statement by the founder of Honda sounds here appropriate: "Success is the 1 percent that is supported by 99 percent failure". Walt Disney went through similar experience in his early days. And there are numerous examples both in the West as in Asia or anywhere for that matter. It seems to be what life is all about: trying, failing, being resilient, trying again, and in some instances succeeding . . . Now, effective boards can help executives and employees to swiftly learn from those mistakes through learning and honest plus fair feedback systems in the organization, or can attempt to limit those failures by following some procedures. Being committed to fulfil the fiduciary duties of care, loyalty and prudence allow boards to advise and supervise executives. Determining the risk appetite at beforehand to avoid too risky attempts could have turned things differently for the unfortunate.

A steering board will connotate the analytical tools but also synthesize contradictions and dialectically integrates them to make informed decisions that benefit the organization. At the same time, a deep-seated narrative of the organizational purpose is clearly and consistently communicated by this board, speaking to the hearts of the stakeholders involved, both customers and employees, as well as suppliers, distributors and the community at large. An eco-system only survives when the different elements are balanced, as in a *yin* and *yang* synthesis. That is also true for an organization where boards are the ultimate arbiters and guardians to secure its survival. An effective board provides the space for executives, employees and partners to thrive and to be creative, to get excited to make innovative products or services, and thus to prosper. Kiichiro Toyoda, the founder of Toyota, strongly believed in an open debate seeking consensus through hierarchy, whereby each person who fulfils his or her duties thoroughly will generate great power through gathering together, whereby a chain of such power will lead to a ring of power. Indeed, the contribution of a good team – as a well-functioning boardroom – is greater than the sum of the contribution of each individual member. When a problem arises, everyone is accountable, and all its members have the responsibility and the authority to find a solution. When everyone feels that power, and uses it responsibly, they know that they count, and change will occur, behaviour will become less self-centred. A unit or even an organization that aims to maximize only its profits, and engages in exploitative behaviour, can easily trigger further self-centred and destructive behaviour, undermining any meaningful narrative.

What does make a board successful? Fulfilling its purpose and mission-vision, a board must have the right people and team, the right information and right structures and processes in place. Assessing a board's stewardship is evaluated by its success in meeting its mandated goals on strategy, CEO selection, and installing an organizational culture that can be perceived as balanced and harmonious to a certain extent. Governance puts up the first barricades against threatening risks from whatever nature. Second, governance safeguards continuity and sustainability by preparing for the future.

Concretely, the [supervisory] board's fiduciary obligation includes monitoring the executives' performance and advising the CEO. Compliance to rules and regulations is obviously necessary but a boardroom does much more. Good corporate governance transcends fulfilling the minimal legal requirements. Boards are also providing connections and a broader perspective to the world, giving meaning and sense to the organization, instilling a worthy organizational culture. Above all, context matters and gives credit to a practicality and action: the reality of board effectiveness is found in the interaction where lofty governance principles meet the practical and often ambiguous details in properly governing an organization within its unique socio-cultural and industry specific environment. Creating, sharing and capturing value allows individuals and organizations to thrive. In creating value, mindful leaders show confident humility while accepting uncertainty as a potential and not as threat. Allowing an entrepreneurial and creative spirit to blossom, will probably result in innovations. And when leadership does succeed, we should applaud for their efforts and courage to take those risks. Indeed, an effective board and its leadership function as a steward and guardian, and in their efforts to wisely steer the organization, they will possibly succeed to enrich their shareholders and serve stakeholders in a thriving community.

Epilogue: The Relevance of Leadership in a Changing World

The concept of leadership is a much-used word when discussing the strength of an organization both in terms of its competitive positioning and in terms of its adaptive capability. Books and journal articles give ample advice on beefing up the overall leadership within an organization.

Leadership as an academic discipline has evolved over decennia, thereby shifting a focus on the importance of individual leadership (the CEO as "our" hero) to a more multilayered focus on the importance of embedding leadership and leadership skills throughout the entire organization. Clearly, this book belongs to the latter tradition. In this epilogue, I want to make four reflections on the importance of leadership at the Board level of companies and why, for me, this book adds additional value to the overcrowded scene of leadership books.

Firstly, Peter and Tanri explicitly embed the importance of leadership within the context of the Boardroom. This might seem logical, but many writings on corporate governance focus perhaps too much on compliance issues in general and the fiduciary duties of board members. The authors rightfully claim that leadership is much more and that board members must fully embrace the leadership challenge to make their organizations future-proof.

Secondly and by focusing on the level of the "boardroom", a more holistic picture of what makes an organization successful is created. And this is much needed. Many discussions on leadership zoom in at the managerial level of an organization, whether this is on senior/top, middle, or frontline management. Developing leadership at the Board level and upgrading corporate governance may create the much-needed leverage to really change organizations. A more strategic and effective Board will be an essential and positive lever management teams can use to make better decisions and implement strategic choices. We sometimes forget that what happens (or not happens) at the Board level creates the context in which the "rest" of the organization must work. It is an essential part of what the late management guru Sumantra Ghoshal called the "smell of the place", which refers to the level of vitality within an organization. Effective boards instill confidence in the organization and ensure that management is empowered to take action and work in unison, thereby creating healthy organizations.

The third reflection relates to the contextualization the authors are offering. The book focuses on developing guidelines for effective leadership in Southeast Asia in general, focusing specifically on Indonesia. This bracketing allows for offering specific advice and guidelines to companies and organizations operating in this context. The dominance of family-owned businesses and state-owned enterprises with their dual-tier board structure calls for adapting generally accepted norms for corporate governance and leadership. This is exactly what this book tries to do.

Much of the mainstream literature on leadership is developed using examples and research from an Anglo-Saxon context. In this context, one-tier boards are much more common, CEOs are often very "powerful," combining different roles (Chairman/president), and stock markets tend to have a more dominant position in the governance of enterprises. Of course, some general principles (transparency, fairness, accountability & responsibility) are valid in all contexts. But, how to translate them? How to bring them into practice and embed these general principles in the functioning of Indonesian and Southeast Asia? The cases discussed in the book learn that some companies like Telkom had some success whereas others like Garuda, the national carrier, face serious challenges. The authors also emphasize the different leadership challenges that distinguish family business from a state-owned enterprises.

My final reflection stresses the importance of effective boards in volatile times. The strength and the health of an organization can only be adequately assessed when it is "under pressure". In stable times, any board will do. In fast-changing and volatile environments, the pressure on boards mounts as well. And it is exactly here that Peter and Tanri ask the one million dollar question: "Is your Boardroom future-proof?". In the midst of geopolitical shakeups, technological evolution, and the push to become a truly sustainable company, many organizations are challenged in unprecedented ways. Especially the ESG (Environmental, Social & Governance) reality will have a huge impact on how companies and enterprises are managed, whatever their institutional context. Successful companies need to go beyond shareholders' primacy and must build strategies based on stakeholder engagement and societal stewardship. These trends are pushing Boards to the limits and call for more leadership in the Boardroom. There is a clear need for mindful board members, as the authors claim. And mindful is probably the correct word to use here. It goes beyond taking into account what is happening in the broader environment. Mindful action also calls for a different mindset, reflective practice, and openness to experiment (and build a better future).

Understanding the dynamics of successful organizations is like being on a quest. It probably never ends. Organizations are open and social systems that cannot be managed or governed using simple theories and recipes. Hence, this book invites you to start your own leadership journey and become more mindful of your role in the functioning of a company. Enjoy the ride!

Prof. dr. Koen Vandenbempt
Dean of the Faculty of Business and Economics at the University of Antwerp,
Belgium
April 2022

Bibliography

Abbott, K.W. & D. Snibal, (2000), "Hard and soft law in international governance", *International Organization*, Vol. 54(3): 421–456.

Adams, R.B.; Hermalin, B.E. & M.S. Weisbach, (2010), "The role of boards of directors in corporate governance: A conceptual framework and survey", *Journal of Economic Literature*, Vol. 48(1): 58–107

Addy, C.; Chorengel, M; Collins, M. & M. Etzel, (2019), "Calculating the Value of Impact Investing. An evidence-based way to estimate social & environmental return", *Harvard Business Review*, Jan-Febr: 102–109

Adegbite, E., (2015), "Good corporate governance in Nigeria: antecedents, propositions and peculiarities", *International Business Review*, Vol. 24: 319–330

Agrawal, A. & CR Knoeber, (1996), "Firm Performance and Mechanisms to control agency problems between managers and shareholders", *Journal of Financial and Quantitative Analysis*, Vol. 31(3): 377–397

Aguilera, R.V., (2005), "Corporate governance and director accountability: an institutional comparative perspective", *British Journal of Management*, Vol.16 (S39-S53)

Aguilera, R.V. & A. Cuervo-Cazurra, (2004), "Codes of good governance worldwide: what is the trigger?", *Organization Studies*, Vol. 25(3): 415–443

Aguilera, R.V. & A. Cuervo-Cazurra, (2009), "Codes of Governance", Corporate Governance: An International Review", Vol. 17(3): 376–387

Aguilera, R.V. & R. Crespi-Cladera, (2016), "Global corporate governance: on the relevance of firms' ownership structure", *Journal of World Business*, Vol. 51: 50–57

Aguilera, R.V.; Desender, K.A. & L.R, Kabbach de Castro, (2012), "A bundle perspective to comparative corporate governance" in Clark,Th & D. Branson (Eds), *The Sage Handbook of Corporate Governance*, Chapter 17: 379–405

Aguilera, R.V.; Desender, K.A.; Bednar, M.K. & J.H. Lee, (2015), "Connecting the dots: Bringing external corporate governance into the corporate governance puzzle", *Academy of Management Annals*, Vol.9(1): 483–573

Aguilera, R.V. & K. A. Desender, (2012), "Challenges in measuring of comparative corporate governance: a Review of the main indices", *Research Methodology in Strategy and Management*, Vol. 8: 289–321

Aguilera, R.V.; Filatotchev, I.; Gospel, H. & G. Jackson, (2008), "An organizational approach to comparative governance: costs, contingencies, and complementarities", *Organizational Science*, Vol. 19(3): 475–492

Aguilera, R.V. & G. Jackson, (2002), "Hybridization and Heterogeneity across National Models of Corporate Governance", *Economic Sociology: European Electronic Newsletter*, ISSN 1871-3351, Vol.3 (2):17–22

Aguilera, R.V. & G. Jackson, (2003), "The cross-national diversity of corporate governance: dimensions and determinants", *Academy of Management Review*, Vol. 28(2): 447–483

Aguilera, R.V. & G. Jackson, (2010), "Comparative and International Corporate Governance", *The Academy of Management Annals*, Vol. 4(1): 485–556

Anderson, A. & P.P. Gupta, (2009), "A cross-country comparison of corporate governance and firm performance: Do financial structure and legal system matter?", *Journal of Contemporary Accounting and Economics*, Vol. 5: 61–79

Andiani, S. & B. Frensidy, (2015), "The effect of Price Earnings Ratio and Institutional Ownership on Stock Returns of LQ45 Stocks in Indonesia Stock Exchange (2008–2013)", Working Paper presented at International Accounting Conference in Bandung, Nov 2015.

Amman, M.; Oesch, D. & M.M. Schmid, (2011), "Corporate Governance and Firm Value: International evidence", *Journal of Empirical Finance*, Vol. 18: 36–55

Aoki, M., (2001a), *Towards a comparative institutional analysis*, Cambridge-MA, MIT Press.

Aoki, M., (2001b), *Information, corporate governance, and institutional diversity*, Oxford, Oxford, University Press.

Argüden, Y., (2009), *Boardroom Secrets. Corporate Governance for Quality in Life*, Hamsphire, Palgrave Macmillan.

Arora, A.; Harrison, A.; Plotkin, C.L.; Magni, M. J. Stanley, (2022), "The new B2B growth equation", *McKinsey & Company*, February.

Arryman, A. & Y. Indrayadi, (2005), "A Model of Corporate's Board Supervision over procurement processes: Case of an Indonesian State-Owned Enterprise", Working Paper presented at 1st International Conference on Operations and Supply Chain Management, Bali.

Attig, N.; Guedhami, O. & D. Mishra, (2008), "Multiple large shareholders, control contests, and implied cost of equity, *Journal of Corporate Finance*, Vol. 14: 721–737

Atilano, J.; López, P. & J.M.S. Santos, (2014), "Does corruption have social roots? The role of culture and social capital", *Journal of Business Ethics*, Vol. 122: 697–708. DOI: 10.1007/s10551-013-1789-9

Badaracco, J.L., (2013), *The Good Struggle. Responsible Leadership in an Unforgiving World*, Cambridge MA, Harvard Bus School Press.

Badaracco, J.L., (2016), *Managing in the Gray. Timeless questions for resolving your toughest problems at work*, Cambridge MA, Harvard Business School Press.

Bailey, C. & A. Shantz, (2018), "Creating an ethically strong organization", *MIT Sloan Management Review*, Summer.

Bainbridge, S.M., (2003), *Agency, Partnership and Limited Liability Companies*, New York, Foundation Press.

Balasubramanian, B.; Black, B. & V. Khanna, (2010), "The relationship between firm level corporate governance and market value: a study of India", *Working Paper at the University of Michigan Law School*, 4-1-2010

Ball, R., (2001), "Infrastructure requirements for an economically efficient system of public financial reporting and disclosure", Brookings – Wharton Papers on Financial Services, 127–169

Ball, R.; Robin, A. & J.S. Wu, (2003), "Incentives versus standards: properties of accounting income in four East Asian countries", *Journal of Accounting and Economics*, Vol. 36: 235–270

Balsmeier, B. & D. Czarnitzki, (2011), "Ownership concentration, Institutional Development and Firm Performance in Central and Easter Europe", *Discussion Paper No.10-1096 at ZEW* (Centre for European Research)

Barth, J.; Lin, C.; Lin, P. & F. Song, (2009), "Corruption in bank lending to firms: cross-country micro evidence on the beneficial role of competition and information sharing", *Journal of Financial Economics*, Vol. 91: 361-388

Barton, D. & M. Wiseman, (2015), "Where boards fall short. New data shows that most directors do not understand the company's strategy", *Harvard Business Review*, January-February: 98–104

Baughn, C.; Bodie, N.; Buchanan, M. & M. Bixby, (2010), "Bribery in International business transactions", *Journal of Business Ethics*, Vol. 92: 15–32

Bazerman, M. H., (2014) "Becoming a first-class notice", *Harvard Business Review*, 92(7–8): 116–119.

Bazerman, M. H. & M.R. Banaj, (2004) "The social psychology of ordinary ethical failures", *Social Justice Research*, 17(2):111–115.

Bazerman, M.H. & A.H. Tenbrunsel, (2011), "Ethical Breakdowns. Good people often let bad things happy. Why?", *Harvard Business Review*, April: 58–65

Bebchuk, L., (2009), "Long-term performance is key", *Harvard Business Review*, September: 40–47
Bebchuk, L., (2021), "Don't let the Short-Termism Bogeyman scare you", *Harvard Business Review*, January-February: 42–47
Bebchuk, L.; Kraakman, R. & G. Triantis, (2000), "Stock pyramids, cross ownership, and dual class equity: the creation and agency costs of separating control from cash flow rights", in Morck, R.K. (ed), *Concentrated Corporate Ownership*, Chicago, University of Chicago Press.
Bebchuk, L. & J. Fried, (2004), *Pay Without Performance. The Unfulfilled Promise of Executive Compensation*, Harvard University Press, Cambridge MA.
Bebchuk, L.; Cohen, A. & A. Ferrell, (2004), "What matter in corporate governance?", Working Paper Harvard Law School.
Bebchuk, L. & A. Cohen, (2005), "The costs of entrenched boards", *Journal of Financial Economics*, Vol. 78: 409–433.
Bebchuk, L.; Cohen, A. & A. Ferrell, (2009), "What matters in corporate governance", *Review of Financial Studies*, Vol. 22: 783–827.
Bebchuk, L. & A. Hamdani, (2009), "The elusive quest for global governance standards", *University of Pennsylvania Law Review*, Vol. 157 (5):1263–1317 http://www.law.upenn.edu/lrev/.
Bebchuk, L. & M. Weisbach, (2010), "The State of Corporate Governance Research", *The Review of Financial Studies*, Vol. 23(3): 939–961.
Bennedsen, M.; Hoffmann, A.; Hoffmann, R.; Hrnjic, E. & Y. Wiwattanakantang, (2013), *East meets West: Rotschild's Investment in Indonesia's Bakrie Group*, INSEAD, Case no 113-065-1.
Berglof, E. & E. Perotti, (1994), "The Governance structure of Japanese financial keiretsu", *Journal of Finance Economics*, Vol. 36: 259–284.
Berle, A.A. & G.C. Means, (1932), *The modern corporation and the private property*, New York, Harcourt Brace; and (1967), Columbia University Press.
Bertini, M; Pineda, J.; Petzke, A. & J-M. Izaret, (2021), "Can we afford sustainable business?", *MIT Sloan Management Review*, Fall, Vol. 63(1): 25–33
Bertrand, M., Johnson, S., Samphantharak, K. & Schoar, A., (2008). Mixing family with business: A study of Thai business groups and the families behind them. *Journal of Financial Economics*, 88(3), 466–498
Bettenmann, D.; Giones, F.; Brem, A. & P. Gneiting, (2022), "Break out to Open Innovation", *MIT Sloan Management Review*, Winter, Vol. 63(2): 39–43
Bhagat, S. & B. Black, (2002), "The non-correlation between board independence and long term firm performance", *Journal of Corporation Law*, Vol.27: 231–274
Bhagat, S. & B. Bolton, (2008), "Corporate Governance and Firm Performance", *Journal of Corporate Finance*, Vol. 14: 257–273
Biondi, Y. & A. Reberioux, (2012), "The governance of intangibles: Rethinking financial reporting and the board of directors", *Accounting Forum*, Vol. 36: 279–293
Björnberg, A. & C. Feser, (2015), "CEO succession starts with developing your leaders", *McKinsey Quarterly*.
Black, B.S.; Jang, H. & W. Kim, (2006), "Does corporate governance affect firms' market values? Evidence from Korea", *Journal of Law, Economics and Organization*, Vol.22(2): 366–413
Bloomfield, S., (2013), *Theory and Practice of Corporate Governance. An integrated approach*, Cambridge, Cambridge University Press.
Boesso, G. & Kumar, K. (2005). Drivers of corporate voluntary disclosure: A framework and empirical evidence from Italy and the United States, *Accounting, Auditing & Accountability Journal*, 20(2),269–296.
Boubakri, N.; Guedhami, O. & D. Mishra, (2010), "Family control and the implied cost of equity: Evidence before and after the Asian financial crisis", *Journal of International Business Studies*, Vol. 41: 451–474

Bower, J.C. & L.S. Paine, (2017), "The error at the heart of corporate leadership", *Harvard Business Review*, May June: 50–60.

Bradley, C.; Hirt, M. & S. Smit, (2018), *Strategy beyond the Hockey Stick. People, Probabilities, and big moves to beat the odds*, New York, Wiley & Sons - McKinsey & Company.

Brown, R.A., (2006), "Indonesian Corporations, Cronyism, and Corruption", *Modern Asian Studies*, Vol. 40 (4): 953–992

Brown, L.; Caylor, M., (2006), "Corporate Governance and Firm Valuation", *Journal Accountancy Public Policy*, Vol.25: 409–434

Bruno, V. & S. Claessens, (2010), "Corporate Governance and Regulation: can there be too much of good thing?", Journal of Finance Intermediation, Vol.19: 1789–1825

Bushee, B.J., (1998), "The influence of Institutional Investors in Myopic R&D Investment Behavior", *The Accounting Review*, Vol. 73(3): 305–333

Bushman, R.M. & A.J. Smith, (2001), "Financial Accounting Information and Corporate Governance", *Journal of Accounting and Economics*, Vol. 32: 237–333

Campos, J.E.; Lien, D. & S. Pradhan, (1999), "The impact of corruption on investment: predictability matters", *World Development*, Vol. 27 (6): 1059–1067.

Carter, C.B. & J.W. Lorsch, (2004), *Back to the Drawing Board. Designing Corporate Boards for a complex world*, Boston MA, Harvard Business School Publishing.

Chacar, A. & B. Vissa, (2005), "Are emerging economies less efficient? Performance persistence and the impact of business group affiliation", *Strategic Management Journal*, Vol. 26: 933–946.

Chalmers. D., (2022), *Reality+. Virtual Worlds and the Problem of Philosophy*, Dublin, Allen Lane – Penguin.

Chambers, P. & P. Verhezen, (2016), "Case studies in Indonesia", in Verhezen, P.; Williamson, I.O.; Crosby, M. & N. Soebagjo, *Doing Business ASEAN markets. Leadership challenges and Governance solutions across borders*, London, Palgrave MacMillan: 89–108

Chang, S., (2003), "Ownership structure, expropriation, and performance of group-affiliated companies in Korea", *Academy of Management Journal*, Vol. 46(2): 238–254

Chang, Y.C.; Kao, M-S. & A. Kuo, (2014), "The Influences of governance quality on equity-based entry mode choice: The strengthening role of family control", *International Business Review*, Vol. 23: 1008–1020.

Charan, R. (1998), *Boards that work. How corporate boards create competitive advantage*, San Fransisco, Jossey Bass.

Charan, R., (2005), *Boards that deliver. Advancing corporate governance – from compliance to competitive advantage*, San Fransisco, Jossey Bass.

Charan, R., (2016), "The secrets of Great CEO Selection", *Harvard Business Review*, December: 52–59.

Charan, R., Carey, D. & M. Useem, (2014), *Boards that Lead. When to take charge, when to partner, and when to stay out the way*, Cambridge (MA), Harvard Business Review Press.

Chen, K.C.W.; Chen, Z. & K.C.J. Wei, (2009), "Legal protection of investors, corporate governance, and the cost of equity capital", *Journal of Corporate Finance*, Vol. 15: 273–289.

Chen, CJP; Ding, Y. & C. Kim, (2010), "High-level politically connected firms, corruption, and analyst forecast accuracy around the world", *Journal of International Business Studies*, Vol. 10: 1505–1524.

Chen, V.Z.; Li, J. & D.M. Shapiro, (2011), "Are OECD-prescribed "good corporate governance practices" really good in an emerging economy", *Asia Pacific Journal of Management*, Vol. 28: 115–138 / DOI: 10.1007/s10490-010-9206-8.

Chen, C. & yu, C., (2012). Managerial ownership, diversification, and firm performance: evidence from an emerging market. *International Business Review*. 21. 518–534.

Cheng, J. Y-J; Groysberg, B. & P. Healy, (2020), "Your CEO Succession Plan can't wait", Harvard Business Review, May.
Cheung, Y-L; Jiang, P.; Limpaphayom, P. & T. Lu, (2008), "Does corporate governance matter in China?", *China Economic Review*, Vol. 19: 460–479
Cheung, Y-L; Connelly, J.T.; Estanislao, J.P.; Limpaphayom, P.; Lu, T. & S. Utama, (2014), "Corporate governance and Firm Valuation in Asian Emerging Markets" in Boubaker, S. & DK Nguyen (eds), *Corporate Governance in Emerging Markets*, Berlin, Springer / DOI: 10.1007/978-3-642-44955-0_2.
Chew, D.E. & S.L. Gillan, (2009), *Global Corporate Governance*, New York, Columbia University Press.
Churchland, P.S., (2019), *Conscience. The Origins of Moral Intuition*, New York; London, Norton & Company.
Claessens, S.; Djankov, S. & L.H.P. Lang, (2000), "The separation of ownership and control in East Asian Corporations", *Journal of Financial Economics*, Vol.58: 81–112.
Claessens, S.; Djankov, S.; Fan, JPH. & LHP. Lang, (2002), "Disentangling the incentive and entrenchment effects of large shareholders", *Journal of Finance*, Vol. 57: 2741–2771.
Claessens, S. & B.B. Yurtoglu, (2013), "Corporate Governance in emerging markets: A survey", *Emerging Markets Review*, Vol. 15: 1–33.
Clarke, Thomas, (2007), *International Corporate Governance. A comparative Approach*, London; New York, Routledge.
Coles, J.W.; McWilliams, V.B. & N. Sen, (2001), "An examination of the relationship of governance mechanisms to performance", *Journal of Management*, Vol. 27 (1): 23–50.
Coreynen, W.; Matthyssens, P. & W. Van Bockhaven, (2017), "Boosting servitization through digitization: pathways and dynamic resource configurations for manufacturers", Industrial Marketing Management, Vol. 60: 42–53.
Cyert, R.M. & J.G. March, (1963), *A Behavioral Theory of the Firm*, Englewood Cliffs, NJ., Prentice Hall.
Deci, E. L., & A.C. Moller,(2005), "The Concept of Competence: A Starting Place for Understanding Intrinsic Motivation and Self-Determined Extrinsic Motivation", in Elliot, A.J. & C. S. Dweck (Eds.), *Handbook of competence and motivation* (pp. 579–597). New York, Guilford Publications.
De Haes, S.; Caluwe, L; Huygh, T. & A. Joshi, (2020), *Governing Digital Transformation. Guidance for Corporate Board Members*, Cham, Springer.
Dela Rama, M., (2012), "Corporate Governance and Corruption: Ethical Dilemmas of Asian Business Groups", *Journal of Business Ethics*, Vol.109 (4): 501–519.
Demsetz, H. & K. Lehn, (1985), "The structure of corporate ownership: Causes and consequences", *Journal of Political Economy*, Vol.33: 3–53.
Demsetz, H. & B. Villalonga, (2001), "Ownership structure and corporate performance", *Journal of Corporate Finance*, Vol.7: 209–233.
Desender, K.A.; Aguilera, R.V.; Crespi, R. & M.A. Garcia—Cestona, (2011), "Board characteristics and audit fees: When does ownership matter?", Working Paper.
De Smet, A.; Lund, F.; Weiss, L. & s. Nimocks, (2021), "Boards and decision-making", *McKinsey & Company*, April.
Detert, J. & E. Bruno, (2021), "The courage to be candid", *MIT Sloan Management Review*, Summer, Vol. 62(4): 66–73.
Dhnadirek, R. & J. Tang, (2003), "Corporate governance problems in Thailand: is ownership concentration the cause?", *Asia Pacific Business Review*, Vol. 10(2): 121–138.
Djankov, S.; Lopez-de-Silanes, F.; la Porta, R.L. & A. Schleifer, (2008), "The Law and economics of self-dealing", *Journal of Financial Economics*, Vol. 88: 430–465.

Doidge, C.; Karolyi, G.; Stulz, R., (2007), "Why do countries matter so much for corporate governance?", *Journal of Finance Economics*, Vol. 86: 1–39.

Douma, S.; George, R. & R. Kabir, (2006), "Foreign and domestic ownership, business groups and firm performance: evidence from a large emerging market", *Strategic Management Journal*, Vol. 27: 637–657.

Duckworth, A.,(2017), *Grit. Why passion and resilience are the secrets to success*, London, Vermillion.

Durnev, A. & E.H. Kim, (2005), "To steal or not to steal: firm attributes, legal attributes, legal environment and valuation", *Journal of Finance*, Vol.60: 1461–1493.

Dvorak, T., (2005), "Do Domestic Investors have an Information Advantage? Evidence from Indonesia", *The Journal of Finance*, April, Vol.LX (2): 817–839.

Dweck, C.S., (2006), *Mindset: the new psychology of success*, New York, Random House.

Dyck, A. & L. Zingales, (2004), "Private benefits of control: an international comparison", *Journal of Finance*, Vol. 59: 537–600.

Edmondson, A. & R. Gulati, (2022), "Agility hacks. How to create temporary teams that can bypass bureaucracy and get crucial work done quickly", *Harvard Business Review Special Issue*, Cambridge MA, Harvard University, Spring: 49–53.

Eisenhardt, K.M., (1989), "Agency Theory: An Assessment and Review", *Academy of Management Review*.

Englisch, P., (2021), "Family Businesses have an opportunity to lead on ESG", *Strategy + Business* (PWC), July 28.

Erdmann, D.; Sichel, B. & L. Yeung, (2015), "Overcoming obstacles to effective scenario planning", *McKinsey & Company*, June.

Faccio, M., (2006), "Politically connected firms", *American Economic Review*, Vol. 96: 369–386.

Faccio, M. & L.H.P. Lang, (2002), "The Separation of Ownership and Control: an analysis of Ultimate Ownership in Western European Corporations", *Journal of Financial Economics*, Vol. 65: 365–395.

Faccio, M.; Lang, L. & L. Young, (2001), "Dividends and Expropriation", *American Economic Review*, Vol. 91(1): 54–71.

Fahy, M; Roche, J. & A. Weiner, (2005), *Beyond Governance. Creating Corporate Value through Performance, Conformance and Responsibility*, Sussex, John Wiley & Sons.

Fama, E., (1980), "Agency problems and the theory of the firm", *Journal of Political Economy*, Vol. 88: 288–307.

Fama, E. & M. Jensen, (1983a), "Separation of ownership and control", *Journal of Law and Economics*, Vol. 26: 301–325.

Fama, E. & M. Jensen, (1983b), "Agency problems and residual claims", *Journal of Law and Economics*, Vol. 26: 327–349.

Fan, J.P.H. & T.J. Wong, (2004), "Do external auditors perform a corporate governance role in emerging markets? Evidence from East Asia", *Journal of Accounting Research*, Vol. 43: 35–72.

Fan, J.P.H. & Wei, J.K.C. & X. Xu, (2011), "Corporate Finance and governance in emerging markets: a selective review and an agenda for future research", *The Journal of Corporate Finance*, Vol. 17(2): 207–214.

Farinha, J., (2003), "Dividend policy, Corporate Governance and the Managerial Entrenchment Hypothesis: an empirical analysis", *Journal of Financial Economics*, Vol. 60(1): 3–45.

Farinha, J. & O. Lopez de Foronda, (2005), "The relation between dividends and insider ownership in different legal systems: International evidence", *Working Paper Universidade do Porto*, DP 2005-09.

Farrar, J., (2005), *Corporate Governance. Theories, Principles, and Practice*, Melbourne, Oxford University Press.

Felton, R.F.; Hudnut, A. & V. Witt, (1995), "Building a stronger board", *The McKinsey Quarterly*, 2: 163–175.

Fich, E. & A. Shivdasani, (2006), "Are busy boards effective monitors"", *Journal of Finance*, Vol. 61: 689–724.

Filatotchev, I.; Lien, Y.C & J. Piesse, (2005), "Corporate governance and performance in publicly listed, family-controlled firms: Evidence from Taiwan", *Asia Pacific Journal of Management*, Vol. 22: 257–283.

Filatotchev, I.; Strange, R.; Piesse, J. & Y.C. Lien, (2007), "FDI by firms from newly industrialized economies in emerging markets: Corporate governance, entry mode and location", *Journal of International Business Studies*, Vol. 38(4): 556–572.

Filatotchev, I; Jackson, G. & C. Nakajima, (2013), "Corporate governance and national institutions: a review and emerging research agenda", *Asia Pacific Journal of Management*, Vol. 30(4): 965–986.

Francis, J.; Khurana, I & R. Pereira, (2005), "Disclosure incentives and effects on cost of capital around the world", *Accounting Review*, Vol. 80: 1125–1162.

Freeman, E., (1984), *Strategic Management: A Stakeholder Approach*, Boston, Pitman.

Frydlinger, D.; Hart, O. & K. Vitasek, (2019), "A new approach to contracts. How to build better long-term strategic partnerships", *Harvard Business Review*, Nov-Dec: 116–125.

Garcia-Castro, R.; Aguilera, R.V. & M.A. Ariño, (2013), "Bundles of Firm Corporate Governance Practices: A fuzzy set analysis", *Corporate Governance: An International Review*.

Ghazali, N.A.M., (2010), "Ownership structure, corporate governance and corporate performance in Malaysia", *International Journal of Commerce*, Vol. 20(2): 109–119.

Gill, A., (2003), "Corporate Governance Issues and Returns in Emerging Markets", in Litan, R.; Pomerleano, M. & V. Sundararajan, *The future of domestic capital markets in developing countries*, Brookings Institution Press. http://www.jstor.org/stable/10.7864/j.ctt12814q.16

Gillan, S.; Hartzell, J. & L. Starks, (2003), "Explaining corporate governance: Boards, bylaws, and charter provisions", *Working Paper, University of Texas at Austin*.

Gillan, S. & L. Starks, (2003), "Corporate Governance, Corporate Ownership, and the Role of Institutional Investors: A global perspective", *Journal of Applied Finance*, Fall-Winter, pp.4–21.

Gilson, R.J., (2006), "Controlling shareholders and corporate governance: complicating the comparative taxonomy", *Harvard Law Review*, Vol. 116(6): 1641–1679.

Gino, Fr., (2019), "Cracking the Code of Sustained Collaboration. Six new tools for training people to work together better", *Harvard Business Review*, Nov-Dec: 72–81.

Globerman, S.; Peng, M.W. & D.M. Shapiro, (2011), "Corporate governance and Asian companies", *Asia Pacific Journal of Management*, Vol. 28: 1–14.

Gompers, P.A.; Ishii, J. & A. Metrick, (2003), "Corporate Governance and Equity Prices", *Quantitative Journal of Economics*, Vol.118: 107–155.

Granovetter, M., (1985), "Economic action and social structure: the problem of embeddedness", *American Journal of Sociology*, Vol. 91(3): 481–510.

Granovetter, M., (1995), "Coase revisited: Business groups in the Modern Economy", *Industrial and Corporate Change*, 2(4): 93–130.

Grossman, S.J. & O.D. Hart, (1988), "One share-one vote and the market of corporate control", *Journal of Financial Economics*, Vol. 20: 175–202.

Guedhami, O. & J.A. Pittman, (2006), "Ownership concentration in privatized firms: The role of disclosure standards, auditor choice, and auditing infrastructure", *Journal of Accounting Research*, Vol. 44: 889–929.

Guedhami, O. & J.A. Pittman, (2011). "The choice between private and public capital markets: The importance of disclosure standards and auditor discipline to countries divesting state owned enterprises", *Journal of Accounting and Public Policy*, Vol. 30: 395–430.

Gupta, S., (2018), *Driving Digital Strategy. A guide to reimagining your business*, Boston MA, Harvard Business School Press.

Habib, M. & L. Zurawicki, (2002), "Corruption and foreign direct investment", *Journal of International Business Studies*, Vol.33(2): 322–340.

Habir, M., (2016), "Corporate Governance in the Indonesian Banking sector", in Verhezen, P.; Williamson, I.O.; Crosby, M. & N. Soebagjo, *Doing Business ASEAN markets. Leadership challenges and Governance solutions across borders*, London, Palgrave MacMillan. 45–64.

Hambrick, D. C., & Quigley, T. J. (2014). Toward more accurate contextualization of the CEO effect on firm performance. *Strategic Management Journal*, 35(4), 473–491.

Harjoto, M.A. & H. Jo, (2009), Why do firms engage in Corporate Social Responsibility?", Working Paper, Santa Clara University.

Hastori; Siregar, H.; Sembel, R. & N.A. Maulana, (2015) "Agency costs, corporate governance and ownership concentration: the case of Agro-Industrial companies in Indonesia", *Asian Social Science*, Vol. 11(18): 311–319.

Hawley, P. (Ed), (2010), *Corporate Governance Failures*, Londen.

Healy, P. & G. Serafeim, (2012), "Causes and consequences of firm disclosure of anti-corruption efforts", *Working Paper Harvard Business School*, 12–077, February 28.

Henry, B., (2017), "Four Simple Rules for Succession Planning", *INSEAD Knowledge Paper*: http://knowledge.insead.edu/family-business/four-simple-rules-for-succession-planning-5856.

Hermalin, B.E. & M.S. Weisbach, (2003), "Board of directors as an endogenously determined institution: A survey of the economic literature", *Economic Policy Review*, Vol.9: 7–26.

Hickel, J., (2020; 2021), *Less is More. How Degrowth will save the World*, London, Windmill-Penguin Books.

Hill, L.A.; Tedards, E. & T. Swan, (2022), "Drive innovation with better decision-making", *Harvard Business Review Special Issue*, Spring. Cambridge MA, Harvard University. 86–93.

Hillman, A.J., Cannella, A.A., & Paetzold, R. L. (2000). "The resource-dependence role of corporate directors: Strategic adaptation of board composition in response to environmental change", *Journal for Management Studies*, 37 (2): 235–255.

Hillman, A. J. & Dalziel, T. (2003). "Board of directors and firm performance: Integrating agency and resource dependence perspectives", *Academy of Management Review*, 28(3): 383–396.

Hirschman, A.O., (1970), Exit, Voice and Loyalty. Responses to decline in firms, organizations and states, Cambridge MA, Harvard University Press.

Ho, K.L. (Ed.) (2005). *Reforming corporate governance in southeast Asia: Economics, politics and regulations*, Singapore, ISEAS Publications.

Hooijberg, R. & N. Lane, (2016), "How Boards both CEO succession", *MIT Sloan Management Review*, Summer: 13–16.

Huber, C.; Leape, S.; Mark, L. & B. Simpson, (2020), "The board's role in embedding corporate purpose: Five actions directors can make today", *McKinsey & Company*, November.

Huber, C., Sukharevsky, A. & R. Zemmel, (2021), "How boards can help digital transformations", *McKinsey Digital*, June.

Huber, C.; Lund, F. & N. Spielmann, (2021), "The postpandemic board agenda: Redefining corporate resilience", *McKinsey & Company*, August.

Hunt, V.; Simpson, B. & Y. Yamada, (2020), "The case for stakeholder capitalism", *McKinsey & Company*, November.

Huse, M., (2007), *Boards, governance, and value creation: The human side of corporate governance*, Cambridge; Cambridge University Press.

Huyghebaert, N. & Wang, L. (2012), Expropriation of minority investors in Chinese listed firms: the role of internal and external corporate governance mechanisms. *Corporate Governance: An international Review*, 20, 308–332.

Jain, P.K.; Kuvvet, E. & M.S. Pagano, (2017), "Corruption's impact on foreign portfolio investment", *International Business Review*, Vol. 26: 23–35.

Jensen, M.C. & W.H. Meckling, (1976), Theory of the Firm: managerial behavior, agency costs and ownership structure, *Journal of Finance Economics*, Vol. 3: 305–360.

Jensen, M.C., (1986), "Agency cost of free cash flow, corporate finance, and takeovers", *American Economic Review*, 76, 323–329.

Jensen, M.C.,(2002), "Value maximization, stakeholder theory, and the corporate objective function", *Business Ethics Quarterly*, 12(2),235–256.

Kahneman, D. & A. Tversky, (1979), "Prospect Theory: An Analysis of Decision Under Risk", *Econometrica*, Vol. 47(2): 263–291.

Kahneman,. D., (2011a), *Thinking, Fast and Slow*, London, Penguin-Pearson.

Kahneman, D., (2011b), *"Beware the inside view"*, McKinsey Quarterly, November.

Kahneman, D. & D. Lovallo, (1993), "Timid Choices and Bold Forecasts: A Cognitive Perspective on Risk Taking", *Management Science*, Vol. 39(1): 17–31.

Kahneman, D. & G. Klein (an interview), (2010), "Strategic decisions: When can you trust your gut?", *McKinsey Quarterly*, March.

Kahneman, D.; Lovallo, D. & O. Sibony, (2011), *"Before You Make That Big Decision"*, Harvard Business Review, June: 50–60.

Kahneman, D.; Rosenfield, A.M.; Gandhi, L. & T. Blaser, (2016), *"Noise. Inconsistent Decision-making"*, Harvard Business Review, October: 38–46.

Kahneman, D.; Sibony, O. & C.R. Sunstein, (2021), *Noise. A Flaw in Human Judgment*, London, William Collins.

Kahler, M. & Lake, D.A. (Eds.) (2003). *Governance in a global economy: Political authority in Transition*, Princeton, NJ, Princeton University Press.

Kang, J-K. & J.M. Kim, (2010), "Do foreign investors exhibit a corporate governance disadvantage? An information asymmetry perspective", *Journal of International Business Studies*, Vol. 41: 1415–1438

Kaplan, R.S. & K. Ramanna, (2021), "Accounting for Climate Change. The first rigorous approach to ESG reporting", *Harvard Business Review*, November-December: 120–131.

Kaufmann, D. & S.J. Wei, (1999), "Does grease money speed up the wheels of commerce", *World Bank Policy Research Working Paper* 2254.

Kaufmann, D.; Kraay, A. & M. Mastruzzi, (2010), "The worldwide governance indicators: Methodology and Analytical Issues", *World Bank Paper*.

Keong Low, C., (2004), "A road map for corporate governance in East Asia", *Northwestern Journal of International Law & Business*, Vol. 25: 165–204

Khalil, S.; Saffar, W. & S. Trabelsi, (2015), "Disclosure standards, Auditing Infrastructure, and Bribery Mitigation", *Journal of Business Ethics*, Vol. 132(2): 379–399

Khanna, T. & K. Palepu, (2000a), "Is group affiliation profitable in emerging markets? An analysis of diversified Indian business groups", *Journal of Finance*, April Vol. 55(20): 867–893

Khanna, T. & K. Palepu, (2000b), "The future of business groups in emerging markets: long-run evidence from Chile", *Academy of Management Journal*, Vol. 43: 268–285

Khanna, T. & K. Palepu, (2006), "Strategies that fit emerging markets", *Harvard Business Review*, Vol. 84: 60–69

Khanna, T. & J.W. Rifkin, (2001), "Estimating the performance effects of business groups in emerging markets", *Strategic Management Journal*, Vol. 22: 45–74

Khanna, V. & Zyla, R., (2013), Survey says . . . corporate governance matters to investors in emerging markets companies, *IFC World Bank Paper*.

Khwaja, A.I. & A. Mian, (2005), "Do lenders favor politically connected firms? Rent provision in an emerging financial market", *Quarterly Journal of Economics*, Vol. 120: 1371–1411

Klapper, L. & I. Love, (2004), "Corporate Governance, investor protection and performance in emerging market", *Journal of Corporate Finance*, Vol. 10: 703–728

Kim, K.A.; Kitsabunnarat, P. & J.R. Nofsinger, (2004), "Ownership and operating performance in an emerging market: evidence from Thai IPO firms", *The Journal of Corporate Finance*, Vol. 10: 322–381

Kim, J.B. & C.H. Yi, (2006), "Ownership structure, business group affiliation, listing status, and earnings management: evidence form Korea", *Contemporary Accounting Research*, Vol. 23(2): 265–276

Kim, J.; Simunic, D., Stein, M. & C. Yi, (2011), "Voluntary audits and the cost of debt capital for privately held firms: Korean evidence", *Contemporary Accounting Research*, Vol. 28: 585–616

Kirkman, B.; stoverink, AC.; Mistry, A. & B. Rosen, (2022), "The four things resilient teams do", *Harvard Business Review Special Issue*, Harvard University, Cambridge MA, Spring: 57–59.

Klein, G, (1998), *Sources of Power: How People Make Decisions*, Cambridge MA, MIT Press.

Klein, G., (2003), *The Power of Intuition. How to use your gut feelings to make better decisions at work*, New York, Currency Paperback.

Klein, G. (2009). *Strengths and shadows: Searching for the keys to adaptive decision-making*, Cambridge MA, MIT Press.

Klein, G., (2014), *Seeing what others don't. The remarkable ways we gain Insights*, London; Boston, Nicolas Brealy Publishing.

Korac-Kakabadse, N.; Kakabadse, A. & A. Kouzmin, (2001), "Board governance and company performance: any correlations?", *Corporate Governance: the International Journal of business in society*, Vol. 1 (1): 24–30.

Kostikov, I. (2003). Governance in an emerging financial market: The case of Russia. In Cornelius, P.K. & Kogut, B. *Corporate governance and capital flows in a global economy*, New York, Oxford University Press, 443–450.

Kraft, T. & Y. Zheng, (2021), "How Supply Chain Transparency boosts business value", *Sloan Management Review*, Fall, Vol. 63(1): 34–40.

Kwok, C. & S. Tadesse, (2006), "The MNC as an agent of change for host country institutions: FDI and corruption", *Journal of International Business Studies*, Vol. 37(6): 767–785.

Kurtzman, J., Yago, G., & Phumiwasana, T. (2004), The global cost of opacity, *MIT Sloan Management Review*, Fall, 38–44.

Kurtzman, J. & Yago, G. (2007). *Global edge: Using the Opacity Index to manage the risks of cross-border business*, Boston, MA, Harvard Business School Press.

Lambert, R.A. & D. Larcker, (1985), "Golden Parachutes, Executive Decision-Making and Shareholder Wealth", *Journal of Accounting and Economics*, Vol (VII): 179–203.

Lambsdorff, J., (2003), "How corruption affects productivity", *Kyklos*, Vol. 56: 457–474.

Larcker, D. & B. Tayan, (2011), *Corporate Governance Matters. A closer look at organizational choices and their consequences*, New Jersey, Pearson.

La Porta, R., Lopez-De-Silanes, F. & A. Schleifer, A, (1999), "Corporate ownership around the world", *Journal of Finance*, 54(2),471–517.

La Porta, R., Lopez-De-Silanes, F., Schleifer, A.& R. Vishny, (2000), "Investor protection and corporate governance", *Journal of Financial Economics*, 58, 3–27.

La Porta, R., Lopez-De-Silanes, F., Schleifer, A.& R. Vishny, (2002), "Investor protection and corporate valuation", *Journal of Finance*, Vol. 57; 1147–1170.
Lawler, E.E.; Finegold, D; Benson, G.S. & JA Gonger, (2002), "Corporate Boards: keys to effectiveness", *Organizational Dynamics*, Vol. 30(4): 310–324.
Leblanc, R. & J. Gillies, (2005), *Inside the Boardroom. How boards really work and the coming revolution in corporate governance*, Ontario, John Wiley & Sons Canada.
Lee, S. & K. Oh, (2007), "Corruption in Asia: Pervasiveness and arbitrariness", *Asia Pacific Journal of Management*, Vol. 24(1): 97–115.
Leong, H.K. (Ed), (2005), *Reforming Corporate Governance in Southeast Asia. Economics, Politics, and Regulations*, Singapore, ISEAS.
Leuz, C., Nand, D. & P. Wysocki, (2003), "Earnings management investor protection: an international comparison", *Journal of Financial Economics*, Vol. 69: 505–527.
Leuz, C.; Lins, K.V. & F.E. Warnock, (2008), "Do foreigners invest less in poorly governed firms?", *ECGI Finance Working Paper*, No.43/2004; Febr 2008.
Levrau, A. & L. Van den Berghe, (2009), "Identifying Key Determinants of Effective Boards of Directors", in Kakadadse, A. & N. Kakadadse (eds), *Global Boards: One desire, Many realities*, London, Palgrave MacMillan, pp.9–44.
Libert, B; Beck, M & J. Wind, (2016), *The Network Imperative. How to survive and grow in the Age of Digital Business Models*, Cambridge MA, Harvard Business Review Press.
Lien, Y-C; Piesse, J.; Strange, R. & I. Filatotchev, (2005), "The role of corporate governance in FDI decisions: evidence from Taiwan", *International Business Review*, Vol. 14(6): 739–773.
Li, J.S., (2003), "Relation-based versus rules-based governance: An explanation of the East Asian miracle and Asian crisis", *Review of International Economics*, 11(4),651–662.
Lins, K.V. & H. Servaes, (2002), "Is corporate diversification beneficial in emerging markets?", *Financial Management*, Vol. 31(2): 5–31.
Lorsch, J. & R. Clark, (2008), "Leading from the Boardroom", *Harvard Business Review*, April: 104–111.
Lovallo, D. & O. Sibony, (2006), "Distortions and Deceptions in Strategic Decisions", *McKinsey Quarterly*, April, Vol. 1: 18–29.
Lovallo, D. & O. Sibony, (2010), "The case of Behavioral Strategy", *McKinsey Quarterly*, March: 30–343.
Low, C.K., (2004), "A Roadmap for corporate governance in East Asia", *Northwestern Journal of International Law & Business*, Vol. 25: 165–204.
Lozano, M.B.; Martinez, B. & J. Pindado, (2016), "Corporate governance, ownership and firm value: Drivers of ownership as a good corporate governance mechanism", *International Business Review*, Vol. 25: 1333–1343.
Lund, F., (2021), "Board and decision-making", *McKinsey & Company*, April.
Luo, Y., (2011), "Strategic responses to perceived corruption in an emerging market: lessons from MNEs investing in China", *Business & Society*, Vol. 50(2): 350–387.
Macey, J.R., (2008), *Corporate Governance. Promises Kept, Promises Broken*, New Jersey, Princeton University Press.
Macey, J.R. (2013), *The death of Corporate Reputation, How Integrity has been destroyed on Wall Street*, New Jersey, Pearson Education FT Press.
Mak, Y. & Y. Li, (2001), "Determinants of corporate ownership and board structure: evidence from Singapore", *Journal of Corporate Finance*, Vol. 7+(3): 235–256.
Mallin, C., (2004), *Corporate Governance*, Oxford, Oxford University Press.
Martin, K.D.; Cullen, J.B.; Johnson, J.L. & K.P. Parboteeah, (2007), Deciding the Bribe: A cross-level analysis of firm and home country influences on bribery activity", *Academy of Management Journal*, Vol. 50: 1401–1422.

Martin, G. P., Gomez-Mejia, L. R., & Wiseman, R. M. (2013). Executive stock options as mixed gambles: Revisiting the behavioral agency model. *Academy of Management Journal*, 56(2), 451–472.

Mauro, P., (1995), "Corruption and Growth", *Quarterly Journal of Economics*, Vol. 110 (3): 681–712.

Mauro, P., (1997), "The effects of corruption on growth, investment, and government expenditure: a cross-country analysis", in Elliott, K. (Ed), *Corruption and the Global Economy*, Washington, DC, Institute for International Economics: 83–107.

McGinn, D., (2016), "The best performing CEOs in the World", *Harvard Business Review*, November: 41–51.

Mehra, M. (2005), "Corporate governance: An alternative model" in Ho, K.L. (Ed.), chapter 1, *Reforming corporate governance in Southeast Asia: Economics, politics and regulations*, Singapore, ISEAS Publications, 3–15.

Meyer, C. & J. Kirby, (2010), "Leadership in the Age of Transparency", *Harvard Business Review*, April: 19–26.

Meyer, E., (2014), *The Culture Map*, New York, PublicAffairs.

Midanek, D.H., (2018), *The Governance Revolution. What every board member needs to know, now!*, Berlin, DeGruyter [The Alexandra Lajoux Corporate Governance Series].

Mo., P.H., (2001), "Corruption and Economic Growth", *Journal of Comparative Economics*, Vol. 29 (1): 66–79.

Mobius, M. (2003). "Corporate governance", in Cornelius, P.K. & Kogut, B. *Corporate governance and capital flows in a global economy*, New York, Oxford University Press, 401–412.

Mobius, M., (2012a), *Passport to Profits. Why the Next Investment Windfalls will be found abroad – and How to grab your share*, Singapore, John Wiley & Sons.

Mobius, M., (2012b), *The Little Book on Emerging Markets. How to make money in the world's fastest growing markets*, Singapore, John Wiley & Sons.

Moldoveanu, M. & D. Narayandas, (2016), "The Skills Gap and the Near-Far Problem in Executive Education and Leadership Development", *Working Paper Harvard Business School* 17–019.

Monks, R.A.G. & N. Minow, (2004), *Corporate Governance*, Malden, Blackwell Publi.

Morck, R.; Schleifer, A. & R. Vishny, (1998), Management ownership and market valuation: an empirical analysis", *Journal Finance Economics*, Vol. 20: 293–316.

Morck, R. & B. Yeung, (2004), "Corporate Governance and Family Control", *Global Corporate Governance Forum – World Bank, Discussion Paper no 1*.

Morewedge, C.K., (2022), "When we don't own the things we use, will be still love them?", *MIT Sloan Management Review*, Winter, Vol. 63(2): 16–18.

Moyo, D., (2021), *How Boards work. And how they can work better in a chaotic world*, London, The Bridge Street Press.

Neves, P. & J. Story, (2015), "Ethical leadership and reputation: combined indirect effects on organizational deviance", *Journal of Business Ethics*, Vol. 127: 165–176. DOI 10.1007/s10551-013-1997-3.

Newell, R. & G. Wilson, (2002), "A Premium for Good Governance", *McKinsey Quarterly*, No.3: 20–23.

North, D., (1990), *Institutions, Institutional Change, and Economic Performance*, Cambridge, Cambridge University Press.

Nonaka, I. & H. Takeuchi, (2019), *The Wise Company. How companies create continuous innovation*, Oxford, Oxford University Press.

Nonaka, I. & H. Takeuchi, (2021), Strategy as a way of life", MIT *Sloan Management Review*, Fall, Vol. 63(1): 56–63.

Notowidigdo, P. & P. Verhezen, (2012), "Leadership and Remuneration in Indonesia", in Verhezen, P.; Riyana Hardjapamekas, E. & P. Notowidigdo, *Is corporate governance relevant? How good corporate governance practices affect Indonesian organizations*, Jakarta, University of Indonesia Press: 217–246

Oberholzer-Gee, F., (2021a), "Eliminate Strategic Overload. How to select fewer initiatives with greater impact", *Harvard Business Review*, May-June: 89–97

Oberholzer-Gee, F., (2021b), *Better, Simpler Strategy. A value-based guide to exceptional performance*, Cambridge MA, Harvard Business Review Press.

Ogwang, T. & D.I. Cho, (2014), "A conceptual framework for constructing a corruption diffusion index", *Journal of Business Ethics*, Vol. 125(1): 1–9

Pacini, C.; Rogers, H. & J. Swingen, (2002), "The OECD convention on combating bribery of foreign public foreign officials in international transactions: a new tool to promote transparency in financial reporting", *Advances in International Accounting*, Vol. 15: 121–153.

Pant, M. & M. Pattanayak, (2007), "Insider ownership and firm value: evidence from the Indian corporate sector", MPRA Paper No.6335.

Papic, M., (2021), *Geopolitical Alpha. An Investment Framework for Predicting the Future*, Hoboken-New Jersey, John Wiley & Sons

Parent, M. & B.H Reich, (2010), Governing Information technology risk, *California Management Review*, Vol. 53(3): 134.

Pearlson, K. & K. Huang, (2022), "Design for Cybersecurity from the start", *MIT Sloan Management Review*, Winter, Vol. 63(2): 73–77.

Peng, C-W. & M-L. Yang, (2014), "The effect of corporate social performance on financial performance: the moderating effect of ownership concentration", *Journal of Business Ethics*, Vol. 123(1): 171–182.

Pfeffer, J. (1972), "Size and composition of corporate boards of directors: the organization and its environment", *Administrative Science Quarterly*, 17, 218–229.

Pfeffer, J. & Salancik, G.R. (1978). *The external control of organizations: A resource dependence perspective*, New York, Harper and Row.

Phan, P.H., (2001), "Corporate Governance in newly emerging economies", *Asia Pacific Journal of Management*, Vol. 18: 131–136.

Pidun, U.; Reeves, M. & N. Knust, (2022), "Setting the Rules of the Road", *MIT Sloan Management Review*, Winter, Vol. 63(2): 44–50.

Polanyi, M., (1966), *The Tacit Dimension*, New York, Doubleday.

Polman, P. & A. Winston, (2021), *Net Positive. How courageous companies thrive by giving more than they take*, Cambridge MA, Harvard Business School Press.

Rajan, R.G., (2010), *Fault Lines. How Hidden Fractures Still Threaten the World Economy*, New Jersey, Princeton Univ Press.

Rajan, R.G. & L. Zingales, (2003), "The great reversals: The politics of financial development in the twentieth century", *Journal of Financial Economics*, Vol.69: 5–50.

Rajan, R.G. & J. Wulf, (2006), "Are perks purely managerial excess?", *Journal of Financial Economics*, Vol. 79: 1–33.

Randhawa, D.S. (2005), "Corporate reforms in the banking sector in Southeast Asia: Economics and institutional imperatives", in Ho, K.L. (Ed.), chapter 4, *Reforming corporate governance in Southeast Asia: Economics, politics and regulations*, Singapore, ISEAS Publications, 51–82.

Redding, G., (1996), "Weak organizations and strong linkages: managerial ideology and Chinese family business networks", in Hamilton, G. (Ed) *Asian Business Networks*, New York, Walter de Gruyter, pp.27–42.

Reddy, K.; Locke, S. & F. Scimgeour, (2010), "The efficacy of principle-based corporate governance practices and firm financial performance. An empirical investigation", *The International Journal of Managerial Finance*, Vol. 6(3): 190–219.

Reese, M. & Weisbach, M. (2002). "Protection of minority shareholder interests, cross listings in the United States, and subsequent equity offerings", *Journal of Financial Economics*, 66, 65–104.

Reimer, D. & A. Bryant, (2022), "The new rules of succession planning", McKinsey & Company, February.

Resick, C.J.; Martin, G.S.; Keating, M.A.; Dickson, W.; Kwan, H.K. & C. Peng, (2011), "What ethical leadership means to me: Asian, American, and European perspectives", *Journal of Business Ethics*, Vol. 101: 435–457. DOI 10.1007/s10551-010-0730-8

Rezaee, Z., (2007). *Corporate governance post-Sarbanes-Oxley: Regulations, requirements, and integrated processes*, Hoboken, NJ, John Wiley & Sons.

Rezaee, Z. (2009), *Corporate governance and ethics*. Hoboken, NJ: John Wiley & Sons.

Richter, A. & C. Weiss, (2013), "Determinants of ownership concentration in public firms: the importance of firm, industry- and country-level factors", *Institutional Review of Law and Economics*, Vol. 33; 1–14.

Roe, M.J., (1994), *Strong managers, weak owners: the political roots of American corporate finance*, Princeton NJ, Princeton University Press.

Roe, M.J., (2002), "Can culture constrain the economic model of corporate law", *University of Chicago Law Review*, Vol. 69(3): 1251–1269.

Roberts, J., McNulty, T., & Stiles, P. (2005), "Beyond agency conceptions of the work of the non-executive director: Creating accountability in the board room", *British Journal of Management*, 16, 5–26.

Roberts, C.M. & M.W. Summerville, (2016), "The Mindful Board", *Organization & People*, January 25.

Rother, M., (2010), *Toyota Kata: Managing People for Improvement, Adaptiveness, and Superior Results*. New York, McGraw Hill.

Roubini, N. & S. Mihn, (2010), *Crisis Economics. A crash course in the future of finance*, London, Penguin.

Salter, M.S., (2012), "How Short-Termism Invites Corruption . . . And what to do about it", *Harvard Business School Working Paper*, April, 12–094.

Schleifer, A. & R. Vishny, (1994). "Politicians and firms", *Quarterly Journal of Economics*, 109, 995–1025.

Schleifer, A. & R. Vishny, (1997), "A survey of corporate governance", *Journal of Finance*, Vol.52: 737–783.

Shell, G. R., (2021), *The Conscience Code. Lead with your values. Advance your career*, New York, Harper Collins.

Shiller, Robert, (2008), *The Subprime Solution. How Today's Global Financial Crisis Happened, and What to Do about it*, Princeton; Oxford, Princeton University Press.

Shiller, R.J., (2012), *Finance and the Good Society*, Oxford; Princeton, Princeton University Press.

Siagian, F.T., (2011), "Ownership Structure and Governance Implementation: Evidence from Indonesia", *Institutional Journal of Business, Humanities and Technology*, Vol. 1(3): 187–202.

Sibony, O., (2019), *You're about to make a Terrible Mistake! How Biases distort decision-making – and what we can do to fight them*, New York; Boston; London, Little-Brown Spark.

Singh, A. & A. Zammit, (2006), "Corporate Governance, Crony Capitalism and Economic Crises: should the US Business Model replace the Asian Way of 'doing business'?", Centre for Business Research, *University of Cambridge, Working paper* No 329.

Siregar, S.V. & S. Utama, (2008), "Type of earnings management and the effect of ownership structure, firm size, and corporate-governance practices: Evidence from Indonesia", *The International Journal of Accounting*, Vol. 43(1): 1–27

Slangen, A.H.; R.J.M. Van Tulder, (2009), "Cultural distance, political risk, or governance quality? Towards a more accurate conceptualization and measurement of external uncertainty in foreign entry mode research", *International Business Review*, Vol.18(3): 276–291

Smith, I.H. & M. Kouchaki, (2021), "Building Ethical Company. Create an organization that helps employees behave more honourably", *Harvard Business Review*, November-December: 132–139.

Sørensen, J.B. & G.R. Carroll, (2021), "Why good arguments make better strategy", *MIT Sloan Management Review, Summer*, Vol. 62(4): 47–53.

Stout, Lynn, (2012), *The Shareholder Myth. How putting Shareholders first harms Investors, Corporations, and the Public*, San Francisco, Berrett-Koehler Publ.

Taleb, N.N., (2005), *Fooled by Randomness. The hidden role of Chance in Life and in the Markets*, New York, Random House Trade Paperbacks.

Taleb, N.N., (2007), *The Black Swan. The Impact of the Highly Improbable*, London, Allen Lane – Penguin.

Taleb, N.N., (2012), *The Antifragile*, London Allen Lane-Penguin.

Taleb, NN, (2018), *Skin in the Game. Hidden Asymmetries in daily life*, New York, Random House.

Tanzi, V. & H. Davoodi, (2001), "Corruption, growth, and public finances", in Jain, A.K. (Ed), *Political Economy and Corruption*, London, Routledge: 89–110.

Thiele, L.P., (2006), *The Heart of Judgment. Practical Wisdom, Neuroscience, and Narrative*, Cambridge, Cambrige University Press.

Tian, J; Coreynen, W.; Matthyssens, P. & L. Shen, (2021), "Platform-based servitization and business model adaptation by established manufacturers", Journal of Technovation, https://doi.org/10.1016/j.technovation.2021.102222

Tinsley, C., Dillon, R. & P. Madsen, (2011), "How to avoid catastrophe", *Harvard Business Review*, April: 90–97.

Tomlinson, B.; Whelan, T. & K. Eckerle, (2021), "How to bring ESG into the quarterly earnings call", *MIT Sloan Management Review, Summer*, Vol. 62(4): 9–11.

Tricker, B., (2015), *Corporate Governance. Principles, Policies, and Practices*, Oxford, Oxford University Press.

Utama, C.A., (2012), "Company Disclosure in Indonesia: Corporate Governance Practice, Ownership Structure, Competition and Total Assets", *Asian Journal of Business and Accounting*, Vol. 5(1): 75–108.

Utama, C.A. & Utama, S., (2014), Determinants of disclosure level of related party transactions in Indonesia, *International Journal of Disclosure and Governance*, 11(1), 74–98.

Van Essen, M; Van Oosterhout, J.H. & M. Carney, (2011), "Corporate boards and the performance of Asian firms: a Meta-Analysis", *Asia Pacific Journal of Management*, September; DOI 10.10007/s10490-011-9269-1.

Verhezen, P. (2008), "Guanxi: Networks or nepotism?" in Zsolnai, L. (Ed.), *Europe-Asia dialogue on business spirituality*, Antwerp; Apeldoorn, Garant, 89–106.

Verhezen, P., (2009), Gifts, Corruption and Philanthropy. The ambiguity of gift practices in business, Oxford; Bern, Peter Lang Publishing.

Verhezen, P., (2010), "Giving voice to a culture of silence: from a culture of compliance to a culture of integrity", *Journal of Business Ethics*, Vol. 96(2): 187–206.

Verhezen, P., (2015), *The Vulnerability of Corporate Reputation. Leadership for Sustainable Long-term Value*, Berkshire, Palgrave Pivot Publishing: http://www.palgrave.com/us/book/9781137547354.

Verhezen, P., (2015), "Fear, Regret or Trust? Transparency to control or transparency to empower", *International Finance Corporation (World Bank) Paper*, No 38, Washington.

Verhezen, P., (2018), "Is Indonesia serious about corporate governance?" *Strategic Review*, Vol. 8 (3): 48–59

Verhezen, P. & Morse, P. (2009), "Consensus on global corporate governance principles?" *Journal of International Business Ethics*, July, 2(1): 84–101

Verhezen, P.; Riyana Hardjapamekas, E. & P. Notowidigdo, (2012), *Is corporate governance relevant? How good corporate governance practices affect Indonesian organizations*, Jakarta, University of Indonesia Press.

Verhezen, P. & N. Soebadjo, (2013), "Is there hope for corporate governance in Indonesia?", *Strategic Review*, Vol. 3(3): 67–73.

Verhezen, P.; Williamson, I.O.; Crosby, M. & N. Soebagjo, (2016), *Doing Business ASEAN markets. Leadership challenges and Governance solutions across borders*, London, Palgrave MacMillan.

Verhezen, P.; Williamson, I.O. & N. Soebagjo, (2018), "Living less dangerously in Indonesia", *Strategic Review*, January-March: 54–67

Verhezen, P. & G. Martin, (2018), Corporate Governance & Ethical Behavior affecting Performance: Propositions and Peculiarities at Indonesian Firms within its Institutional context, *Melbourne Business School Working Paper*, financed by IFC World Bank.

Verhezen, P.; Chambers, P. & S. De Haes, (2018), "Cyber-threats: Facing the Faceless", *Strategic Review*, Vol. 8(2): 24–40

Verhezen, P. & P. Chambers, (2019), "Hacking and the darker side of social media", *Strategic Review*, Jan-March, Vol. 9 (1):25–32 http://sr.sgpp.ac.id/post/hacking-and-the-darker-side-of-social-media.

Verhezen, P. & T. Abeng, (2020), "Boards that Govern and Lead", *Strategic Review*, Vol. 10(2): 42–57.

Wade, M.; Joshi, A. & E. Teracino, (2022), "Six principles to build your company's strategic agility", *Harvard Business Review Special Issue*, Harvard University, Cambridge MA, Spring: 107–111.

Wallace, P. & J. Zinkin, (2005), *Corporate Governance. Mastering Business in Asia*, Singapore, John Wiley & Sons.

Wasef, R.M. & R. Kusumastuti, (2010), "Ownership structure and performance of public companies listed in the Indonesian Stock Exchange", *Journal of Administrative Sciences and Organization*, November, Vol. 17(3): 238–249.

Webb, A., (2016), *The Signals are Talking. Why Today's Fringe is Tomorrow's Mainstream*, New York, PublicAffairs.

Weisbach, M.S., (1988), "Outside directors and CEO turnover", *Journal of Financial Economics*, Vol. 20: 432–460.

Whelan, T., (2021), "US corporate boards suffer from inadequate expertise in financially material ESG matters", *NYU Stern Center for Sustainable Business*, January. https://ssrn.com/abstract=3758584.

Wright, M; Filatotchev, I.; Hoskisson, R. & M. Peng, (2005), "Strategy research in emerging economies: challenging the conventional wisdom", *Journal of Management Studies*, Vol. 42(1): 1–33.

Wu, X., (2009), "Determinants of bribery in Asian firms: Evidence from the World Business Environment Survey", *Journal of Business Ethics*, Vol.87: 75–88.

Wucker, M., (2020), "Is your board risk-ready?", *Strategy + Business*, Summer, Issue 99.

Wyma, K.D., (2015), "The case for investment advising as a virtue-based practice", *Journal of Business Ethics*, Vol. 127: 231–249. DOI 10.1007/s10551-013-2025-3.

Yadong, L. (2005), "Corporate governance and accountability in multinational enterprises: Concepts and agenda", *Journal of International Management*, 11, 1–18.

Yermack, D., (1996), "Higher market valuation for firms with a small board of directors", *Journal of Finance Economics*, Vol. 40: 185–211.

Young, O.R. (Ed.) (1997), *Global governance: Drawing insights from the environmental experience*, Cambridge, MA, MIT Press.

Young, S. & Thyil, V. (2008), "A holistic model of corporate governance: A new research framework", *Corporate Governance*, 8(10), 94–108.

Young, M.; Peng, M.W.; Ahlstrom, D.; Bruton, G.; & Y. Jiang, (2008), "Corporate governance in emerging economies: A review of the Principal-Principal perspective", *Journal of Management Studies*, Vol. 45: 196–220

Xu, Z.X. & H.K. Ma, (2015), "Does honesty results from Moral Will or Moral Grace? Why moral identity matters", *Journal of Business Ethics*, Vol. 127: 371–384. DOI 10.1007/s10551-014-2050-x

Zhou, J.Q. & M.W. Peng, (2010), "Relational exchanges versus arm's length transactions during institutional transitions", *Asia Pacific Journal of Management*, Vol. 27: 355–370

Zingales, L., (1998), *Corporate Governance. The New Palgrave Dictionary of Economics and Law*, London, MacMillan.

About the Authors

Dr. Peter Verhezen is a professor of strategy and corporate governance at the University of Antwerp and AMS (Belgium), and he advises boards on governance and risk. He was a former Associate Professor for global corporate governance at the University of Melbourne and Adjunct Professor at MBS (Australia), and a Harvard Kennedy School Fellow (USA). He worked as senior consultant for corporate governance at IFC–World Bank in Asia Pacific, and as debt negotiator-advisor for IBRA-IMF during the 'Asian crisis'. He founded and ran an IBM spin-off software company in the early nineties for more than fifteen years in Southeast Asia.

Dr. Tanri Abeng is a former CEO of Heineken Indonesia (Bir Bintang), and was the first minister of state-owned enterprises in Indonesia during the Asian crisis. He has served as an elected member of People's Consultative Assembly, and was the board's chairman of the state-owned telco company, PT Telkom, and the state owned gas- and oil company, PT Pertamina. Today he chairs the board of state- owned Bio Farma in Indonesia. He is also the rector of Tanri Abeng University and the Executive Center for Global Leadership in Jakarta-Indonesia.

Index

Abeng, T. 73, 74, 96–98, 104–106
activist agenda 5
advisory capacity 85, 98
agency costs 27, 85
agency problem 4
– of asymmetric information 72
– auditing process 7
– corporate governance and 5, 6, 166
– managers/agents 6
agency theory 6, 32, 133
Akhlak VII, 107
alpha returns 129
Anglo-Saxon
– governance structures XV, 91, 113
– investment model 10, 22
– jurisdictions 85, 166, 170
arm's length system 93
articles of association (AoA) 114
Asian-based Transnational firms 3
Asian financial crisis XIII
– governance standards during 11–12
– Indonesian corporate governance and 30, 35, 37
Asian governance 9–10
– challenges 14–17
– hierarchical management approach 14–15
assessing boardroom 57–60
– enacting functioning boards 59–60
– fiduciary duties 58
– functioning/evaluating 57–58
– good corporate governance principles 59
asymmetric information 4
auditing committee 58
auditing process 7
audit subcommittee 67
Australia Institute of Corporate Directors (AICD) 163
autocar manufacturing 143–144
awards, corporate governance 35

Berle, A. A. 3
Best Buy 160
best corporate governance 35–36
Bezos, J. 117
board(s)/boardroom 1, 43. *See also* assessing boardroom
– audit subcommittee 67–68

– business environment 57
– effectiveness 169–170
– Enron's collapse and bankruptcy 111
– fiduciary duties of care, loyalty and prudence 43, 46–57
– functioning of 2, 28, 66–67
– future challenges 142
– governance 7
– impacting performance 165–175
– improvisation 57–75
– Indonesian 30
– members duties/skills 43, 44, 46, 68, 165 (*see also* fiduciary duties)
– organizational principles 146–148
– performance 65
– processes and procedures 65–72
– purpose/narratives 145–146
– right information 72
– right oversight and guidance 60–63
– right people and team 63–65
– right processes and culture 65–72
– sensitive and inventive 160–161
– steel-cement-foundations 165
– structure and composition 30–32, 67, 104, 165
– technological/digital innovation and implementation 142–144
Board of Commissioners (BoC) 28, 73, 76
– composition of 108
– dual-tier boards role 62
– fiduciary duties of 47
Board of Directors (BoD) 28, 73
– concepts of 77–78
– fiduciary duties of 45, 74, 90
business environment 57, 139–140
business practice on value creation 8–9
business strategies 7–9

Cadbury, A. 24, 91
California Pension Fund (CalPERS) 30
capitalism 2
– entrepreneurial 2–4
– institutional 4–6, 112
– managerial 4–6, 91
capital market 13, 29, 32, 89, 166. *See also* concentrated ownership
CEO/President Director selection 63–65

CEO succession plan 113
certifying board 31
charter 43
Children Investment Fund (CIF) 138
civic law system 23
CO_2 emission firms 125–126, 130, 140
Code of Good Corporate Governance (CGCG) 82
commissioners. *See* Board of Commissioners (BoC)
common law system 23, 84
company affairs 79
competition for international funds 32–33
comply/explain approach 37, 38
concentrated ownership 19, 29, 76, 107
conflicts of interest 29, 35
– commissioner 47–49, 78
controlling shareholders 28
corporate governance
– across borders 10
– attributes 38
– debate 133
– decision-making 141
– definition of 24, 33, 34
– effectiveness of 36
– evolution of 4
– failures in 22–32
– global investment 27
– individual leadership 38
– in Indonesia 35–40 (*see also* Indonesian corporate governance)
– institutional investment perspective 10, 22
– models 11
– structures of 83–84, 87, 101–103
– sustainability obligation 125
Corporate Governance (Sub) Committee 71
corporate governance practices
– benefits of 12–13
– IFC's 13
– lack of 9–10
corporate governance principles 22, 23
– agency problem 27
– in Asian context 32–40
– assessing boardroom 59
– board structure/composition 30–32
– civic law system 23
– common law system 23
– competition for international funds 32–34
– conflict of interest 29
– disclosure and transparency 28

– effective framework 25, 42
– equitable treatment of shareholders 25–26
– expropriation risk 27
– external/technological pressure 148–150
– fund managers 30
– international investors 26–32
– OECD principles of 23, 24–26
– organizational principles and 146–148
– rights of shareholders 25
– stakeholders, role of 26
corporate shared value 119
corruption 29, 30, 36
culture, organization 62, 65–72, 107, 158–161
cybersecurity 149
cyberthreats 56–57

Dasgupta Review 136–137
data privacy 56–57
decision-making process XVI–XVII, 1, 14, 43–46, 48, 49, 52, 65–66, 81. *See also* duty of prudence
decoupling economies 18
de-politization 64
destructive entrenchment 28
Djohan, R. 96
dual-tier board structure
– "combined" approach 93–94
– executive board of 49
– fiduciary duties of 90
– foster collaboration 94
– Garuda's 96–97
– in Indonesia 113
– new (holding) structure 104
– at Pertamina 104
– SOEs structure 103–106
Dutch legal system 23
duty of care 46–47
duty of loyalty 47–48
duty of prudence 48–57. *See also* risk appetite; risk management

eliminating risk 53–55
enacting functioning boards 59–60
enforcement 39
engaged board 30, 31
enlightened ownership and fiduciary duties 120–123
Enron's collapse and bankruptcy 111
entrepreneurial capitalism 2–4

entrepreneurial innovation 91
equity investors 22
ESG (Environmental, Social & Governance) 119, 125. *See also* shared value
– disclosures 129
– issues 159
– non-financial measurements 128
– reporting/impact 119, 125–131
European Green Deal 131
executive board (BoD) 28, 81, 90, 93, 97, 100, 101, 103
executive compensation 86, 113
executives performances 27, 65
expropriation risk 28
external governance 8

family-oriented businesses 10, 15, 17, 37, 64, 86, 125, 130, 160, 178
fiduciary duties 43
– assessing boardroom 58
– board and managers 45–46, 168
– of care 46–47
– determining risk 50
– in Indonesian context 73–75
– of loyalty 47–48
– maximizing shareholder value 120–123
– of prudence 48–57
– re-interpreting 120–123
– risk appetite 50–56
– risk management process 48–49
financial auditing 61
financial theory 134
Fink, L. 126
firm-level corporate governance 29, 37
foreign investors 37–38
four generic corporate governance principles 24–26
Freeman, E. 118
Friedman, M. 120, 124
full time executive director 46
fund managers of governance 30
future-proof. *See* technological and business innovation

Garuda case in Indonesia 95–97
generic (OECD) governance principles 24–26
George, B. 134
Global Financial Crisis 74, 82
global investment 27

good corporate governance 13, 18, 25, 26–32, 113
governance VII, XIII, 1. *See also* corporate governance
– boards 7
– external/internal 8
– principles of 45
– rating agencies 167
– Western *vs*. Asian 9–10
greenwashing 126, 138

Henderson, R. 132, 135–136
hierarchical management approach 14–15
Hohn, C. 138
holding board structures 77, 104

IFC's corporate governance 13
IIRC approach 127
Indonesian Company Law (ICL) 73, 107, 114
Indonesian corporate governance 9, 18, 23, 25, 30, 35–40
– awards 35
– concentrated ownership 19, 29, 76
– deviance in 37
– evidence of 35–36
– fiduciary duties in 73–75
– foreign investors and 37–37
– Garuda case 95–97
– holding board structures 77
– inexperienced corporate bodies 77
– legal rules 35, 44
– ownership and control, separation of 77, 166
– PT Pertamina in 99–100
– roadmap for 37, 41
– state-owned enterprises 76
– structures 83–84
– "Telkom" case in 97–99
– weak legal enforcement 36
Indonesian Financial Services Authority 35
inexperienced corporate bodies 77
information asymmetries 33–34
ING bank 130
innovation. *See* technological and business innovation
institutional capitalism 4–6, 112
institutional investment perspective of governance 22, 35–40
institutional voids 34
institutional weaknesses 32

internal audit 49, 58, 61
internal governance 8
international exchanges 5
international funds competition 32–34
intervening board 31
inventive boards 160–161
investment 27, 83, 86, 150
– in innovative technology XIV, 9
– institutional capitalism 112
– promising projects 150–151
investors 5, 19, 22, 26–32, 37–38, 138
ISO 31000 risk management process 48–49

Jasy, A. 117
Jensen, M. 19–20, 120
jurisdictional context 23–24

kata process 164
Kramer, M. 119
Kyocera 145

Lakatos, I. 136
Largest Investment Management Companies 19
leadership 39
– CEO and succession planning 154–155
– in changing world 177–178
– development of 151–158
– within functioning boards 171
– overseeing top executives 155–158
– retaining talent 152–153
– talent war 152
– technological and business innovation 151
legal history 23–24
limited-liability company
– capitalism 3
– notion of 1–2
London stock exchange (LSE) 3, 5

Mallin, C. A. 24
managerial capitalism 4–6, 91
managerial entrepreneurship 91
maximizing shareholder value 27
– fiduciary duties 120–123
– nexus of contractual agreements 116–117
– nexus of relationships 117
– to "sharing" created value 115–123
Means, G. C. 3
mitigating risk 53–55
modern governance 149–150

monitoring top management 27, 84, 85
MSCI Emerging Markets Index 16
multinational organization (MNO) 2–3

natural capital 124, 126
Nestlé 129–131
New York Stock Exchange (NSYE) 3, 5, 27, 97, 112
nexus of contractual agreements 32, 116–117
nexus of relationships 32, 117
nomination committee 67, 68, 69
Nonaka, I. 145–146
non-executive director 46
non-performing boards 31

OECD's Corporate Governance Principles 23, 24–26, 33
omnichannel 162
open corporate accelerator 143
operating board 31
organizational culture 62, 65–72, 107, 158–161
organizational soul 145–146
organizational values and norms 32
oversight capacity 98
ownership vs. management leadership 5

Paris Climate Agreement 121
passive board 31
Porter, M. 119
premium for firms 11–12
premortem exercise 106–107, 114
preventable operational risks 50, 51
principal-principal problem 28
processes of boards 65–66
promising projects investment 150–151
pro-shareholder ownership 7
PT Pertamina in Indonesian 99–100
– corporate governance structure 101–103
– dual-tier board structure 103–106
– entrenched board 100–101
– entrenchment challenges 106
– managerial entrepreneurs 106–107
– organizational culture at 107
Pucker, K.P. 137
Purnama, B. T. 106

related party transactions 29
relationship-based system 93
reverse governance 35

right decision 97–99, 159
right information 72
right oversight and guidance 60–63
right processes and culture 65–72
risk appetite
– boundaries and 52
– defining 51–52
risk management 113
– absorbing and managing 52–54
– checklist for leading 55
– committee 70–71
– cyberthreats 56–57
– data privacy 56–57
– eliminating/transferring/mitigating 52–55
– external 50
– identification 50
– minimizing threatening 56
– monitoring 55
– organizational culture and 62
– preventable operational 50, 51
– process 48–49
– scenario planning for addressing 51
– strategic guidance 49, 50, 61–62
– supervisory board roles 62
– types of 50
– warning signs 53
risk policy committee 70
roadmap 35, 41
Rother, M. 164
Rothschild, J. 15
Royal Commission 163
RSPO certification 130
rules of thumb 37, 108

Scleifer, A. 24
sensitive boards 160–161
'servitization' of products 143
shared value creation 118, 119, 128, 140, 152
shareholders
– model 32, 34, 45
– primacy 120
– rights and protection 38, 135
– theory 133
short-termism 89, 142, 152, 158–160
signalling effect 29
SinarMas conglomerate group 130
single-tier vs. double-tier boards 44, 84–86
– advantages and disadvantages of 91–93
– "combined" approach 93–94

– corporate governance structure in Indonesia 85
– functioning of board 85
– national carrier Garuda 95–97
– principles of 86–91
– stakeholders 86
– state-owned enterprises 89
– structure of 86
– supervisory board 85, 88
– USA firms 91, 92
Smith, C. 124–125
social responsibility 159
stake-brokers 118
stakeholders
– capitalism 123
– engagement 115–116, 124–125
– single-tier vs. double-tier boards 86
– value creation 118
stake-market 134
state-owned enterprises (SOEs) 10, 68, 74, 76, 89, 98
steel-cement-foundations 165
stewardship governance model 133
stock buybacks 150–151
stock-holders 115, 119, 129
stock options 7
strategy risks 50
structures, organization 83–84
supervisor/monitor 84
supervisory board 28, 37, 88, 90, 93, 96, 98, 100, 101, 103. See also Board of Commissioners (BoC)
– development of effective 108, 109
– issues 141–142
– roles of 62
Sustainability Living Plan 125

Takeuchi, H. 145–146
technological and business innovation 151–152
– addressing longer-term risks 141
– appointing CEO 154–155
– "cultural" sensitivities 142
– development of leaders 141–142
– expertise in boards 159–160
– neoliberal goals 158–159
– organizational culture 158–161
– organizational structures 143
– during pandemic crisis 152
– retaining talent 152–153

– right decision 159
– sensitive and inventive boards 160–161
– social responsibility 159
– top executives, selection of 155–158
Telkom case in Indonesia 97–99
Thohrir, E. 107
thumos 146–148, 162
top executives, selection of 63–65, 155–158
Tragedy of the Commons 121
transferring risk 53–55
triple line reporting 127
trophy board 30
trust 146–148
tunnelling effect 28
two-tier board structure. *See* dual-tier board structure

UK common law system 23
unconditional loyalty 15
unified board 97–99

"universal" governance 36
unprofessional boards 31
US-based MNOs 3

value creation 8–9, 60, 100, 101, 117
value-focused companies 8–9, 48
value maximization 6, 7, 19–20, 123
Vishny, R. 24
volatile, uncertain, complex and ambiguous (VUCA) context 56, 126

Western *vs.* Asian governance 9–10
– challenges 14–17
– corporate governance across borders 10–14
– family-oriented businesses 10
– premium for firms 11–12
– risk factors 12
– state owned enterprises 10
wrongdoing 66

www.ingramcontent.com/pod-product-compliance
Lightning Source LLC
Chambersburg PA
CBHW062137160426
43191CB00014B/2313